Published by J. Mason, 14, City Road; & 66, Paternoster Row.

THE

BRAND OF DOMINIC:

OR

INQUISITION.

At Rome

"SUPREME AND UNIVERSAL".

BY THE REVD W. H. RULE.

LONDON:

PUBLISHED BY JOHN MASON, 14, CITY ROAD,

SOLD AT 66, PATERNOSTER ROW.

MDCCCLII.

THE BRAND OF DOMINIC:

OR,

INQUISITION;

AT ROME "SUPREME AND UNIVERSAL."

BY THE

REV. WILLIAM H. RULE,

AUTHOR OF "MEMOIR OF A MISSION TO GIBRALTAR AND SPAIN,"
"MARTYRS OF THE REFORMATION," &c.

LONDON:
PUBLISHED BY JOHN MASON, 14, CITY-ROAD;
SOLD AT 66, PATERNOSTER-ROW.

1852.

LONDON
PRINTED BY JAMES NICHOLS,
HOXTON-SQUARE.

PREFACE.

To impart correct information, and to assist the general reader in forming his judgment of the Inquisition as it was and as it is, is the object proposed to himself by the Author. He has not attempted to give anything more than a well-authenticated statement of its establishment and progress. Much more might have been related under the title of this little volume; but those countries where the system of the Inquisition was never established, although they were theatres of persecution, are not included. Neither would the Author have been justified in including all persecuting courts or authorities under the single name of Inquisition. He has laboured to be technically exact, and preferred passing over doubtful anecdotes to setting forth as history what is no better than romance; and has also thought it more important to disclose the policy and the power of this member of the Romish Church, than to multiply recitals of the same class, beyond what is really necessary to complete a truthful picture.

The authorities may be described very briefly. As will be seen during the perusal of the following chapters, they are all original. The truth is, that original authorities are much fewer than most readers would expect to find, but that the books used in the course of research, in order to anything like an effective use of those authorities, are too numerous to be recited in the preface to a work of so small volume. Many of them pass unmentioned, but all the sources of authentication are mentioned, either in the text or in the notes. And in every instance the Author has used them for himself. Some of the material is altogether new, and, as he believes, the structure of the work is more perfectly historical than that of most others on the same subject. He has not endeavoured to extenuate the enormity of the Inquisition and its officers, nor is he conscious of exaggeration in any instance. The struggle with Romanism is for life or death, and our strength in the appeal to history consists in sobriety, earnestness, and truth. Neither can he speak of the Inquisition as of an obsolete barbarism, or as of a something that cannot any longer exist. It is a permanent, active, and vigorous institution of the Church of Rome. While the Papacy survives, the Inquisition must live, for the spirit of it is not that of the middle age, but of the Church itself. Many orders have risen and fallen again within the bosom of that Church, because their interests were local, or because, like some of the military societies, they were not so constituted as possibly to be permanent. And special enterprises, like the Crusades, that could not possibly be continued, have had their day, and passed off into the pages of history. But the Inquisition outlives every change, adapts itself to the condition of every country, works quietly amidst the most clamorous professions of liberality, and, while seeming to have been beaten away from the wide field of the Popedom, and forced to retreat within the frontiers of the Papal State, even there the Congregation of the Faith plies its agencies with an impalpable, noiseless, and all-pervading energy that mocks our jealousy, by eluding our vigilance. The Inquisitors are actually conducting a crusade, in union with the Jesuits, against the civil and religious liberties of the world, and are causing that intensely ecclesiastical but worldly spirit, which is erroneously called Ultramontanism, to prevail in countries which very lately seemed to be open for a religious reformation.

The local Inquisitions of the thirteenth century gave place to the more uniformly organized Tribunals of the fifteenth. These were diminished by the awakenings of the civil power in the seventeenth and eighteenth centuries. They seemed to have fallen, together with the Bastilles, in the early part of the nineteenth century; but, during the pontificates of

Leo XII. and his successors, it became increasingly apparent that they had fallen only to be absorbed into one central administration, too truly called, at Rome, the "Supreme and Universal Inquisition." It is not without reason that the Pope is called "Prefect," or Universal Inquisitor. He is really what he professes to be, so far, at least, as his jurisdiction and his influence extend. He is not chief Jesuit, indeed, or chief Dominican, or chief Oratorian, but he is, at the same time, and with equal reality, chief of the Bishops, and chief of the Inquisitors. This is confirmed by facts adduced in the last chapter, and the Author would fail in the discharge of a duty to his fellow-Christians, and to their common Head, the Lord Jesus Christ, if he were not to ask and challenge a searching examination of the results to which those facts conduct him,—*that the Inquisition now exists, and acts throughout Christendom, less repulsively, indeed, but not less effectively, than when it paraded its penitents, and openly burnt its victims.*

W. H. R.

LONDON, *April* 10*th*, 1852.

CONTENTS.

CHAPTER I.

THE

SUPREME AND UNIVERSAL INQUISITION.

CHAPTER I.

BEGINNINGS OF THE INQUISITION.

POPE Alexander III., driven from Rome by the anti-Pope Octavian, has come by sea to France. Henry II. of England, who is in Normandy, and Louis VII. of France, hearing of his arrival, both hasten to give him welcome, and lead him in state on horseback through the town of Couci on the Loire, one monarch walking on either side, and each holding the bridle. Thomas à Becket will soon be there also. He has just been made Archbishop of Canterbury; and is, as yet, on good terms with the King his master. It is two or three years since the first confessors of Christ suffered death for His sake in England;* and about sixteen years ago St. Bernard first came into Languedoc, to lead a crusade against the Albigenses. The King of England has kissed the Pope's foot; and, not presuming to occupy a chair in his presence, has sat down, with his Barons, on the floor, in the abbey of Bourg-Dieu. Thus abject are Englishmen in the twelfth century.

There has been a great religious awakening in the provinces which we now call the South of France and North of Spain; and although Alexander might have enough to do to defend himself against his competitor, whom the Emperor of Germany, and whom almost all Italy, supports, he thinks it expedient to keep up the rage of zeal against heretics, as they are called; and, to do this more effectually, convenes a Council to be holden at Tours, on the 29th day of May, 1163.

On the day appointed, seventeen Cardinals, a hundred and

* "Martyrologia," vol. ii., p. 512.

twenty-four Bishops, four hundred and fourteen Abbots, and a great multitude of Priests and laity, assemble in the church of St. Maurice, with the Pontiff at their head. These Clergy are French and English,—since only these two nations acknowledge Alexander to be their Pope,—and a very few adherents from Italy. Arnoul, Bishop of Lisieux, at his command, delivers a sermon concerning the several interests of the Church, smooth and plausible, and with scarcely any reference to the persons who are intended to be her victims. Forthwith begins the business of the Council. Thomas, the Martyr of Canterbury, as the Romanists now call him, comes to Tours, and is received by the Cardinals in procession, which is an unusual honour, and takes part in the deliberations; but leaves before the close, being much occupied in the affairs of his new dignity in England. Still his heart was with the Council, and whether or not he was present when the following decree was voted, the English Priests were, and it is undoubted that he and they heartily concurred therein. The sentences are worthy to be recited, inasmuch as that was the first act of the Church of Rome that can be correctly called *inquisitorial.**

"In the parts of Toulouse, a damnable heresy has broken out of late, spreading itself by degrees, like a cancer, into the neighbouring places, and now infects great numbers in Gascony and other provinces." And, after descanting on the insidious and destructive character of the new heresy, the fathers proceed to say, "Wherefore we command the Bishops, and all the Priests of the Lord, dwelling in those parts, to keep watch, and under peril of anathema to prohibit that, where followers of that heresy are known, any one

* When we say *inquisitorial*, we speak with reference to the forms, rather than to the principles, of the Inquisition. The flames of persecution had been burning hotly for more than six centuries before the Council of Tours, and the saints of the Most High were pursued with violence, but not yet made the subjects of secret judicial inquest. Soldiers were employed to put down heresy with fire and sword, and Magistrates enforced the laws of Justinian and his successors, or other laws like them, in open court. Between persecution in general, and that particular method of persecution which is called "the Inquisition," the historian must carefully distinguish; and by preserving the distinction in the volume we are now beginning, many flagrant persecutions will be passed over without notice. Their history must be sought elsewhere; in the "Martyrologia," if the reader pleases, and in the "Martyrs of the Reformation."

in the country shall dare to afford them refuge, or to lend them help. Neither shall there be any dealings with such persons in buying or selling; that, all solace of humanity being utterly lost, they may be compelled to forsake the error of their life. And whoever shall attempt to contravene this order, shall be smitten with anathema as a partaker of their iniquity. But they, if they be taken, shall be thrown into prison by Catholic Princes, and be deprived of all their goods. And forasmuch as they frequently assemble together from various parts into one hiding-place, and have no reason why they should be together, except their consent in error, and yet dwell in the same abode, let such conventicles be attentively searched; and if they be found guilty, let them be forbidden with canonical severity."* An attentive search could not be conveniently conducted without some regulations for the guidance of the spies; and, this necessity being felt, rules of Inquisition were soon suggested.

The next General Council was holden at Rome (A.D. 1179) in the church of the Lateran,—the mother church, as it is called,—where Alexander, having so far overcome his antagonist as to be able to return to the seat of government, presided on a lofty throne, surrounded by the Cardinals, Prefects, Senators, and Consuls of the city. In three solemn sessions the affairs of the Papacy were brought under review; many canons were recorded, and, amongst others, one that renewed the regulations of Tours in regard to heretics, named the sects most obnoxious to the hatred of the Church, and determined that all who bestowed the slightest kindness on sectarians should undergo equal punishment, and that the *relaxed*, or persons informed against as under suspicion of heresy, should be outlawed.† We note the peculiar term, *relaxatos*, "relaxed," because it eventually became established in the jargon of the "Holy Office;" and we also mark the part taken by informers, whose successors were the "familiars" of the same tribunal. And the concurrence of the secular with the ecclesiastical power in this Council gave another weighty precedent for their subsequent union in the exercise of inquisitorial jurisdiction.

Lucius III., successor of Alexander, also a wanderer, being driven out of Rome by the violence of the Romans, held a Council at Verona (A.D. 1184), at which the Empe-

* Concilium Turonense.

† Concilium Lateranense III.

ror Frederic I. was present, and there condemned all heretics, and smote them with a perpetual curse; including under that fulmination all unlicensed Preachers, and all who taught concerning the eucharist, baptism, and remission of sins, and other chief points of doctrine, differently from the Church of Rome. "And because the severity of ecclesiastical discipline is sometimes despised by those who do not understand its virtue, we ordain," says the decree, "that they who shall be manifestly convicted of the aforesaid errors, if they be Clerks or religious persons, shall be divested of every order and benefice, and given over to the secular power, to receive suitable punishment: unless the culprit, so soon as he is discovered, shall make abjuration in the hands of the Bishop of the place. In like manner the layman shall be punished by the secular Judge, unless he make abjuration. They who are only found suspected shall be also punished, unless they can prove their innocence by a suitable purgation; but they who relapse after abjuration or purgation, shall be left to the secular judgment, without being heard again. The property of condemned Clerks shall be applied, according to law, to the churches that they served. This excommunication against heretics shall be renewed by all the Bishops on the great solemnities, or when occasion presents itself, under penalty of suspension from their episcopal functions for three years. We add, by the advice of the Bishops, and on the representation of the Emperor, and the Lords of his court, that every Bishop shall visit, once or twice every year, himself, or by his Archdeacon, or by other qualified persons, those parts of his diocese where it is commonly reported that heretics are living, and shall swear in three or four men of good character, and even, if he thinks it desirable, all the people of the neighbourhood, binding them, if they can discover where there are any heretics, or persons who hold private meetings, or that lead a different life from the faithful in general, to denounce such persons to the Bishop or the Archdeacon. The Bishop or the Archdeacon shall then call the accused before him; and if they do not clear themselves, following the custom of the country, or if they relapse, they shall be punished by the judgment of the Bishops. But if they refuse to swear, they shall at once be judged heretics." Barons, Governors, Consuls, and all other secular authorities, are then required to render effectual aid for the detection and punishment of heretics and their accomplices, whenever required so to do, under the penalties of excommunication and interdict. "All the fautors of heretics shall be noted with perpetual infamy, and, as such, excluded from being advocates, witnesses, or discharging any public functions."*

Here we find the concurrence of the civil and ecclesiastical powers for the extirpation of heresy. The Church employs excommunication and other censures: the Emperor, the Lords, and the Magistrates, are to inflict temporal penalties. Bishops are to inform themselves, personally, or by commissaries, of persons suspected of heresy, following common report, or receiving special information. The various degrees of suspected, convicted, penitent, and relapsed, are marked, and must be visited with correspondent penalties. And after the Church has spent her spiritual weapons, she leaves the subjects of her displeasure to be smitten by the secular arm. This is the theory of the Inquisition, which may be considered as then established, although, as yet, a distinct tribunal was not erected: we may therefore say, that in the period of twenty-one years, from the Council of Tours to that of Verona, the general plan was formed. Thenceforth it only awaited the usual process of legislation and experience to reach the horrible perfection of the sixteenth century.

Hitherto the Bishops had been acknowledged as guardians of the faith, and intrusted with the duty of making inquisition. But, notwithstanding the bond of canonical obedience, and the expedients employed for detaching the secular Prelates and Clergy from the interests of their native countries, they were never all so absolutely devoted to the Roman See as to overlook every consideration of patriotism and humanity. A humane, or perhaps an aged, Bishop could not incessantly endure the groans of dying heretics, nor dip his hands every day in blood. The aged Priest, although a dotard in bigotry, might not have either strength or courage to brave the dangers that would be incurred in so rude a service. The ruler of one diocese might be as gentle as his neighbour was severe in the government of the next, and the inequality of their administration would detract from the force of discipline. And in almost every province there was a prevalent persuasion, that Bishops held the crozier by a

* Lucius III., epist. 1183.

Divine right, and that they were not justly required to coerce and slay their flocks at the pleasure of a distant and overbearing chief. And besides all this, it became evident, that so great a work as the extirpation of heresy could not be efficiently performed, even by the most willing servants, unless there were some charged with the oversight of them all. It was not enough that each episcopal court should take cognisance of heresy, and that every Magistrate should be at the command of his Diocesan to burn the culprits he condemned. It was found that, in those numberless imprisonments and executions, there was more than enough labour to provide work for a distinct ecclesiastical department; and accordingly, Pope Innocent III., whose fury still breathes in two ponderous folios of Epistles, almost each one of those missives being full of threatening and slaughter, resolved to take the matter into his own hands, and no longer trust it entirely to the "natural inquisitors," the Bishops.

He therefore sent two commissaries into the South of France, to represent his plenary authority in the dioceses where the Albigenses and Waldenses were numerous, and require every Bishop, Priest, or layman to assist in the horrible service on their requisition, under peril of ruin in this world, and, in the world to come, damnation. These two envoys were Cistertian Monks, brother Rainier and brother Guy; but the order of St. Bernard was not sufficiently savage to furnish chief Janizaries to the Sultan of the West, and we have not much to record concerning their operations. For a few years others were appointed, who did their utmost to revive the zeal of the multitude against the Albigenses and Waldenses of Aquitaine, Narbonne, and other provinces; but, while the eloquence of their sermons drew some applause, their cruelties provoked indignation; and, at length, one of them, Peter of Castelnau, was killed by a soldier in the neighbourhood of Toulouse. Innocent III. declared him a martyr, gave him the title of Blessed, and called on the Church to devise some more effectual method for the inquisition and punishment of heresy. The crusade against heretics was raging, it is true, and Simon de Montfort was laying waste the county of Toulouse. Cities were besieged, taken, and sacked. Hundreds of martyrs had been already cut to pieces, or burnt upon the field of battle; but it was evident that relays of volunteer troops could not always be levied, and that there was a point beyond which Princes and Barons would not be carried, in slaughtering their subjects and impoverishing their estates, to satisfy the vengeance of the Church.

Again, in the church of the Lateran, or, as it was also called, the palace of Constantine, Innocent convened a Council. Being a man of words, no less than of deeds, he chose to be the Preacher, and delivered two vehement sermons, one at the opening, and the other at the close, of a session of twenty days. The sermons are preserved; but contain nothing remarkable beyond exhortations to take up the Cross, and go to Jerusalem. On the word "passover," he founded all his doctrine. That word signifies a passage from one place to another. He, like St. Paul in his text, desired to celebrate a passover, a "passage of the Holy Land," there to storm the Holy City, and kill the infidels. The chapters of this Council—fourth of Lateran—are very copious, but contain little more than a verbal repetition of the acts of similar assemblies, and of letters apostolic concerning heretics; but more was done at that Council than appears on the face of the record.

Foulques, Bishop of Toulouse, came from amidst the ruins of a desolated diocese to make his appearance in the Council, and brought with him a youthful zealot, a Spaniard, Domingo de Guzman. His mother, Juana, whose imagination seems to have been as fiery as that of many of her daughters in the present generation, had dreamt that she was going to be delivered of a dog, carrying a brand to set the world on fire. Her child was precisely to her taste. He made rapid proficiency in the school of Palencia, then one of the best in Europe, soon obtained preferment in the Church, was chosen by the Bishop of Osma, his own Diocesan, to accompany him on an inquisitorial journey into France, and signalised himself there by great address in dealing with heretics, some of whom he converted, by means of an argument written on prepared paper, that would not burn, although put three times into the fire, his own peculiar element. At Toulouse, the scene of that performance, he had conceived the design of raising a new order of Preachers, a sermon being in those days the approved preliminary to a burning, as we shall shortly see; and one of his adherents, Pierre Cellan, gave him some houses to serve himself and his other companions for endowment, and for a first monastery. Domingo was just the man to serve Innocent; and although this Pope had already engaged the Council to determine that no new orders should be established, but that the old ones should be mended, he did not hesitate to give the hopeful Prior of St. Romain authority to prepare a set of rules. "The oracle" had spoken otherwise in the Lateran, but in the Vatican he pronounced otherwise again, yet prudently shaded his fallibility from immediate observation by refraining from the publication of a Bull.

Nevertheless, Fray Domingo proceeded to establish his fraternity, obtained a church and cells in Toulouse, and, on the accession of a new Pope, in the year following, applied to him for the document that should invest him with full authority. Honorius III., favourable to a scheme of so vital importance to the Papacy, received the application graciously. This son of a dreaming mother, when at the Pontiff's feet, related a vision with which he had been honoured since his arrival at the threshold of the Apostles. He said, that when praying, one night, in a church, he had seen Christ, angry, and holding in His uplifted hand three javelins, to be launched against sinners,—one to destroy the proud, another the avaricious, and a third the voluptuous. He declared that he had seen the Holy Mother embrace the feet of her Son, imploring mercy, and had heard Him acknowledge that her intercession had appeased His wrath; but that He had two servants there, whom He would introduce to her. One was Dominic, (as we call him,) and the other was Francis, afterwards famous as founder of the Franciscans, whom he did not then know, but met him in the church next morning. Honorius was confirmed, by the recital, in his sentiment of approbation, and granted Dominic two Bulls; one declaring that he and his brethren were champions of the faith, and true lights of the world, and the other empowering them to possess property, and perform their intended functions. Not to contradict the Council which prohibited the creation of new monastic orders, he called them Canons regular. The Bulls were dated September 12th, 1217.

At this time Dominic somewhat resembled a Bishop *in partibus*, having a title, but not a throne. He was commissioned to be a champion of the faith, and all the members of his order were to be champions of the faith; but as yet he had no troop of familiars, nor any fixed tribunal before which to summon the suspected. However, he determined to begin his work without loss of time, and, on the same day, making a speech to those who came with the usual congratulations, told them that the Pope had conferred on him a new office; and assured them that he was determined to defend the faith manfully, and that, if spiritual and ecclesiastical weapons should be insufficient, he had made up his mind to call the secular power to his aid, and to excite and impel Catholic Princes to take up arms against heretics, that their memory might be utterly blotted out. From that time he sent out Preachers, whose business was to inflame the populace, who received repeated assurances of protection from the Pope, and were, doubtless, worthy to be called Inquisitors. Meanwhile, Dominic pursued the organisation of a system, and soon formed a "third order,"* called the "Militia of Christ," to fight as crusaders against heretics. These assisted the Dominicans of the first order in searching out heresy, and, being considered part of their family, were called *familiars*. Honorius gave them his formal approbation, and first we find them active in Italy about the year 1224. But not only in Italy. For in this year the Emperor Frederic II., in a decree published at Padua, speaks of "the Inquisitors whom the Apostolic See had appointed in any part of the empire." And "we declare," said he, "that the Friars Preachers and the Friars Minors, deputed in our empire for the affair of faith against heretics, are under our special protection."

The Holy Office was not yet erected; but the ground was opened, and the Clergy, especially the Dominicans, were busily laying the foundations. And the pontificate of Gregory IX. was to be distinguished by a visible advancement of the fabric. At Toulouse, which had been conquered by the crusaders, and where the last Count had preserved his title, with a shadow of power, by abandoning the faith of his ancestors, a Council was holden in the year 1229; and, although its chapters generally resemble those of previous assemblies of the kind, there is a specialty of character in them which indicates the near approach of a settled Inquisition. It was decreed, in substance, that the Bishops should

* He had founded a second order of women.

appoint a Priest, and two or three laymen of good repute, in every parish, whom they should swear to seek out heretics exactly, and frequently, in houses, in caverns, and in all places where they might be concealed; and, after having taken precaution, in order that none might escape, they should give immediate notice to the Bishop, the Lord of the place, or his bailiff. The Lords were required to search in villages, houses, woods, or other hiding-places; and if any one of them was known to allow a heretic to take refuge on his domain, he should himself be punished. Negligent bailiffs were to be chastised, and houses wherein the guilty had found shelter were to be pulled down. Yet none should suffer as a heretic until condemned by the Bishop, or by an ecclesiastic having power to act. Any one might apprehend a heretic. Converted heretics, although reconciled to the Church, were not to live in a village suspected of heresy, "and, to show that they detest their former error, they shall wear two crosses, of a different colour from their dress, one on the right, and the other on the left, breast." But they could never be admitted to any public office, except by dispensation of the Pope. Persons converted against their will were to suffer perpetual imprisonment. An exact list of all the inhabitants was to be kept in every parish; and all males above fourteen years, and females above twelve, should swear to the Bishop, or his delegate, that they utterly renounced heresy, held the Catholic faith, and would persecute and denounce heretics. All who refused to swear thus would be dealt with as suspected of heresy; and so would all who failed to confess and to communicate three times every year. And at this Council of Toulouse, *for the first time*, the laity were forbidden to read the holy Scriptures of the Old and New Testament. An aged person might possess a Latin Psalter, a Breviary, or the Hours of the Virgin; "but," said the fathers of the Council, "we most strictly forbid them to have the above-said books translated into a vulgar tongue."

The reader shall not be wearied with tracking the Dominicans in their inquisitorial itinerancy. Neither shall we transcribe, or even abbreviate, the chapters of Council after Council, and the Papal Briefs which were issued to instruct them in their vocation, to give sanction to their procedure, or to exact the concurrence of the civil power with their violence. It is enough to say, that the Provincials of the Dominicans were gradually invested with an authority closely resembling that of the Inquisitors-General in later times, and that their operations extended just so far as the Papal power could prevail. Happily for Germany, frequent misunderstanding, or open conflict, between the Pope and the Emperor hindered the progress of Inquisitors in the empire; but they found entire support in France and Spain, and in most of the Italian states. Even the republic of Venice received the Inquisitors; but insisted on associating her own Magistrates with them in every case, and gained the point, much to the annoyance of those Papal delegates. When the objects of their pursuit escaped to other countries, they pursued them into every accessible retreat. Refugees in the island of Sardinia, for example, found themselves beset with the emissaries of St. Dominic from Rome. These emissaries even established themselves in the remote region of Servia; and, as if to crown the opprobrium of their spurious Christianity in Asia, they prowled about in the territories occupied by the crusaders in Syria and Palestine, endeavouring to preserve the godless garrisons with the attendant rabble that held precarious possession, from influences unfavourable to the priesthood. We now proceed to examine one of the records of the Inquisition of Toulouse, probably the most ancient document of the kind extant.

CHAPTER II.

THE INQUISITION OF TOULOUSE.

At the prayer of St. Louis, King of France, in the year 1255, Alexander IV. constituted the Provincial of the Dominicans and the Guardian of the Franciscans in Paris Inquisitors-General for all that kingdom. And in the beginning of the fourteenth century we find regular tribunals, jurisdiction conducted with accord of three several authorities,—the civil in the Magistrates, the ordinary ecclesiastical in the Bishops, and the pontifical in the Inquisitors,—with a rigorous administration of prison-discipline and capital punishment, publicly inflicted. This is what it is usual to call *the ancient Inquisition.*

Philip Van Limborch, Professor of Theology among the Dutch Remonstrants, and author of a general history of the Inquisition, obtained a manuscript which had been taken from the archives of the Inquisition of Toulouse, a city wrenched from the Counts of that title by the crusaders of the twelfth and thirteenth centuries, and made by Dominic the cradle of his order and seat of the earliest of those tribunals. The document was a parchment volume, held between two covers, or pieces of wood. On each of these covers was cut the title: L. SENTENCIARUM, "Book of Sentences;" that is to say, of sentences passed on culprits in the Inquisition of Toulouse. Each record was subscribed in the handwriting of one of the Notaries at least, of whom four had made the original reports, and thus authenticated the fair copies, adding to the signature a seal of office. Limborch gives the *fac-simile* of each seal, and preserves in his reprint of the volume the barbarous orthography of the yet more barbarous Latin, in order that every letter of his original may be expressed, merely putting syllables at length, instead of abbreviations. His edition is a folio of the size usually given by the Wetsteins,* of four hundred and twenty pages, with the folios of the manuscript exhibited in the margin. I have carefully examined this very remarkable evidence of the doings of the first Inquisition, and will endeavour to give, I think for the first time in our language, an idea of what they were.

What is now called, after the Portuguese, an *Auto da Fé*, or "Act of Faith," was then called a "General Sermon of Faith," because the proceedings of each of those gaol deliveries were opened by a sermon, and the same custom continued down to the latest of them. The "sentences" which the Inquisitors delivered at fourteen "sermons" are preserved here, syllable by syllable, as the Notaries drew them up. The first is dated on the first Sunday of Lent, 1308.† It was holden in the cathedral of St.

* The imprint is "Amstelodami, apud Henricum Wetstenium. CIↃ IↃ C XCII."

† The authenticity of the MS. is tested by the accuracy of the dates. There are two errors, however, which strengthen the proof. For 1308, the scribe wrote 1307, by putting VII instead of VIII. And by the

Stephen; and for the others the same building or a market-place was chosen, where a great crowd of spectators might be assembled. A Seneschal, a Judge, a Serjeant-at-arms, and a civil Governor, representing the Sovereign, swore on the holy Gospels faith to the Lord Jesus Christ and to the holy Roman Church, promising to defend them with all their might, to pursue and take—if they could—all heretics in belief, and their aiders and abettors, and accuse and present them to the Church and the Inquisitors. They swore, engaging that they would not give office of any sort to the aforesaid pestilential persons, nor to any reputed to be such, nor admit the like into their family, their friendship, their service, or their counsel, if they knew it; and if they came to know of having unwittingly harboured any, they would instantly put such away. And then they reiterated the vow of obedience to God, the Church, and the Inquisitors.

A company of "Consuls," or civil Magistrates, next approached, and were adjured after the same manner, word for word.

But the Archbishop of the province and the neighbouring Bishops were not well content; for between them and the Roman delegates there had been jealousy from the beginning. It was by dint of negotiation, no doubt, that they obtained a place at the "sermons" as something more than mere spectators; and, at length, the Archbishop was able to exercise an official power, and authorise some of his Bishops to be present. They, when prevented by business, or deterred by humanity, sent "canonical commissaries" to act as advocates of the persons accused, if there was any ground for palliation, or any space for pity.

The oaths being taken, the two Inquisitors for all the kingdom of France gave sentence of excommunication against all that had any way hindered or opposed them and their subordinates in office, either openly or secretly.

The "House of Inquisition" in Toulouse—and there was another such house in Carcassonne, and, most probably, others in other places—was emptied of its tenants, who appeared in companies in the cathedral. They are said, in this Book of Sentences, to have been "brought out of the

omission of an I at the seventh sermon, he makes it 1315 instead of 1316. De Morgan's tables help me to verify the dates and the records at the same time.

wall" (*educti de muro*), a phrase which indicates the kind of dungeons wherein they had been literally *immured*, models of those which later historians have described in other countries. Some of them were sentenced to wear crosses; and others, by an act of grace, were excused from carrying that badge, yet were to do heavy penance. Take a sentence for each class, as we find it in the book: and first, of penitents marked with crosses.

"In the name of the Lord, Amen. We, the aforesaid Inquisitors of heretical pravity," (Brother Bernard Guy, and Brother John de Belna, of the order of Preachers,) "and the Commissary-delegate of the aforesaid Archbishop of Toulouse, and I, the aforesaid Brother Bernard Guy, by virtue of commission from the reverend Fathers and Lords in Christ, G——, and R——, and G——, Bishops," (the names of the sees are obscure and unimportant,) "in what pertains to them concerning the undermentioned persons of their dioceses." Then follow fifty-seven names, with designations, showing that whole families had been seized by the Inquisitors, and that the Gospel had penetrated beyond the Pyrenees into Spain. "These men and women, immured by way of penance for crimes of heretical pravity which they had committed, and in humble obedience to the mandates of Us and of the Church, having been in the wall now for many years, We, willing mercifully to mitigate their pain and penance, by grace release them from the prison of the wall. But we enjoin on them, all and each, under obligation of the oath they have rendered, that, in exchange for the said penance and prison, they henceforth perpetually wear two crosses of yellow felt on every garment, except the shirt," (of size prescribed,) "one on the breast, and the other on the back, between the shoulders, without which appearing they must not be seen either within doors or out of doors. If the crosses be torn, or worn out, they must be mended or renewed; and as long as these persons live they must, every year, visit the church of St. Stephen of Toulouse, on the festival of the saint, and the church of St. Saturnine of Toulouse, in the octaves of Easter, and hear high mass and sermon in each. They must also confess thrice every year, before Christmas, Easter, and Whitsuntide, and communicate in those festivals, unless they abstain by counsel of their Priest. On every Sunday and feast-day they must hear full mass in their parish church, and a sermon whenever there is one in the parish where they are, unless lawfully excused. They must abstain from work on feast-days, and never bear any public office. They must keep a lenten fast at Advent, refrain from divinations and lots, and take no interest on money. They must also persecute heretics, by what name soever they be called, as well as their believers, abettors, receivers, and defenders, and fugitives for heresy. With all their power they must honour the Catholic faith, ecclesiastical persons, the rights of churches, and the office of the Inquisition. They must also make pilgrimage, according to directions contained in letters which will be given to them; but which we command them to ask for, keep, and follow the directions they contain. We and ours, and our successors in the office of the Inquisition, retain plenary power to throw the above persons, or any of them, into the aforesaid wall again, even without any new cause, or to increase or diminish, to mitigate or remit, this punishment to any of them, as we, or any of our successors, may think fit."

Sometimes it was thought expedient to impose a dreary penance, quite enough to make life burdensome, but without the yellow crosses. This is designated "arbitrary penance without crosses." But the penitents at large were a privileged class, reconciled to their Church, restored to her bosom, hugged in her cold embrace, and envied by the fellow-prisoners whom they left behind.

On Sunday, April 23d, 1312, on the feast of St. George the Martyr, and "for the honour of the holy Roman Church," Bernard Guy and a fellow-Inquisitor, with the usual array of ecclesiastical and civil forces, held a sermon in the accustomed place. The number of their victims was not unusually large; but we can count the company of prisoners this day before them the more easily, because the Notary happened to set down their names with a mark (¶) of separation. Here are men, women, and children, whole families, dragged into their presence, garbed in wretchedness, and stricken with despair. An officer of the Holy Office reads over a catalogue of eighty-seven names: "Thou, Raymund Vasco; and thou Bernarda Wilhelma, formerly wife of such an one; and thou, ——; and thou, ——; and thou, ——;" on to the end. "So gravely and in so many ways have you offended in the damned crime of heresy, as has been read and repeated to you intelligibly in the vulgar tongue; you all being personally before us in this day and place, to receive penance, and to hear your definitive sentence peremptorily pronounced upon you, and desiring, as you say, with good heart and unfeigned faith, to return to the unity of the Church, and now again publicly abjuring all heresy, and all favour and belief of heretics of every sect, and all stubbornness, and belief, and rite, and favour of heretical pravity, and promising to keep and defend the orthodox faith, and to persecute heretics, and detect and bring them out wherever you know them to be; and swearing that you will simply and faithfully obey the prescribed mandates of the Church, and ours, for the benefit granted to you of absolution from the excommunication with which, for the said faults, you were bound; if, indeed, you return to the unity of the Church with all your heart, and keep the commandments we have enjoined upon you, the most holy Gospels of God being placed before us, that our judgment may proceed from the presence of God, and our eyes may see equity." The reader is breathless. This long-protracted sentence should end kindly. The penitents have much to do. They are to be very active in persecution. They have promised to render large service to the Church, which will require great readiness and diligence. They are absolved. Brother Bernard invokes the God of mercy and equity. The ever blessed Gospel is before him. But, no! hear it out. The reader finishes in these words: "Sitting at this tribunal, and having the counsel of good men, learned in civil and canon law, we condemn you, by sentence in this writing, to *perpetual prison of the wall*, there to perform healthful penance with bread of grief and water of tribulation."

The "benefit of absolution" is not yet exhausted. Three men, one of them aged, and three women, two of them widows, receive sentence thus: "And because you have offended more largely and more gravely, and therefore deserve weightier punishment, we determine that you shall be perpetually shut up in closer wall and straiter place, in fetters and chains." The sentence then draws to its close in the usual form, and ends with a threat of yet sorer punishment on any who may be found to have suppressed the least fact when under examination.

From very copious notes of the examination of Waldenses,

although they cannot be regarded as faithful records, much might be extracted to throw light on the domestic habits and ecclesiastical position of that long-persecuted people. At another Sermon we find, amidst many companions in suffering and confession, Hugo de Cernon. From childhood he had witnessed the piety of his father, who did not refuse hospitality to the wandering Barbe. The Inquisitors extorted the names of thirteen persons whom he had seen as guests at various times, or had himself entertained after his father's death. He had prayed with them before dinner and after,* on bended knees, leaning on a seat, "according to their manner and rite of praying." He had heard their discourse and received their exhortations, and learnt, as they are charged with maintaining, that judicial oaths are forbidden in the New Testament. They denied the fable of purgatory. The Inquisitors represent him as saying that he had twice confessed his sins to those Waldenses, and received absolution and penance from them, "although he knew that they were not Priests ordained by a Bishop of the Roman Church."† Juliana, wife of Vincent Vertelperio, had been guilty of the same crime of hospitality; for she and her husband had suffered some of their Pastors to sleep in their house, and they had joined in family prayer in the same simple manner. The alleged confessions of these Waldenses are so exceedingly alike, that one cannot help regarding them as forced or fabricated answers to a uniform set of questions, with the addition, now and then, of some trifling incident that is only noticed because it may serve to aggravate the case. Juliana, for example, had accepted a needle from one of them, and this is noted down. In another house the custom of family prayer, first learnt from a visiter, had been continued. The

* The Inquisitor Eymeric, describing the marks by which Waldenses might be known, after some incredible accusations of licentiousness, adds what bears a beautiful appearance of truth: "When they take their places at table, they say, 'May He who blessed the five barley loaves in the wilderness for His disciples, bless this our table!' And when they rise, they repeat that passage of the Revelation: 'Blessing, and glory, and wisdom, and thanksgiving, and honour, and power, and might, be unto our God for ever and ever! Amen.' They always [say this] raising their hands and eyes towards heaven." (Directorium Inquisitorum, p. 441.)

† That they certainly were not, but by Bishops of their own. The tale of confession is extremely improbable. Allix, on the Ancient Churches of Piedmont, demonstrates the dishonesty of inquisitorial reports.

offence of one man chiefly consisted in his having carried money and clothing from some humane persons to Waldenses that were lying in "the wall." For such aggravations of their guilt many, in these fourteen Sermons, were delivered over to the secular arm, and burnt alive.

The case of a Priest named John Phillibert, even so far as it can be gathered from the "Book of Sentences," is remarkable. When officiating in the parish of St. Lawrence, in Burgundy, he was chosen, together with another person, to go in search of a fugitive Waldense. Like Saul of Tarsus, he received letters from the Chief Priest, the Inquisitor of heresy, empowering him to call in help, if help were necessary, to arrest the man, and bring him back. With what success he performed that journey into Gascony, is not stated; but his communication with the persecuted Christians had produced such an effect on him, that he went to visit them, not as a familiar of the Inquisition, but as an inquirer after truth and peace. The Waldenses welcomed him into their society. He was introduced into an extensive circle, visited from house to house, and from town to town. He shared in their hospitality as freely as if he had been a Barbe. He prayed in companies gathered to meet him, and attended in congregations where the word of God was preached. This was, of course, unpardonable in the sight of the Inquisitors, who maintained that the Waldensian Ministers were mere laymen, not having been ordained by any Bishop of the Roman Church.* They invited him to join their company, which he readily consented to do; for, notwithstanding his knowledge that the Inquisitors persecuted them, he believed them to be good people. But so far were those honest Christians from flattering their convert, that one, Cristino, told him that it would be better for him to be a swineherd than a Priest, in mortal sin, singing mass.

Even the partial defection of a Priest could not escape the vigilance of the Inquisitors. Like many of his order in those ages, he continued to serve at the altar after he had ceased to believe in the doctrine of the mass; but his conscience, more scrupulous than enlightened, could not be reconciled to a judicial abjuration; and when Friar Guy, of Rheims, Inquisitor of heresy in Burgundy, required him, on

* "— Qui non erant nec sunt sacerdotes ordinati per aliquem episcopum *Romanæ Ecclesiæ*, sed erant layci."

some occasion, to swear upon the Gospels, he refused, and, on twice repeating the refusal, was arrested, and placed under observation. The persecution continued. Ere long he was summoned into the presence of the same Inquisitor, in the Archbishop's palace at Besançon; and, in the presence of ten or twelve witnesses and a Notary, submitted to be sworn, but avowed his correspondence with the Waldensians, and his belief that the Inquisitors, in persecuting them, were sinning against God. What means were employed to overcome his constancy, we know not; but he wavered so far as to swear, that he renounced the Waldensian sect, and promise that he would help to seize its followers wherever he could find them. Perhaps the dread of scandal, as they would call it, induced the Inquisitors to release him from durance without penance, and allow him to return into Gascony, where he again joined the Waldenses, visiting their congregations from place to place, eating and drinking in their houses, and everywhere uniting in their secret worship. Often, at night, he listened to their readings of the Gospels and Epistles in the vulgar tongue, followed by earnest expositions and exhortations. Still, pursuing that fatal policy of concealment and consequent equivocation which so frequently injured the work of God far more than the utmost violence of its enemies could have done, he continued to officiate as a Romish Priest. During fourteen years he thus dissimulated, sometimes elevating the host, and sometimes visiting imprisoned brethren, and conveying food and clothing into their prisons,* at the hazard of his life.

At length, in October, 1311, he was again arrested in Toulouse, and brought into the presence of the Inquisitor. The register of his abjuration at Besançon was produced; and, as there could be no mercy for one relapsed, he was finally condemned. And this is the sentence: "Since the Church has nothing more that for thy demerits she can do against thee, We pronounce and declare by these presents that thou, John Phillibert, Presbyter, aforesaid, art to be degraded from thy holy orders; and, when degraded, art to be given over to the secular court and judgment, and from

* It is notorious enough that, until a very recent period, the prisons of Europe have been open to casual visiters, and that the prisoners depended on visiters, chiefly or entirely, for their daily food. And the Inquisition had not yet its secret dungeons.

that time we hereby leave thee to that court, affectionately praying the same, as the canonical sanctions advise, to preserve thy life and limb unhurt, and allowing thee, if thou wilt worthily repent, the sacrament of penance and the eucharist." And from this we may fairly infer that he had not repented, but that at last, as he had so often been exhorted in the discourses of the Waldenses of Gascony, he preferred suffering death to making shipwreck of his conscience.

And he quickly suffered martyrdom. His diocesan, the Bishop of Auch, had died; so that there was no one empowered to degrade him, except the Pope. But Pope John XXII., then at Avignon, himself a Frenchman, and formerly Bishop in the very province of Toulouse, gladly issued a Bull authorising the Archbishop to degrade John Phillibert, and give him over to the secular arm. On Sunday, June 15th, 1320, the Archbishop proceeded to the cathedral; and, surrounded by a multitude of Clergy of all degrees, "zealous for the orthodox faith," and by a greater multitude of laity, had the delinquent Presbyter brought from prison, attired in his robes, and set him on high in view of all, to hear the records of previous examinations read, and the Papal warrant of degradation. While this was done, one Raymund Fish sat by to take notes of the formalities. The form of degradation, as prescribed by the Metropolitan, was after this manner. The martyr being clad in robes of all the orders, with all sorts of sacred vessels and sacramental symbols placed on the credence, they took a chalice and paten from his hand, to divest him of power to say mass. They stripped him of the sacerdotal stole, to signify that, among the Waldenses, he had lost the robe of innocence, and, therewith, the office of the priesthood. With the dalmatic they removed "the ornament of the diaconate, the garment of gladness, and the vesture of salvation." Taking from his hand a book of the Gospels, they deprived him of "power to read the office in the Church of God." The Deacon's robe was taken from his shoulders, and, with it, the power of exercising the functions of the Deacon's office. And the instruments of that office, a chalice, paten, pitcher (*urceolus*), water, and finger-cloth, were taken from him, to denote that he was prohibited their future use. In like manner the tunic of sub-Deacon was removed, showing that, with the ornament of that office, he had lost the use of it unto righteousness and health. From his left arm they took the maniple of the sub-diaconate, and ministry thereby designated. They made him deliver up the book of Epistles, out of which he had learned more than it liked them he should know, and thus took away the faculty of reading the Epistles in the Church. The instrument with which the Acolyth lights candles being snatched away from him, he learned that he should thenceforth have no authority to light them. So with the pitcher, again removed, passed away his authority to mingle water with sacramental wine. With the book of exorcisms, too, they took from him the power which the Church professes to bestow on her meaner Ministers, to cast out devils,—a service which their superiors may well be excused from. And his Reader's book being taken, his lips were closed from reading in the congregation. Lastly, they took out of his hand the keys of the church, inasmuch as he might not open nor enter the church again. Then, in the name of the Holy Trinity, Raymund Fish declared that he was deposed and degraded from every ecclesiastical order, honour, benefice, and privilege. "And, nevertheless, we pronounce and say to the noble man, Lord Guyard Guy, Seneschal of Toulouse, here present, that he may receive thee, now degraded, into his jurisdiction. Yet we instantly require and pray him that he would so temper his sentence concerning thee, *that thou mayest not be in peril of death, nor suffer mutilation of limb*." The Presbyter Phillibert had thus dwindled down, step by step, from the superhuman dignity of Priest into the vile estate of a layman. Yet one vestige of his former dignity remained. The sacerdotal crown was on his head; and to destroy this a barber was employed, whose razor reduced him to perfect baldness, and thus he stood before the crowd with the last mark of ignominy on him. Seized by the executioners, he was then dragged out of the cathedral, and thrown into the flames; and we may hope that the more truthful boldness of his latter days indicated the presence of that faith that God crowns with glory. But the Notary made no note of the victim's words after they had consigned him to the mercy of Guyard Guy.*

* Concerning this matter of "degradation" a brief note may not be unimportant. For information the canonists refer us to the Sixth Book of the Decretals, tit. ix., cap. 2. We find there the first legal document

Not only did they burn the living, but the dead. In their examinations of the Waldenses and other reputed heretics, they obtained information of many who had died in their fellowship, and then issued formal sentences of condemnation. One such sentence will suffice for all. "Considering that the crime of heresy, because of its vastness and enormity, ought, according to both canonical and civil sanctions, not only to be punished in the living, but also in the dead; having God before our eyes, &c., &c., we declare and pronounce the aforesaid" (two men and four women) "to have been receivers, believers, helpers, and abettors, when they were alive, of the Waldensian heretics; and that they died without repenting of the crime of Waldensian heresy which they had committed; and we condemn, as such, the said deceased men and women, and their memory. And we command, in sign of

on the subject, which has great historical value. It is a letter from Boniface VIII.—who began to reign in 1294, and continued a little more than eight years—to the Bishop of Bourges, who did not know how to perform the ceremony of degradation. That ceremony, therefore, must have been novel, or it would have been provided for. But it was novel in France, and it was introduced there *together with the Inquisition.* Boniface gives general directions, leaving the Bishop to work them into form. The Archbishop of Toulouse appears to have drawn up his own form, using the liberty, as to ritual, which every Bishop then enjoyed, although such appeals to the Pope as that of the Bishop of Bourges tended to curtail the liberty. The act, however, having relation to the priesthood only, of which the Pope was chief, there was a reason why he might give the general instruction to use "these, or like words" (*hæc vel similia*); and the Archbishop, thus fortified, could truly say that the form we have abridged in the text, was lawfully delivered (*à jure tradita*). But let it now be well noted that there is an established form of degradation, with a very full rubric, and that throughout the Romish Church it is in force. It will serve either to save the honour of the Church, by depriving criminous Clerks of their sacerdotal character before they are subjected to the sentence of civil law, or to consign heretical Clerks to civil punishment on the judgment of a Church court, or Inquisition. *This is now quite practicable in Italy and Spain.* An analysis of the present "Form of Degradation" would show that it is thoroughly inquisitorial; but it is enough to say that the concurrence of other Bishops with the one officiating, or deputing to officiate, is dispensed with in a cause of heresy (*in causa hæresis*), that the secular Magistrate is *required to be present*, that the old request for *mercy* is retained in *the very words* used by the Archbishop of Toulouse in the year 1320, and that the last sentence of the rubric, which closes all, is, "Which being done, the ministers of the secular court take the degraded person into their custody, and depart." (*Quo facto, ministri sæcularis curiæ degradatum sub sua custodia recipiunt, et discedunt.*)

perdition, that the bones of the said William and Michael, and of the said women, if they can be distinguished from the bones of the faithful, be extumulated or exhumed from the sacred cemeteries, cast out thence, and burned." This sentence was passed at Toulouse, at the Sermon celebrated on Sunday, under the octaves of the Nativity of the Blessed Mary, Virgin, 1322. And the Roman hyenas have ever since employed themselves, on all possible opportunities, in digging for carcases of heretics. Up to the year 1831, it may be confidently affirmed, that the bodies of deceased Protestants in Spain were liable to the grossest outrage, which the populace were instructed to think it became them, as "good Catholics," to perpetrate. A royal decree then made the interment of an English Protestant lawful, where burial-grounds could be purchased and enclosed; but where that is not the case, there is no assurance that the grave will not be violated.

Assuming universal control, the Inquisition of Toulouse laid its hands on books, as well as persons; and we find it stated that, on the 28th of November, 1319, at the requisition and mandate of Bernard Guy, two large waggon-loads of Hebrew books, being as many as could be found on searching the houses of the Jews, were drawn through the streets of Toulouse, with a procession of servants of the royal court, and a crier going before, proclaiming with a loud voice that the books, said to be copies of the Talmud, contained blasphemies against Christianity, and, having been examined by persons learned in the language, were to be burnt. And they were burnt accordingly. Gregory IX., a zealous persecutor of the Jews, had commanded the Talmud to be burnt, which was done by the Chancellor of Paris in the year 1230, before an assemblage of Clergy and people; and, after an interval of thirteen years, there was another solemn burning of that work at Paris, and probably in other parts of France, by order of Innocent IV. The works of Raymund Lully, father of oriental learning in Christendom, who gave his life for Christ in Africa, where the Moors stoned him to death, were burnt by order of Gregory XI. in the year 1376. This was a revival of the old pagan custom of burning the sacred writings; and the allegation that there were blasphemies in the Talmud, and heresies in other books, however true it may have been, was insufficient to justify the method taken to silence, rather than to refute. Here, however, we mark the beginning of the literary persecution which is conducted by the Congregations of the Inquisition and the Index, as earnestly as at their first establishment.

Another incident from this "Book of Sentences," and we have done with the Inquisition of Toulouse.

On Sunday, June 28th, 1321, the sound of a trumpet was heard in the market-place of Castrum de Cordua, a town in the diocese of Alby. It was to summon the inhabitants to that place, in order to hear a Sermon, or proclamation of the two Inquisitors and their Assistants, and a Commissary and other representatives of the Bishop, whose letters patent, addressed to the Consuls, or Magistrates, were there produced and read. The Consuls and their Councillors hastened to the spot, bringing with them a petition, which was to be read in reply to the Bishop's pastoral, and the sentence of the Inquisitors. The fact was, that when the Inquisitors had proceeded to exercise their vocation there, and imprisoned some of the inhabitants, the townsfolk turned out in a body, attempted to break into the dungeons, and poured forth volleys of threatening against their priestly assailants. The Inquisitors fled in terror from the town, and published an anathema, which was followed by the fearful consequences of such a sentence, until the people were obliged to sue for mercy. The humble and reverent supplication, therefore, recited the offence and its penalty, and offered, on the part of the inhabitants in general, submission to whatever penance and retribution the Inquisitors might think proper to ordain. Piteously did they implore for absolution and release from the ban laid upon them, promising and swearing devout and perpetual obedience to the Inquisitors and their successors, to perform whatsoever it might please them to enjoin; and called on the Notaries of the Inquisition there present to register the vow. And the whole multitude of Consuls and Councillors, of men and of women, raised a dolorous cry, in token of repentance, and in affirmation of the prayer. Then the Inquisitors and Commissary deigned to accept the supplication, made the Magistrates, one by one, swear to fulfil the conditions of pardon, and, holding up a book of the Gospels in sight of the people,—for it seems that they did not yet swear them on a crucifix,—required the whole multitude to raise their hands in abjuration of all purpose to resist the Inquisition. The whole multitude then sang, mournfully, a penitential psalm; and, as the last notes died away, the Commissary pronounced a solemn absolution of all and each of the "university" of people in that place. This done, the penance was enjoined. Considering the clemency of holy Church, and the penitential humiliation of both Magistrates and people, they ordained that the town should build a chapel, without prejudice of the parish church, of a form and magnitude prescribed, and to be well furnished and endowed. It should be intituled with the name of Peter the Martyr,—that Dominican Inquisitor-General who lost his life, in the cause of the Inquisition, by the hand of an assassin between Milan and Como, in the year 1252, and whom the fraternity worship as their peculiar Saint,—and three others, placing pictures of all of them over the altar, and as many images of them in wood or stone. Outside the building were to be exhibited three stone statues, one of the Bishop, and two of the Inquisitors. The building, its sacred vessels and sacred pictures, with every ornament and appurtenance, was to be completed on the site chosen, to be of the magnitude and material required, and to be ready by the time appointed, under a heavy fine, which fine would be repeated every two years until the finishing of the work. Added to this was a heavy tax, levied on the town for the solace of the Bishop and Inquisitors, and recoverable at their discretion. And to bind them the more certainly, a deed, engrossed in readiness, was signed and sealed upon the spot. The deed, moreover, empowered the Inquisition to do its pleasure in the town thenceforth, and thus gave it a legal sanction under the hand and seal of the Magistrates themselves. After such an event we cannot but say that the Tribunal was fully established in the kingdom of France; and with this humiliating fact must close our notice of the Inquisition of Toulouse, merely observing that the followers of our Lord Jesus Christ were not the only persons subjected to punishment, but others, accused of immorality and witchcraft. Multitudes of Beguins, as they were called, whose only offence was, that they desired to revert to the most rigorous discipline of the Franciscan order, as they understood it, were accused of the most disgusting impurities, yet far too monstrous to be credible, and burnt alive as heretics.

CHAPTER III.

LAWS AND CUSTOMS.

During about two centuries and a half, the Inquisition was advancing towards an established form. At Toulouse, indeed, it soon became complete, although not yet independent of the Bishops, as in after-times. There, at Carcassone, and probably at a few other places, the Inquisitors had *houses*, that is to say, prisons, and courts, for the exercise of their juridical authority. At first they proceeded arbitrarily, using all means within reach for the accomplishment of their purpose, but without any code of instructions. From time to time the Popes issued Bulls or Briefs, just as circumstances might require, and generally with respect to some particular district or case; but as every such document had the full authority of the Apostolic See, it was carefully preserved, and afterwards referred to as of universal sanction. And as the canon-law in general depends on such documents, so does the ever-growing code of the Inquisition for the most part. The *secret* began, as being necessary in the management of affairs that could not be divulged with safety; and the pontificate of Boniface VIII., from 1294 to 1303, is more particularly marked as the time when secret examinations became an acknowledged part of inquisitorial jurisprudence, and gave those courts, at once and for ever, a character of their own. Terror, and sometimes actual torture, were made use of, to assist the Notaries to fabricate reports of confession. And it is remarkable that the evidence preserved in the Tolosan "Sentences" from 1307 to 1323, entirely consists of alleged confessions, which would not have been the case if any method of humane and fair investigation had been followed. First, familiars and other informers gave the Inquisitors intelligence enough to convict their subject of heresy; and, this being done, the accused person was required to confess; and we have already seen that the most trifling word or action was considered sufficient evidence of his being a heretic, or of having aided, abetted, sheltered, or approved of heretics.

The action of the ancient Inquisition was various and

intermittent. In France it appears as the sequel of the crusades of Bernard and Montfort; and after the first zeal of the Kings, who obtained the annexation of Toulouse to their territories, by the ruin of its Counts and the depopulation of the towns, had passed away; and when the Clergy could more effectually resist the encroachment of a tribunal which represented the person of the Pope, with derogation of episcopal rights, the people and Parliaments also resisted the interference of an alien and cruel power. Nor would the Kings willingly allow the Court of Rome to meddle with their domestic affairs. Perhaps the "Gallic liberties" would not have been obtained for the Clergy, but for a reaction provoked by the Inquisition; and the "liberties of the kingdom of France" resulted from the same cause.* In Spain, also, notwithstanding the vigorous support of many of the Kings reigning over the four kingdoms then comprehended in that peninsula, the Inquisitors made unequal progress, everywhere encountering opposition. If our dates be correct, more than a hundred and sixty years elapsed before an "act of faith" was celebrated in Castile. Then, however, those exhibitions became very frequent everywhere; and, at length, Nicholas Eymeric, made Inquisitor-General of Aragon in the year 1356, collected from the civil and canon laws all that related to the punishment of heretics, and formed the "Directory of Inquisitors," the first and indeed the fundamental code, which has been followed ever since, without any essential variation. To give a correct idea of what the Inquisition really is, we will borrow a general description from this Directory of Eymeric, expounded as it is by his commentator Peña, and sanctioned by the approbation of

* Some of these twenty privileges, as they were published in the reign of Louis XII., are obviously opposed to the Inquisition. For example: "1. The King of France knows no superior in temporals." "4. The King of France, without consulting the Pope, may impose subsidies on Ecclesiastics or on churches, under the name of loan, gift, or charity, for defence of the kingdom." "6. The King of France cannot be excommunicated, nor declared excommunicate, by any dignitary in the realm." "11. The King has cognisance of civil causes between ecclesiastical persons, while they act in spiritual causes, or causes thereunto relating." "12. The King alone makes constitutions or laws in the kingdom of France." "15. The Pope does not legitimate nor restore in the kingdom of France, but the King only." "19. No one authorises the bearing of arms in the kingdom of France, but the King only." (Stylus Supremæ Curiæ Parlamenti Parisiensis. Parisiis, MDLI., pars 4.)

Gregory XIII. It exhibits the practice of the Inquisition at the time of its sanction in 1578, and republication in 1587; and the theory of the Inquisition, which, under some necessary variations of practice, remains unchanged. This authority instructs practitioners to the following effect. To avoid the dryness of a verbal transcript, I shall employ my own words, but be careful to represent the true sense of the "Directory."

Prosecution.

In a cause of heresy you should proceed quietly and simply, without formality and noise of pleadings. There should be no delay, no interruption, no appeal, and as few witnesses as possible. It is the peculiar and high privilege of the tribunal of the Inquisition, that its Judges are not obliged to follow forensic rules; and therefore the omission of what common right requires does not annul the process, so that nothing essential to the proof be wanting.

There are three ways of proceeding in cases of heresy: by accusation, by information, and by inquiry.

The Inquisitor will seldom make use of *accusation*, inasmuch as it is unusual, dangerous to the accuser, and tedious. He will therefore discourage accusations, and advise accusers to refrain from bringing a charge, and to content themselves with information. Or, if an accuser persists, he may prepare the charge officially at the instance of the party; but private persons are very seldom permitted to undertake formal accusations, since an Attorney, or Fiscal, of the Holy Office does this by virtue of his ministry, and therefore runs no risk of punishment if the charge should turn out to be false. (This provides impunity to false accusers.)

It is most usual to proceed on *information*. One person informs against another, not to involve himself in the affair, but to avoid the excommunication denounced on those who will not inform, or through zeal for the faith. The information must be reduced to writing, and attested by an oath on the four Gospels, and must contain circumstances of time and place. The Inquisitor may receive the information in private, with no other witness than his Secretary. The obligation to inform is absolute, notwithstanding oath, bond, or promise to the contrary. There may be previous admonition to the suspected person, but that is not necessary. The information may appear groundless at first sight, but the Inquisitor must not cancel it on that account: for what cannot be brought to light to-day, may be made clear to-morrow. (Christ came not to condemn the world, but to save: not so the Inquisitor.)

When there is no informer, resort may be had to *inquiry*. This may be general, according to the Council of Toulouse, setting the population to hunt for heretics wherever they are likely to be found; or it may be undertaken by the Inquisitor alone, when there is a common report that such an one has said or done anything against the faith. The Inquisitor may question persons concerning the reputation of that person; and if he can elicit that there is any ill report against him, he may call him up. Or if he only entertain suspicion, in the absence of all such report, he may proceed in the same way, but cautiously. There ought to be two witnesses to confirm the suspicion; but their evidence will be valid, even if they cannot say that they have ever heard him utter an erroneous opinion, but can only testify that they have heard it from others. Neither need they say what they have heard; for it will suffice if they declare that people talk suspectingly about him. By common right, no criminal is required to give evidence against himself; but in a cause of heresy there is this obligation,—the person accused must furnish all the particulars, to enable the Fiscal to make out the charge. All the Doctors agree to this. (For their only business is to make sure of their victim.)

Witnesses.

In causes of heresy, testimony of all sorts of persons is admissible. They may be excommunicate, accomplices, infamous, or convicted of any crime. Heretics, too, may give evidence; but only against the culprit is it valid, never in his favour. This provision is most prudent, nay, it is most just: for since the heretic has broken faith towards his God, no one ought to take his word; and it should always be presumed that, say what he may, he is actuated by hatred to the Church, and a desire that crimes against the faith may go unpunished. The testimony of infidels and Jews may be taken also, even in a question of heretical doctrine. The testimony of false witnesses is also taken, if against the accused person, even although a previous favourable testimony may have been retracted. And note that, if the first declaration was against him, and the second favourable, the first only must be accepted. The Judge must never give credit to such retractations; for if he do, heresy will be committed with impunity. Domestic witnesses—wife, for example, children, relatives, and servants—may have their testimony accepted against him, and then it has great value; but it never must avail to his advantage. All moralists agree that, in case of heresy, a brother may declare against his brother, and a son against his father. Father Simancas would have excepted fathers and children from this law: but his opinion is not admissible; for if a man may kill his father if he be an enemy to his country, how much more may he inform against him if he be guilty of heresy! The son of a heretic, who has informed thus, is exempted from the anathema launched against the children of heretics, and this is *in reward of his information.* The reason of all this is, that nothing but the force of truth would so overcome natural feelings, as to lead one member of a family to delate another. And as heresy is generally best known at home, such evidence is very necessary. (The testimony of a parricide has a special value.)

Every witness who appears against a heretic must be examined and sworn by the Inquisitor, in presence of a Secretary or Scribe. Having put to him the usual questions, he must bind him to secrecy. There may be one or two men, of gravity and prudence, present at the examination; but this is by no means desirable. The criminal must not see the witnesses, nor know who they were. Eymeric weakly said that there should be more than two witnesses to establish a fact; but practice, and the general opinion of the Doctors, allow Inquisitors to condemn a culprit on the evidence of any two whom they can trust; and, seeing that his case has been attentively examined, this is all that he should wish. (If his enemies have *diligently* sought to kill him, he should be thankful for their diligence!)

When the culprit is informed of the charges against him, the names of witnesses should be concealed; or, if there be any particulars in the charges that would help him to guess the names, the testimony given by one person should be attributed to another; or names should be substituted of persons that were not witnesses: but, after all, it is best to suppress all names; and this is the general practice, safest to informers, and to the Christian public. (A lie is lovely in the Holy Office, if it helps to homicide.)

False witnesses, who have caused the death of an innocent person, must not suffer any severer punishment than perpetual confinement. Some have thought otherwise, and Leo X. authorised the delivery of such offenders to the secular arm, to be put to death; but the Councils of Narbonne and Toulouse, after grave deliberation, mention no such punishment; the Council of Burgos condemns them to penance with *sambenito;* and false witnesses are not put to death by the Inquisition at Rome, nor anywhere else. However, in any special case, the Judges may consult the Inquisitor-General. A witness, suspected of falsehood, may be put to the torture; "and I," says Eymeric, "was present in a case at Toulouse in 1312, where a father, who had informed against his son, was laid on the rack, and there declared that his information was false." (Reward nine hundred and ninety-nine false witnesses, to keep up the practice. Let one of a thousand be punished for a blind.)

Examination of the Culprit.

The Inquisitor must require the culprit to swear that he will answer every question truly, even to his own damage. He must ask his name, birth-place, residence, and so on. Has he heard speak of such and such points of heresy? Or has he spoken of them? The answers shall be written down, and the culprit shall sign them. He must also ask him if he knows why he is imprisoned, whom he supposes to have caused his apprehension, who is his Confessor, when he confessed last, and so on. He must not question him in such a manner as to suggest subterfuges, or provide escape, but let his interrogatories be vague and general. "Too much prudence and firmness," says Peña, "can never be employed in the interrogation of a prisoner. The heretics are very cunning in disguising their errors. They affect sanctity, and shed false tears, which might soften the severest Judges. An Inquisitor must arm himself against all these tricks, always supposing that they are trying to deceive him." (An Inquisitor, therefore, must be no less hardened than depraved.)

Manifold are the tricks of heretics. They equivocate, use mental reservation, elude the question, affect surprise, shuffle, answer evasively, feign submission, pretend to be fainting, counterfeit madness, or counterfeit modesty. But the Inquisitor must rebut this tenfold craft, paying them in their own coin, according to the words of the Apostle, *Cum essem astutus, dolo vos cepi:* "Being crafty, I caught you with guile." Let him proceed thus with such:—

Press them to give direct answers to your questions. If you are not satisfied with the declaration of a prisoner,—even having employed the jailer, or secret spies, to extract from him beforehand,—speak gently, let him understand that you know all, and discourse with him after such a sort as this: "Be assured, my child, that I am very sorry for you: they have imposed on your simplicity, and ruined you. You have been in error, no doubt; but your deceiver is more to blame than you. Be not a partaker of other men's sins, nor think of acting the part of a teacher, when you are but a learner. Confess the truth. You see that I know it well already; but I want you to save your character, and enable me to set you at liberty as soon as possible, and let you return home in peace. But, tell me, who led you first astray?" Give him good words, but keep firm, and take it for granted that the fact of his heresy is certain. Perhaps the evidence will be incomplete, and the heretic may persist in declaring that he is innocent. In that case do you put general questions; and when he denies something that you happen to have taxed him with, turn over the notes of a former examination, and say, "It is clear that you are not telling the truth. Do not equivocate any longer." And so he will fancy that you have other evidence against him. Or you may turn over a bundle of papers, seem to be reading them, and, when he denies anything, start, as with surprise, and ask how he can deny that, seeing that it is as clear as day. Read your papers, turn over the leaves, and say, every now and then, "Ah! did I not say so? Confess the truth." But be careful not to go into particulars, lest he see that you know nothing about them.

Or if he be still obstinate, tell him that you had hoped to finish his case, as you are just going to take a long journey, and know not when you shall return; but, as he will not confess, you must leave him still in prison. He is evidently out of health, and not able to bear close confinement. You are very sorry, but cannot help it, and so on. Or you may multiply questions, and renew the examination from time to time, until he has been made to contradict himself for want of memory or self-possession; and when his answers are confused, the Doctors agree that you may put him to the torture. This method is almost sure to succeed, and he must be clever that does not fall into the snare. (Clever indeed! The father of lies contrived the snare.)

Or you may seem to relent, when the prisoner persists in his denial. Relax your severity, give him better food, send people to visit him, encourage him, advise him to confess, and promise that the Inquisitor will forgive him, or, at least, that they will interest themselves on his behalf. Indeed, you may promise him pardon, and you may pardon him in effect; for in the conversion of a heretic all is pardoned, and penances are favours. So tell him that, if he will confess, he shall have more than he could himself desire: and so he will; for you will save his soul. The Doctors are not agreed as to this dissimulation, which is not allowed in civil courts; "but I," Peña, "believe that it may be used in tribunals of the Inquisition, because an Inquisitor has far more ample powers than other Judges, and may dispense with penitential and canonical punishments at his pleasure. So that as he does not promise total impunity to the guilty, when he says that he will pardon him, he can fulfil the promise by forgiving him some of the canonical penalties, which depend entirely on himself." Still some Doctors are not satisfied with this opinion; but the fraud is useful for the public good; and as it is lawful to extort the truth by torture, it must be lawful, reasoning *à fortiori*, to do so by dissimulation (*verbis fictis*). However, for greater security of your conscience, you may employ vague terms, capable of a double interpretation. (How *tender* must this conscience be!)

Or you may gain over some friend of the prisoner, and let him talk with him frequently alone, and get the secret. If it be necessary, you may authorise the friend to feign himself of the same opinion, and even to prolong his conversation, until it shall be too late at night for him to go home, and then he shall stay in the prison, "having witnesses concealed in some convenient place, that they may hear the conversation, and, if possible, a Clerk, who shall note down all that the criminal says, while the person you have bribed draws from him his most hidden thoughts." But the spy, although he may pretend to be also a heretic, must not say so in so many words; for that would be a lie, which is, at least, a venial sin; and sin is not to be committed on any account. In short, whatever tricks you allow, you must be careful not to sanction an untruth. By such contrivances as these, you may get at all you want, without touching the rack, and your sagacity will search out the truth, according to the wise sentence of a poet:

> "Sed quoniam variant animi, variabimus artes;
> Mille mali species, mille salutis erunt."

(And still the Inquisitor preserves a tranquil conscience.)

Defence.

When you have extracted a confession, it will be useless to grant the culprit a defence. For although in other courts the confession of the criminal does not suffice without proof, it suffices here. Heresy is a sin of the soul, and therefore confession may be the only evidence possible. However, for the sake of appearance, you may allow him to consult an Advocate, to object to witnesses, to object to one or more of the Judges, or to appeal. (In no other court is so much trouble taken to save the soul. *Holy* Office!)

As for the Advocate, *you* are to choose him; and, besides possessing other good qualities, he must be zealous for the faith. Swear him to keep the secret, and to engage his client to confess. But the prisoner must not communicate with his Advocate, except in presence of the Inquisitor. But recollect that there is a chapter in the Decretals (*Si adversus*, lib. v., tit. 7, *De Hœret.*) which forbids Advocates to plead for heretics in any cause; and therefore you must not allow one to a notorious heretic, but only where the suspicion is not yet proved. And when an Advocate is granted, he must swear that he will abandon his client so soon as the heresy is proved. (The Advocate being a zealot, and the law framed for vengeance, conviction is pretty certain.)

As for objecting to witnesses, heretics must not fancy that this is easily admitted, since both honest men and rogues, excommunicate, heretics, criminals, perjured persons, and any others, are allowed to bear witness against heretics. Only on one account, that of capital hatred in the witness towards the prisoner, may the latter be suffered to object; and, even in such a case, various methods are devised to weaken the objection, or to prevent it. (Of course: capital hatred is a capital qualification.)

If he appeal to the Pope, observe that all the laws agree that a heretic has no right to appeal. Thus the Emperor Frederic decided; and thus the Council of Constance determined, that the appeal of John Huss was illusory and vain. Truly some laws appear to countenance appeals; but these may be easily disposed of. Note, also, that if the prisoner appeals from you on one point, you can appeal against him on some other. Or you can dispute the legality of the appeal. Or you can grant it under protest. But in no case should the Inquisitor appear at Rome to answer for his judgment, but let the Inquisitors-General, who are there, represent you. (The prisoner may have a friend at Rome.)

CHAPTER IV.

LAWS AND CUSTOMS (CONTINUED).

Torture.

WHEN you subject a prisoner to torture, in order to compel him to confess, observe the rules following:—

Torture is inflicted on one who confesses the principal fact, but varies as to circumstances. Also on one who is reputed to be a heretic, but against whom there is only one witness of the fact. In this case common rumour is one indication of guilt, and the direct evidence is another, making altogether but semi-plenar proof. The torture may bring out full proof. Also, when there is no witness, but vehement suspicion. Also, when there is no common report of heresy, but only one witness who has heard or seen something in him contrary to the faith. Any two indications of heresy will justify the use of torture. If you sentence to torture, give him a written notice, in the form prescribed; but let other means be tried first. Nor is this an infallible means for bringing out the truth. Weak-hearted men, impatient of the first pain, will confess crimes that they never committed, and criminate others at the same time. Bold and strong ones will bear the most severe torments. Those who have been on the rack before, bear it with more courage; for they know how to adapt their limbs to it, and they resist powerfully. Others, by enchantments, seem to be insensible, and would rather die than confess. These wretches use, for incantations, certain passages from the Psalms of David, or other parts of Scripture, which they write on virgin parchment in an extravagant way, mixing them with names of unknown angels, with circles and strange letters, which they wear upon their person. "I know not," says Peña, "how this witchcraft can be remedied; but it will be well to strip the criminals naked, and search them narrowly, before laying them upon the rack." While the tormentor is getting ready, let the Inquisitor and other grave men make fresh attempts to obtain a confession of the truth. Let the tormentors terrify him by all means, to frighten him into confession. And after he is stripped, let the Inquisitor take him aside, and make a last effort. When this has failed, let him be put to the question by torture, beginning with interrogation on lesser points, and advancing to greater. If he stands out, let them show him other instruments of torture, and threaten that he shall suffer them also. If he will not confess, the torture may be continued on a second or third day; but as it is not to be repeated, those successive applications must be called *continuation.* And if, after all, he does not confess, he may be set at liberty. Rules are laid down for the punishment of those who do confess. Innocent IV. commanded the secular Judges to put heretics to torture; but that gave occasion to scandalous publicity, and now Inquisitors are empowered to do it, and, in case of irregularity, (that is, if the person dies in their hands,) to absolve each other. And although nobles were exempt from torture, and, in some kingdoms, as Aragon, it was not used in civil tribunals, the Inquisitors were nevertheless authorised to torture, without restriction, persons of all classes.

And here we digress from Eymeric and Peña, in order to describe, from an additional authority, of what this torture consisted, and probably still consists, in Italy. Limborch collects this information from Juan de Rojas, Inquisitor at Valencia.

There were formerly five degrees of torment, as some

counted, (Eymeric included,) or, according to others, three. First, there was *terror*, including the threatenings of the Inquisitor, leading to the place of torture, stripping and binding; the stripping of all their clothing,—both men and women!—with the substitution of a single tight garment, to cover part of the body, being an outrage of every feeling of decency; and the binding often as distressing as the torture itself. Secondly came the stretching on the rack, and questions attendant. Thirdly, a more severe shock by the tension and sudden relaxation of the cord, which is sometimes given once, but often twice, thrice, or yet more frequently. Limborch here refers to Dillon's account of the Portuguese Inquisition at Goa, whose words we borrow. "During the months of November and December, (1675,) I heard, every morning, the cries of those who were put upon the rack, which is so cruel a torture, that I saw divers persons, both of the one and of the other sex, who were distorted and maimed by it, and, among others, the first companion they had assigned to me in the prison. In this holy tribunal no respect is made of quality, age, or sex, and all are indifferently submitted to the torture, when the interest of the Inquisition so requireth it."

Isaac Orobio, a Jewish physician, related to Limborch the manner in which he had himself been tortured, when thrown into the Inquisition at Seville, on the delation of a Moorish servant whom he had punished for theft, and of another person similarly offended. "After having been in the prison of the Inquisition for full three years, examined a few times, but constantly refusing to confess the things laid to his charge, he was at length brought out of the cell, and led, through tortuous passages, to the place of torment. It was near evening. He found himself in a subterranean chamber, rather spacious, arched over, and hung with black cloth. The whole conclave was lighted by candles in sconces on the walls. At one end there was a separate chamber, wherein were an Inquisitor and his Notary seated at a table. The place, gloomy, silent, and everywhere terrible, seemed to be the very home of Death. Hither he was brought, and the Inquisitor again exhorted him to tell the truth before the torture should begin. On his answering that he had already told the truth, the Inquisitor gravely protested that he was bringing himself to the torture by his own obstinacy; and that if he should suffer loss of blood, or even expire, during the question, the Holy Office would be blameless. Having thus spoken, the Inquisitor left him in the hands of the tormentors, who stripped him, and compressed his body so tightly in a pair of linen drawers, that he could no longer draw breath, and must have died, had they not suddenly relaxed the pressure; but with recovered breathing came pain unutterably exquisite. This anguish having past, they repeated a monition to confess the truth, before the torture, as they said, should begin; and the same was afterwards repeated at each interval.

"As Orobio persisted in denial, they bound his thumbs so tightly with small cords, that the blood burst from under the nails, and they were swelled excessively. Then they made him stand against the wall on a small stool, passed cords round various parts of his body, but principally round the arms and legs, and carried them over iron pulleys in the ceiling. The tormentor then pulled the cords with all his strength, applying his feet to the wall, and giving the weight of his body to increase the purchase. With these ligatures his arms and legs, fingers and toes, were so wrung and swollen, that he felt as if fire were devouring them. In the midst of this torment the man kicked down the stool which had supported his feet, so that he hung upon the cords with his whole weight, which suddenly increased their tension, and gave indescribable aggravation to his pain. Next followed a new kind of torment. An instrument resembling a small ladder, consisting of two parallel pieces of wood, and five transverse pieces, with the anterior edges sharpened, was placed before him, so that when the tormentor struck it heavily, he received the stroke, five times multiplied, on each shin-bone, producing pain that was absolutely intolerable; and under this he fainted. But no sooner was he revived, than they inflicted a new torture. The tormentor tied other cords round his wrists, and, having his own shoulders covered with leather that they might not be chafed, passed round them the rope which was to draw the cords, set his feet against the wall, threw himself back with all his force, and the cords cut through to the bones. This he did thrice, each time changing the position of the cords, leaving a small distance between the successive wounds; but it happened that, in pulling the second time, they slipped into the first wound, and caused such a gush of blood, that Orobio seemed to be bleeding to death. A physician and surgeon, who were in waiting, as usual, to give their opinion as to the safety or danger of continuing those operations, that the Inquisitors might not commit an irregularity by murdering the patient, were called in. Being friends of the sufferer, they gave their opinion that he had strength enough remaining to bear more. By this means they saved him from a *suspension* of the torture, which would have been followed by a repetition, on his recovery, under the pretext of *continuation.* The cords were therefore pulled the third time, and this ended the torture. Then he was dressed in his own clothes, carried back to prison, and, after about seventy days, when the wounds were healed, condemned as one *suspected* of Judaism. They could not say *convicted*, because he had not confessed; but they sentenced him to wear the *sambenito*—a vestment which we will describe presently—for two years, and then to be banished for life from Seville."

To describe the many refinements of a purely diabolical cruelty which Inquisitors have invented, would fill a chapter of horrors, and swell this little volume beyond its limit. They have applied water, perpetually dripping on the bare head, until it has tormented the sufferer to madness; or poured it down his throat, until his stomach has been distended, inducing extreme anguish. They have applied fire, scorching, and almost suffocating, their victim, who has lain before it, bound hand and foot, in the horror of a lingering death. Thumb-screws and the rack are proverbial. Enough of torture for the present chapter. Occasions will occur to refer the reader to these general statements, and to notice, in particular cases, some of the diabolical refinements which Eymeric would have marked as irregular; but the tormentor being allowed a discretionary power, there is no limit to the variety of his methods beyond the poverty of his invention, or the power of endurance in his patients.

Fugitives and Rebels.

No one who thought himself in danger of inquisitorial treatment would remain to be taken, if he could escape; nor, if he were absent, would he return to be thrown into the dungeons. If the Inquisitor caught an ill report of an absent person, his Directory instructed him to wait with patience, even for a year or two, until the unsuspecting culprit might return. If he did not come back, it would then be his duty to issue a citation, requiring him to appear within a time fixed; and if he came not,—and who would come on such a summons?—the Inquisitor was to declare him excommunicate. If he lay unmoved under the lash of excommunication for one year, he should be pronounced a rebel.

Or if a person fled, whether he had been convicted on his own confession, or by witnesses, or had been delated and summoned to appear, or had been known to favour heretics, he was to be summoned to present himself before the Holy Office, under pain of excommunication. At the expiration of a year from the publication of the anathema, he should be condemned as a heretic, on presumption of guilt, although there had never been inquisition made. If he were an Ecclesiastic, the Bishop of his diocese would give a sentence of degradation; but the degraded Priest, or the layman, was then to be given over to the secular arm, by a mandate from the Bishop and Inquisitor unitedly. The document would set forth that the said Bishop and Inquisitor, having heard an ill report of him, had "gone down to see and to inquire, whether the rumour that had reached their ears were true, and whether he was walking in darkness, or in light." On the testimony of witnesses they had detected him in heresy. His confession had confirmed the evidence, and he had consented to do penance. But, seduced by an evil spirit, shrinking from the wine and oil which the Samaritan Inquisitors wanted to shed upon his wounds, he had broken prison, the wicked spirit had caught him away, and hidden him, they knew not where. They had summoned him to return, by papers put up on many church-doors; but, blinded by insane counsel, he had contumaciously refused to come. They, for their part, obeying the exigence of justice, had excommunicated him. He, for his part, had refused the salutary medicine of their curse; and for one full year the malignant spirit had carried him from place to place, but whither they could not tell. Mercifully and kindly the holy Church of God had waited, all that time, to clasp him in her bosom, and nourish him from the breasts of her clemency; but he still refused to come. Then she had invited him to come in order to receive the sentence due for such contumacious heresy; but, insensible to his mother's clemency, he had still refused. Now, their patience being exhausted, and justice urging for the exaltation of the Catholic faith, and the extirpation of heresy, in that day, hour, and place, they gave sentence in the usual manner, leaving him to the secular arm, with the usual deprecation of injury to life or limb. And the secular and ecclesiastical authorities were required to seize him, if they could.

He was then to be burnt in effigy; and if any one, in endeavouring to apprehend the living man, for the honour of the Church, should happen unfortunately to kill him, the homicide, sanctified by a righteous intention, was to be forgiven. His absence, and default of judicial defence, did not diminish the power of the sacred Tribunal to take his life.

Absolution.

It would sometimes happen that the accused person was as good a "Catholic," as they say, as the Inquisitors themselves. The witnesses could not prove so much as one suspicious word or deed. After the exhaustion of all arts, and the application of torture, there had not been a syllable of confession; but, on the contrary, the innocence of the sufferer was manifest. What then? In such a case, the Inquisitor was to grant a written absolution, setting forth that, having come down to inquire, &c., &c., he had not found any legal proof of guilt, and, therefore, he fully released him "from the present charge, inquisition, and judgment." But if he had declared him to be innocent, such a declaration would have made his act invalid. The Inquisition presumes on guilt, in every case, but never thinks of innocence. And the Inquisitor was required to avoid every word that might imply formal justification, in order that a terror might evermore hang over the person who had been once suspected; and that the way might be left open for further prosecution, should it seem desirable. How unlike an absolution in the court of heaven! Nay, how unlike humanity!

Canonical Purgation.

Evil-speaking is not heresy. Ill-natured neighbours, or dishonest debtors, might whisper that such an one was a heretic. On this rumour the Inquisitors might found a process; but, there being an utter want of evidence, not even a word whereon to rest suspicion of the calumniated person, it would become necessary to finish the case. The report could not be refuted without violation of secret, and discovery of slanderers, to the discouragement of all the familiars and friends of the Holy Office. The slandered person was then required to produce such a number of compurgators as the Inquisitors might choose, and of the class that it pleased them to prescribe. The compurgators being found, the subject of calumny was brought into some public place, probably at the celebration of a Sermon, and, after having sworn that he had never fallen into the heresy which report charged on him, the compurgators were all to come forward, and swear that they, from certain knowledge, believed him to be innocent. From that time the compurgators were held answerable for his religious reputation; and if he should fall into heresy, would inevitably share his fate. This made it almost impossible for any one to find compurgators, at least in sufficient number, and of the sort required. In this default, he was sentenced at once as a heretic, and punished accordingly.

Abjuration.

But even so, it was not often thought expedient to allow the chance of escape by expurgation. The Inquisition classified the degrees of suspicion under three heads,—*light*, *vehement*, and *violent*. The person suspected lightly was brought out before the multitude, made his abjuration, received an order to do penance, and so obtained release, with an admonition that, if again suspected, he would fare worse. Abjuration after *vehement* suspicion was followed by some ignominious penance, such as standing at the church-door on festivals, and visiting certain sanctuaries. *Violent* suspicion was to be visited more severely. Suspicion became violent when the pleasure of the Inquisitors had been, in any way, resisted. Numberless circumstances might arise to provoke their vengeance on a person whom they had not even accused of heresy; but whose bearing, in their litigation with him, served as a pretext for violent suspicion. *Sambenito*, and perpetual imprisonment, with bread and water, were the usual remedies employed for the health of their "dear son," who was bidden not to despair; but, by meek submission, merit indulgence at some future, but uncertain, time. But, on any second offence, violent suspicion would be counted equivalent with proof, and his body would then be burnt for the salvation of the soul.

CHAPTER V.

LAWS AND CUSTOMS (CONCLUDED).

Fines and Confiscation.

HERE is a grave question: it is the hundred-and-fourth of the knots which Eymeric, the Canonists assisting him, undertook to loose. "May an Inquisitor exact the expenses from those against whom he proceeds; and may he condemn them, by sentence, to pay these expenses?" *Respondemus quod sic, &c.* Assuredly he may, if his income be narrow, as it generally is, and insufficient for his office. "Who goeth a warfare any time at his own charges?" Most just, then, is it, that holy Inquisitors, men devoted to a work so pious, should have whereupon to subsist; and none can be so proper to maintain them as the heretics, for whose benefit they labour. The customs of countries, indeed, are various, and the methods of maintaining the affluence and dignity of the Holy Office are diverse; but, whether its revenue be granted by the temporal authority, or otherwise obtained, it is most just that spiritual delinquents should be made to pay. And as to confiscation of goods, so soon as the Inquisitor pronounces a sentence of heresy, the life of that sinner ceases to be his own; and, therefore, it is no longer possible that he, already dead, should possess house, or land, or moveables. The sins of the fathers, too, are to be visited upon the children; and, therefore, the children of a heretic are incapable of any other inheritance than poverty and infamy. Still, as the Church is always merciful, she may, of her free grace, take care of the children, binding the boys as apprentices to a trade, putting out the girls to service, and even feeding the infant, or the sickly children; but she must feed them scantily, that they may be sensible of the visitation, in their own persons, of their father's iniquity. As for wives, they share the fortune of their husbands, unless fidelity to the Holy

Office should have entitled them to indulgent consideration, after the perpetual imprisonment, or the fiery death, of their rejected husbands. The legislation on this point is careful, diffuse, and somewhat intricate; but we need not study it too closely. A penitent, be it noted, cannot have his property restored. Indigence will be a salutary penance, and justice demands the pelf in recompense to his converters.

Disability and Infamy.

Every man, of whatever estate, loses all office, benefice, right, and dignity, so soon as he incurs inquisitorial punishment. His memory is to be accursed. His progeny is to be infamous. Some have asked, whether children begotten in the time of his innocency, when, as yet, he had not fallen away from the holy Catholic Church, are to be involved in the dishonour. The Doctors have taken this case into consideration, and unanimously determine that, as the end of punishment is prevention of crime, the terror of infamy ought always to be before the eyes of every parent, in order that natural affection, compassion towards children who might suffer by his fault, may keep his faith right. When a man is heretical, his sons, his daughters, and their children must all be infamous; when a woman, her sons and daughters. Men need harder binding to the Romish altar. Women can be held in softer bonds. Offending fathers, be it also noted, have no more authority at home. They cannot demand honour or obedience from their children. Offending husbands have no more control over their wives, who are instructed, thenceforth, to forsake the nuptial bed. Those dutiful women, of course, are honoured by the fathers of the Holy Office.

Perpetual Imprisonment.

This is a healthful penance, graciously imposed on all convicted heretics who have repented satisfactorily, and have not relapsed. The relapsed are uniformly burnt. As to the mode of inflicting the penalty of perpetual imprisonment, it has been various: a solitary dungeon, a private house hired for that purpose, a monastery. Sometimes the captive has been maintained by the Bishop, by the Inquisition itself, or by a trifling charge on his confiscated property. Sometimes he has had to work at his trade, yet in profound seclusion from all except his keeper, with an occasional visit of an Inquisitor who came to ask how he behaved. Sometimes his friends have been permitted to visit him; but this indulgence could only be allowed when the public were thought free from heresy, and the Inquisitor was in full power. For Ecclesiastics, monasteries have been, and still are, the cheapest and most convenient prisons. Before being indulged with this commutation of a severer penalty, the heretic was to make a solemn abjuration at a "Sermon," or "Act of Faith," in presence of the people. In the days of its glory, the Inquisition sometimes used to parade the perpetual penitents before the public on feast-days. The sentence prescribed to be read by the Inquisitor was almost literally the same as one quoted above from the "Book of Sentences" of the Inquisition of Toulouse. And here we must stay, for a moment, to speak of prisons in general.

In civil jurisprudence imprisonment served for custody alone, until the Inquisition enlarged its use, and made it also penal. But although, in common practice, the end of justice is attained by the safe custody of an accused person, and severities, after trial and sentence, are penal, the canon-law, on the contrary, makes imprisonment for custody harder than imprisonment for penalty. The doctrine and practice of canon-law may be shortly told.

Clement IV., intent on "the extermination of heretics," commanded "all the powers of the world, the Lords temporal of provinces, lands, cities, and all other places," the diocesan Bishops, and the Inquisitors of heretical pravity then deputed, or thereafter to be deputed, from the Apostolic See, to make inquest, pursue, arrest, and keep in strait and careful custody those children of iniquity, despite all appeal or prayer for pity. This you may find in the Sext* Decretals, *De Hæreticis.* The Council of Vienne, under Clement V., directed that, for the glory of God, the augmentation of His faith, and the happier transaction of the business of the Inquisition (*eo prosperetur felicius*), Bishops and Inquisitors, putting away all fleshly love, hatred, fear, or other temporal

* Commonly so called, from the title of the SEXTUS *Decretalium Liber.* It is preceded by the *five Books of Gregory IX.*, and followed by the *Clementines* and the *Extravagantes.* These constitute the Text of Canon-Law, since enlarged or modified by whatever is published "under the ring," or "under the lead," by successive Popes.

affection, should, by their sole authority, cite, arrest, and imprison heretics, laying iron manacles upon their hands, and iron fetters upon their feet. Moreover, they were to deliver them into hard and strait prison, there to be examined and, if necessary, put to torture.

Degrees of guilt required correspondent measures of suffering or degradation in the prison. The palace of the Inquisition, therefore, or the *Holy House*, had extensive accommodation for all classes of delinquents;—rooms well ventilated, light and air being admitted through iron grating, and sufficiently large for the occupant to move about, with bed, seat, fire-place, and a few conveniences;—or close, dark cells, with little air, small space, a heap of straw, no fire-place, and scarcely any kind of convenience;—or, deeper still, no light, scarcely space enough to move or stand upright;—a "little-ease," a mis-shapen pit, wherein the living body sank into the hollow of an inverted cone, and was fed with just enough to keep up the functions of nature, just to prevent death, and no more. Then were added, in due proportion of weight and number, those manacles, fetters, chains, and other contrivances of torment. The sworn jailer might not speak to the suffering "child of iniquity," however summoned. To no call, or entreaty, or sigh, or shriek, was the "faithful and industrious" keeper to give an answer by word or sign. No communication, no respite, no sort of pity! The Inquisitor would come, or send, when so it pleased him, to put question, tempt with a promise, or terrify with a threat. The durance being thus made perfect in solitude and in despair, there could not be collusion with other criminals, nor corruption of the keepers, nor intelligence from the outer world, nor chance of any sort for defeating the ends of "justice." Gradually, from the healthy and convenient chambers, down into the horrible pit, the "inquisite" who refused to deny Christ, to discover brethren, or to confess crimes not committed, was made to descend; and, being still obstinate, was taken to the rack, or handed over for the stake.

This discipline, if necessary, having been exhausted, and yet nothing proven, or if recantation had been extorted, and, if extorted, thought sufficient, the Inquisitors might sentence to perpetual imprisonment. And this imprisonment might be tolerably easy, if in confinement, vexation, and disgrace there can be ease. It was even possible, that, after the endurance of some years, the penalty might cease, and the prisoner become a penitent at large. Or, if the Inquisitor, offended, dissatisfied, or otherwise moved to severity, so chose, he might aggravate the hardship of the place, plunge his victim into the profoundest dungeon, and be only restricted to one limit,—that he should not deprive him of life, but keep the breath in his body. If, however, death should happen, the Inquisitor would be held guilty of an irregularity; for which irregularity he must atone, not by being whipped or strangled, but by mentioning the matter in secret to a brother Inquisitor, and getting instant absolution from all censure ecclesiastical.

Delivery to the secular Arm.

The secular arm (*brachium sæculare*) is the civil power, subservient to the vengeful pleasure of the ecclesiastical. "Penitents" who repent them of having yielded to the fear of temporal death, and, to escape the death eternal, confess Christ again, or persons brought a second time under accusation; reputed heretics, whose endurance is accounted pertinacity; "negative heretics," who persist in denying what the Inquisitors think they should confess, there being "full proof" against them;—are delivered over to the secular arm. But the delivery is conducted with ceremony. "God-fearing men" are sent by the Inquisitors to converse with the doomed offender, to speak to him of the nothingness of this world, the miseries of life, and the glories of heaven. They tell him, that, since he cannot escape temporal death, he ought to be reconciled with God. If he will not heed their exhortations, he must feel the fire; but if he will confess, be absolved, and receive the host, the Church will graciously receive him to her bosom; and although he must die for the good of his soul, the secular arm will strangle him as promptly as possible, that he may be spared the flames, which, in that case, will but consume a dead body, not a living one. This errand of grace accomplished, the messengers report accordingly, and the Inquisitors tell the Magistrate that the person whom they condemned *is ready.*

At the time and place appointed, instruments of death being prepared, the person to be killed is brought forward, himself only, or with others, as we shall presently show. If a Priest, he is degraded according to the form already described. The Inquisitors and others being in their proper places, a paper is read, containing a recitation of his case, and concluding thus:—"Having been informed, after all, that you are fallen again into the same errors, and having examined this information carefully, we find that you are indeed relapsed. Since, however, you return again to the bosom of the Church, abjuring heresy, we grant you the sacraments of penance and the eucharist which you humbly ask; but Holy Mother Church cannot do anything more in your favour, because you once abused her kindness. Therefore we declare you relapsed, put you away from the jurisdiction of the Church, and leave you to the secular Judges, whom we efficaciously beseech (*efficaciter deprecantes*) so to moderate their sentence, that no shedding of blood nor peril of death may follow."

Here, again, is an important question, how the Inquisitors can make this request, at the same time that they deliver the heretic for the very purpose of having him killed, and are directed to excommunicate and punish as a heretic, if they can, the Magistrate who shall refuse to kill him. The difficulties of conscience are instantly obviated. First, they have not in so many words delivered him to the secular arm, but only *left* him to it: secondly, the Magistrate cannot understand them to mean that he shall not be killed, whatever they may say, because it is unlawful to plead or to intercede for a heretic: thirdly, whatever the Magistrate may or may not understand them to mean, they have pronounced words of intercession that will effectually save them from the "irregularity" of shedding blood or killing in any way. To kill, let us remember, is murder in most cases; but Inquisitors being exempted from the operation of ordinary laws, and never intending to kill any person, because the Church does not so intend, if it should happen that any one dies in their hands, not by their intention, but through his own obstinacy, it being remotely possible that they might have prevented it, they have fallen into "irregularity." But this accident happened in the service of the Church, who, therefore, empowers them to confess to each other, and to absolve each other. When the Magistrate kills a heretic, a schismatic, or a rebel, he does his duty, and they bless him. But the deed is *his*, not *theirs*. They never kill, except by accident. Excellent Church! that can so nicely manage conscience, and so liberally remit the pains of hell, and so exquisitely absolve from even the slightest taint of criminality.

It is not necessary to our present purpose to transcribe the various written forms, nor to describe the varieties of ceremonial, observed in the execution of different classes of heretics, or prepared for adaptation to diversities of circumstance. One contingency, however, has to be provided for; and that is, the apparently sincere repentance of a pertinacious heretic when on the verge of death. On this point Eymeric descants with his accustomed coolness, thus:—"And while the secular court is fulfilling its office, a few upright men, zealous for the faith, may go to the criminal, and exhort him to return to the Catholic faith, and renounce his errors. And if, after the sentence is past, and he is given over to the secular court, while they are taking him away to be burnt, or when he is tied to the stake, or when he feels the fire, he says, that he is willing to turn and repent, and abjure his heresy, I should think that he might, in mercy, be received as a heretic penitent, and immured for life, according to some passages in the Decretals," (which are cited,) "although I imagine this would not be found very justifiable, nor is great faith to be placed in conversions of the sort. And, indeed, such an occurrence took place in Barcelona, where three heretics impenitent, but not relapsed, were delivered to the secular arm, and when one of them, a Priest,* had the fire lit round him, and was already half burnt on one side, he begged to be taken out, and promised to abjure and repent. He was taken out, and abjured. But whether we did right or not, I cannot say. One thing I know, that fourteen years afterwards he was accused, and found to have persisted in his heresy all the time, and infected many. He

* During the pontificate of Benedict XII., which was from the year 1334 to 1342, a sect of Beghards, as Eymeric calls them, sprang up in Catalonia. We only hear of them by the report of their enemies; but the fact now before us indicates something far more vigorous than heresy. Fray Bononato, according to our informant, was the leader of those Spanish dissidents. It was he whom they bound to the stake at Barcelona. He repented of the recantation, and resumed his ministrations in secret. A congregation assembled in a private house in Villa Franca, a town between Barcelona and Tarragona, but it was discovered; his "accomplices," as they were called, were thrown with him into the flames, and the house was rased to the ground. (Direct. Inquis., p. 266.)

then refused to be converted; and, as one impenitent and relapsed, was again delivered to the secular arm, and consumed in fire." Consumed in fire, of course, that being the natural punishment of heretics, from its resemblance to hell, and according to the saying of our Lord,—"If a man abide not in Me, he is cast forth as a branch, and is withered, and men gather them, and cast them into the fire, and they are burned." And the impenitent having been burned in presence of the civil authorities and a great multitude of people, who have been edified by this lively image of the last judgment, the Inquisitor or Bishop proclaims a general indulgence from the flames of purgatory to as many as took any part in the solemnities of the day, even as spectators only, or had in any way assisted the Holy Office in their labour of love.

As for those who have betaken themselves to flight, and refused to return to be punished in their proper persons, their effigies are handed over to the civil magistracy to be burnt, in signification of the punishment awarded to them, as rebels, and awaiting them, if they should be caught.

Subjects of Inquisitorial Jurisdiction.

The tribunal claims right of jurisdiction over the following persons. All heretics without exception. All who blaspheme God and the saints. They who utter words of blasphemy when extremely drunk are not to be condemned at once, but watched. If half drunk, they are entirely guilty. They who speak blasphemously or heretically in their sleep are to be watched; for it is likely that their lips betrayed the heresy that was lurking in their heart. All who speak jestingly of sacred things. Wizards and fortune-tellers. Worshippers of the devil: and it seems that, while the Inquisition was in its glory, and the Reformation had scarcely dawned, people were known to offer sacrifices to the evil one, kneel down to him, sing hymns to him, observe chastity and fast in honour of him, illuminate and cense his images, insert names of devils in the litanies of saints, and ask them to intercede with God. Such was the condition of many who had known no other Church on earth but that of Rome! But to return. They who called on Satan to do his proper works of mischief were not guilty of heresy, according to some doctors, if they commanded him; but were guilty if they besought him. They might command, without much impropriety, (we should say,) one who had rendered so long and so faithfully his best service to their Church. To accept that service is not heresy. Astrologers and alchymists. Infidels and Jews: for, although Jews are not subject to the Church, according to the saying of St. Paul, that he did not judge them that were without, Jews become subject if they speak against Christianity; for, in so doing, they commit an ecclesiastical offence. The Church may avenge her own quarrel; she cannot avenge that of Christ. All who harbour, or show kindness to, heretics, being themselves orthodox; very near relatives, however, having slight indulgence allowed them, in some cases, if the Inquisitors so please. All who look ill on an Inquisitor,—those ugly looks being indications of heresy, and injurious to the Holy Office. Experienced Inquisitors could detect a heretic by a characteristic unsightliness about his eyes and nostrils. Persons in civil office who hinder, or who refuse to help, the Inquisition and its agents, or who help or allow an accused person to conceal himself, or to escape. Any one who gives food to a heretic, except he be actually dying with hunger; for, in that case it is allowable to feed him, that he may live to take his trial, and, haply, to be converted.

The general reader has now before him a sufficiently distinct sketch of the science, and the practice too, of inquisition and punishment of heresy. Those whose taste or whose duty may lead them to study this branch of Romish legislation are referred to Eymeric himself, or to Farinacius, a Roman jurisconsult, whose folio saw the light in Rome about thirty years later, and was also circulated throughout Europe for the instruction of that host of practitioners which had spread itself over every province of the Popedom, with or without the name of Inquisitor. We now proceed to mark the progress of the "Holy Office" in those countries where it was formally established, and shall then give our attention to the present state of the same tribunal.

CHAPTER VI.

FRANCE.

WITHIN a very short chapter may be compendiated the history of the French Inquisition. After the crusade preached by Bernard, and headed by such Princes as could be persuaded to engage in it, from time to time, Gregory IX. wrote a letter, still extant, to the Minister of the Friars Minors in Navarre, and to the Master of the Friars Preachers in Pamplona, reminding them that he had given the sword of the word of God into their hands, which, according to the sentence of the Prophet, they were not to keep back from blood; but, after the example of Phinehas, "zealot of the Catholic faith," were to proceed against them, and, if necessary, (*si opus fuerit*,) were to call in the help of the secular arm. They, the Monks, might kill if they could; that is to say, if they could get the faithful to renew the crusade; but, if not, the fire of mad fanaticism being nearly spent, were to call in the secular authority to kill for them. Strange it is, then, that, in the face of this epistle, which any one who can read Latin may peruse in Bzovius (A.D. 1235), any one should dare to say that the Inquisition was established to prevent the people from killing the heretics, and to substitute a humane court, thrifty of life, in order to save the Albigenses from being slaughtered. On the contrary, the two Inquisitors are exhorted to "cry havoc, and let slip the dogs of war."

But the dogs were by that time glutted; and it became, indeed, necessary to call in royal authority to do the work. Obedient to the summons, Louis IX. (Saint Louis) prayed Alexander IV. to establish Inquisitors over all his realm. The fiction of a secular origin to the sanguinary scheme thus received some colour; and the Prior of the Dominicans at Paris was invested with authority to be Inquisitor-General of the whole kingdom of France and the county of Toulouse. How that Inquisition proceeded, we have learned in a preceding chapter from the "Book of Sentences" archived at Toulouse; and, if Papal authorities could have prevailed over all other, the Gallican Church would soon have been laid prostrate under their feet, as is evident from the instances already cited. The Clergy, however, resisted the Roman innovation; and, when Frenchmen fled from their dwellings through fear of the Inquisition, the Priests allowed them to take refuge in the churches, where, by right of asylum, they were safe. Nicholas IV., indeed, willing to sacrifice anything to the reigning passion for destroying heresy, gave a Bull empowering the officers of the new institution to drag fugitives from the altars, and, in so doing, to set at nought one of the proudest, yet most unreasonable and even dangerous, privileges of the Church herself. For a time, no doubt, sanctuary was broken; no consideration of humanity or of sanctity could suffice to shield a suspected person from the rage of his pursuer: but the relations of the civil and ecclesiastical jurisdictions, and the rights of the Bishops and Archbishops to an independent administration within their own provinces, were too closely studied, and too earnestly contended for, to allow the Pontiffs to exercise, by their delegates, the Inquisitors, an absolute power, even over heretics. The ecclesiastical history of France is full of controversy between Church and State, and between the Clergy and their alien Pontiff; and, from this complication of interests, it resulted that the Inquisition, as a permanent court, is less conspicuous there than in some other countries, and that civil officers and dragoons did in France what familiars have done elsewhere.

During four or five centuries the contending powers of the Inquisition and the King or Parliament, or both King and Parliament united, found an alternate ascendancy, each change of position depending on the usual efforts of intrigue, or interest, or force. At one time we find Philip the Fair subjecting Fulco, a blood-thirsty Inquisitor in Aquitaine, to an inquest by Commissioners, and requiring heretics to be sent to royal prisons, and not to the dungeons of the "Holy House," and to be released forthwith, unless the Seneschal concurs in the prosecution. But Philip is excommunicated, and France put under interdict. Then heresy, so called, spreads. Gregory XI. urges King Charles V. to issue edicts, and send Commissioners, to hold up the falling Inquisition. The obedient King hastens to prove his loyalty to Rome, thunders threatenings, dispatches auxiliaries to the Sergeants of the Faith, crams the royal jails with suspected people, and causes new prisons to be built and filled, in order that nothing may be wanting to preserve the faith. Still the spark of truth smoulders in the ashes of the martyrs, the breath of Reformation quickens it after long darkness, and another missive from Clement VII. renews inquisitorial severities. But when a successor in the Popedom, Paul IV., repeats the experiment of a Bull to revive the Inquisition again, the Parliament of Paris refuses to register it; and, by that refusal, its power is annulled. But Popes and their abettors laugh at Parliaments when it seems possible to laugh with impunity; and, after this rebuff (A.D. 1559), when continental Europe is mad against the Reformation,—which appears, just in the last year of Mary, to have been crushed in England,—Henry II., advised by Cardinal Caraffa, purposes to establish the Inquisition with new formality in France, in imitation of Philip of Spain. His Ministers, however, dissuade him from an attempt which may raise a civil war; and he is content to ask for a Prelate or Doctor to be delegated from the Pope to conduct an ambulatory tribunal, disguised under some other name, but effecting the same purpose.

In the beginning of the seventeenth century, therefore, we find that portion of the canon-law which relates to this department of government enforced in Spain; and the Directory of Farinacius, the latest guide printed in Rome, was then published in France under the direct sanction of Louis XIII., to serve, of course, as a guide to the Inquisitors, who persisted in exercising their vocation. But early in the reign of his successor, Louis XIV., when a Nuncio of Innocent X. presumed to condemn a tract written in France in opposition to a decree of the Congregation of the Holy Office in Rome, the Parliament of Paris arose in indignation, and declared that the Congregations of the Court of Rome had no jurisdiction within France, nor had the Pope any right to publish such decrees. This disagreement grew into a formal controversy concerning the relative rights of the King and of the Pope, until, in the year 1682, the high Clergy sided with the Crown; and, at their Assembly in Paris, made the memorable declaration, that they had power to manage their own affairs independently of the Roman See. After this the Inquisition, although desired by some politicians to be retained as an engine of regal government, could no more exist. The Gallican Clergy, at that moment half emancipated, gave a solemn judgment that Kings hold their authority independently of Popes, who cannot justly have any power over them. The Supreme Council of the Spanish Inquisition, on the other side, launched a censure condemning this proposition of the Assembly of the French Clergy as heretical; but their interference was regarded with contempt. Yet the same Clergy that maintained a principle without which no nation can be safe, were at the height of rage against the Huguenots; and the Parliament of Paris, and the provincial Parliaments, were carrying on as horrible a persecution as the world ever saw. The dragonnades were filling France with slaughter; persecution culminated in the revocation of the Edict of Nantes, in the third year after the publication of the famous "Four Articles" of the Metropolitan Assembly; and the French history of that time tells, in every sentence, what universal history confirms, that, without the truth of Christianity and the love of Christ, ecclesiastical independence and national dignity are but a mockery. And it is certain, that the Gallican Clergy would never have opposed the Inquisition, if the Courts of Paris and Rome had not been at variance on a question of temporal emolument and regal or pontifical prerogative.

CHAPTER VII.

SPAIN—THE MODERN INQUISITION ESTABLISHED.

"Better and happier luck* for Spain was the establishment which took place in Castile, about this time, of a new and holy tribunal of severe and grave Judges, for the purpose of making inquest and chastising heretical pravity and apostasy, diverse from the Bishops, on whose charge and authority this office was anciently incumbent. For this

* It is the Father Juan de Mariana of the Company of Jesus who here speaks. It is but fair that admirers of the Inquisition should speak in these pages, which are furnished chiefly from their own lawyers and original historians. If "luck" be a heathenish word, the fault lies in the Spanish *suerte*, for which the translator cannot find a better English representative.

intent the Roman Pontiffs gave them power and authority, and *order was given* that the Princes, with their favour and their arm, should help them. These Judges were called Inquisitors, because of the office which they exercised of hunting out and making inquest, a custom now very general in other provinces, as in Italy, France, Germany, and even in the kingdom of Aragon. Castile, henceforth, would not suffer any nation to go beyond her in the desire which she always had to punish such enormous and wicked excesses. We find mention, before this, of some Inquisitors who exercised this office, at least for a time, but not in the manner and force of those who followed them.

"The chief author and instrument of this very salutary grant was the Cardinal of Spain," (Mendoza,) "who had seen that, in consequence of the great liberty of past years, and from the mingling of Moors and Jews with Christians in all sorts of conversation and trade, many things went out of order in the kingdom. With that liberty it was impossible that some Christians should not be infected: many more, leaving the religion which they had voluntarily embraced as converts from Judaism, again apostatised and returned to their old superstition, an evil which prevailed in Seville more than in any other part. In that city, therefore, secret searches were first made, and they severely punished those whom they found guilty. If their delinquency was considerable, after having kept them long time imprisoned, and after having tormented them, they burnt them. If it was light, they punished the offenders with the perpetual dishonour of all their family. Of not a few they confiscated the goods, and condemned them to imprisonment for life. On most of them they put a *sambenito*,* which is a sort of scapulary of yellow colour, with a red St. Andrew's cross, that they might go marked among their neighbours, and bear a signal that should affright and scare by the greatness of the punishment and of the disgrace; a plan which experience has shown to be very salutary, although, at first, it seemed very grievous to the natives.

"What caused most surprise was, that the children should pay for the crimes of the parents; that the accuser should not be known nor made known, nor confronted with the accused, nor that there should be any publication of wit-

* SAMBENITO. *Saco bendito*, or "blessed sack!"

nesses; which was all contrary to what had ever been observed in other tribunals. Besides this, it seemed to them a new thing, that sins of that kind should be punished with death; and, worst of all, that by those secret huntings out, they were deprived of the liberty of hearing and speaking among themselves, since they had in cities, towns, and villages persons appointed to give notice of all that passed,—a thing which some regarded as most heavy servitude, and bad as death. Hence there were various opinions. Some thought that such delinquents ought not to be punished with death; but, this excepted, they confessed that it was just for them to be chastised with some other kind of punishment. Among others of this opinion was Hernando de Pulgar, a person of acute and elegant genius, whose history of the affairs and life of the King Don Fernando" (Ferdinand) "is in print. Others, whose opinion was better, and more to the point, judged that those were not worthy of life who dared to violate religion, and to change the most holy ceremonies of their fathers; but that they ought to be punished and put to death, with forfeiture of goods and infamy, without caring for their children. For it is well provided by the laws, that, in some cases, children should bear the punishment of their fathers, in order that love towards their own children may make them more careful; that, by the judgment being secret, many calumnies, tricks, and frauds be avoided; that none be punished except those who confess their crime," (imprisonment and the torture, whereby confession is extorted, being no punishment in the eye of this *holy tribunal*,) "or are clearly convicted of it; and that sometimes the ancient customs of the Church be changed, according to what the times may require. And since liberty in sinning is greater, it is just that the severity of the punishment should be greater also. The event has shown this to be true, and the advantages are larger than could have been expected.

"That these Judges might not make an ill use of the great power given to them, neither by bribery nor oppression, very good laws and instructions" (of which the reader has now some knowledge) "were prepared from the beginning, and time and larger experience have given rise to many more. What makes more to the purpose is, that for this office are sought persons of mature age, *very upright and very holy*, (!) chosen out of all the province, as those into whose hands are placed the estates, honour, and life of all the natives. At that time was nominated for Inquisitor-General Fray Tomás de Torquemada, of the order of St. Dominic, a very prudent and learned person, and who had much influence with the King and Queen," (Ferdinand and Isabella,) "from being their Confessor, and Prior of the monastery of his order in Segovia. At first he had only authority in the kingdom of Castile; four years later it was extended into Aragon. Here they removed from the office, which they were there discharging after the ancient manner, the Inquisitors Fray Cristóbal Gualbes, and the Master Ortés, of the same order of Preachers. The said chief Inquisitor, at first, sent his Commissaries to various places as occasions presented themselves, not having as yet any fixed tribunal. In latter years the chief Inquisitor, with five persons of the Supreme Council in the court," (Madrid,) "where are the other supreme tribunals, manages the most grave matters touching religion. Causes of lesser moment, and affairs of first instance, are in charge of each two or three Inquisitors, stationed in the different cities. The towns where the Inquisitors now reside (A.D. 1623) are Toledo, Cuenca, Murcia, Valladolid, Santiago, Logroño, Sevilla, Córdova, Granada, Llerena; and—under the crown of Aragon—Valencia, Zaragoza, and Barcelona.

"The said chief Inquisitor published edicts wherein he offered pardon to all who would present themselves of their own accord. With this hope they say, that seventeen thousand persons, of both sexes and of all ages and ranks, were reconciled, two thousand persons burnt, and a larger but uncounted number fled into neighbouring countries. From this beginning the establishment has risen into so great authority and power, that there is not another in all the world more terrible to the wicked, nor more useful to Christendom; a very opportune remedy for all the evils that were impending, and with which other countries were troubled shortly afterwards; a gift from heaven, without which, no doubt, the wisdom and prudence of men would have been insufficient to prevent or bring succour amidst perils so great as we have experienced, and still are experiencing in other parts." *

Setting aside the eulogy of this Priest, we have accepted

* Historia General de España, libro xxiv., capitulo 17.

his compendium of a long and wearisome tale, as very characteristic of the Inquisition and of Spain. But the Instructions of Torquemada and the Constitution of the Supreme Council deserve a more distinct recital.

As for the Council, it was at first a compromise; but forthwith became a veritable combination of the regal and ecclesiastical jurisdictions for the extirpation of heresy, with a predominance, however, of the latter. To establish this statement, and show the spirit of Rome, as exemplified in the Inquisition, we must relate the facts. By a Bull of Gregory IX., dated May 26th, 1232, Dominican Friars were appointed Inquisitors in Aragon; and from that time inquisition of heretical pravity went onward in the four kingdoms of Aragon, Navarre, Castile, and Portugal, Granada being in possession of the Moors. No inconsiderable part of the Spanish population consisted of Jews, or persons recently converted from Judaism to the Romish Church. They were the most industrious, and therefore the most wealthy, people in the country, and had risen to a position of extensive influence. Their learned men occupied stations of great importance, as physicians, agents of government, and even officers of state; while the "New Christians," or Jews professedly converted to Christianity, were intermarried with the highest families in Spain; and all this had taken place in spite of the enmity of the Clergy, popular bigotry, and the adverse legislation of Cortes or Parliaments in the several kingdoms. But the wealth which procured the Jews and New Christians their social influence, was at the same time an occasion of great suffering. The "Old Christians," less industrious, and therefore not so affluent, were frequently their debtors. And although usury was checked, and debts often repudiated, the Jews maintained the usual advantage of creditors; but the Christians of pure blood, finding themselves involved in long reckonings, became increasingly impatient, and, under a cloak of zeal for the "Catholic" religion, were incessantly embroiling them with the magistracy, or stirring up the populace against them. Llorente estimates the number of Jews who perished in the streets, under the fury of mobs, at upwards of one hundred thousand in the year 1391. To evade persecution multitudes submitted to be baptized. More than a million changed name in the fourteenth century. After those tumults, controversial

Preachers, such as San Vicente Ferrer, declaimed for Popery against Judaism; and in the first ten years of the fifteenth century, a second multitude of converts threw themselves under shelter of the Church, to the discouragement of their brethren, and to their own perplexity at last; for they were placed under the keenest vigilance of the Inquisitors, without being able to display any honest attachment to the Church whose most grievous yoke they had put on.

Then the Church gloried over the declension of Judaism. In presence of Benedict XIII., Anti-Pope, a Spaniard, then wandering in Spain, because he was not owned at Rome, a formal disputation was carried on for sixty-nine days, between Jerome of Santa Fé, and other converts, (or, as the Jews not unreasonably called them, apostates,) on the one side, and a company of Rabbis on the other. Such a controversy, in the presence of even a half-Pope, could only come to the prescribed conclusion; and after seeing persuasion and corruption exhausted to bring over the Hebrews to his sect, but without much success, Benedict abruptly closed the debate, pronounced them vanquished, and gave them notice of severer measures. The richer from interest, the poorer from bigotry, and the priesthood from instinct, poured contempt even on the proselytes, whom they classified according to their supposed degrees of heterodoxy. Some were called *converts*, to note the newness of their Christianity. Others had the title of *confessed*, to tell that they had confessed that Judaism was false. Sometimes they passed under the epithet of *marranos*,—from *maran atha*,—or, as the Spaniards misinterpreted the words, *accursed*. The whole were spoken of as a generation of *marranos*, or were branded with that worst of names, which means all evil that can be concentrated in the imagination of a Papist,—*Jews*. Goaded by this ungenerous persecution, the proselytes groaned for deliverance; a few even dared to renounce the profession of a faith they had never held, and many resumed the practice of Jewish rites in private. This opened a new field to the zeal of the Inquisitors; but the labour of suppressing a revolt so widely spread, so rapidly extending, and even infecting the Romish families with whom the unsound converts were united, was more than the Inquisitors could undertake without recruited forces, and a more perfectly organised tribunal.

While matters stood thus with the Old Christians, the

New, and the remnant of unperverted Jews, Ferdinand and Isabella made progress in reconquering the kingdom of Granada. And as Mohammedanism fell in the south of Spain, the Moriscoes, a middle class, not less dangerous to the purity of Romish faith than the Jewish converts, absorbed the care of a new body of Inquisitors, who were anxious to watch over that uneasy population. No other country in Popedom was at that time more deeply imbued with disaffection to the worship and doctrines of the Church of Rome.

At this juncture one Fra Filippo de' Barberi, a Sicilian Inquisitor, came to the court of Ferdinand and Isabella (A.D. 1477), who were now the rulers of that island, to solicit the confirmation of some privileges recently granted to the Holy Office there; and, having observed the anxieties and peril of the Church within the enlarged and united dominions of the "Catholic Sovereigns," under whose rule nearly all Spain was comprehended, advised that the creation of one undivided court, constituted and acting like that of Sicily, would be the only means of deliverance from the Marranos, Moriscoes, Jews, and Mussulmans. The hint was quickly taken. The Dominicans first of all, and after them the dignitaries of the secular Clergy, crowded around the throne to pray for a reformation of the Inquisition after the Sicilian model. They appealed, directly, to the covetousness of Ferdinand, by offering him the proceeds of confiscations which would be rapidly effected, in pursuance of the laws of their Church to that intent provided. They appealed to the piety of Isabella, and were careful that tales of Jewish murders and Jewish desecrations should be invented, and poured incessantly into the royal ear. Ferdinand had no scruple, and sincerely prayed the Pope to sanction such a movement; and swiftly as couriers could bring it, came the desired Bull. The Queen could not reprove the zeal of the Priests and Monks; for she, too, was zealous. She could not gainsay the authoritative urgency of the Nuncio, a bitter bigot. She could not quench, in the bosom of her husband, the thirst of gold. But she had brought him half his kingdom as her dower, and by that accession he had been able to conquer great part of Granada. To her conscience and judgment some deference was therefore due, and she was allowed to try gentler measures. During two or three years her Orator and her Confessor wrote books, and

Preachers were permitted to publish arguments, and disputants to enter into conferences, for the conviction of the Jews. Cardinal Mendoza published a Constitution in Seville (A.D. 1478), containing "the form which should be observed with a Christian, from the day of his birth, as well in the sacrament of baptism as in all other sacraments which he ought to receive, and of what he should be taught, and ought to do and believe as a faithful Christian, every day, and at all times of his life, until the day of his death. And he ordered this to be published in all the churches of the city, and put in tables in each parish, as a settled constitution. And also of what the Curates and Clerks should teach their parishioners, and what the parishioners should observe and show to their children." Thus does Hernando del Pulgar, in his chronicle of the greater part of the reign of the Catholic Sovereigns, describe what some too hastily call a Catechism. It was merely a standard of things to be believed and things to be done, set forth by authority, read from the altar, and hung up in the church, not at all resembling the familiar compositions now called Catechisms. The King and Queen also—*not the Cardinal*—commanded "some Friars, Clerks, and other religious persons to teach the people." But no honest Jew could be convinced that idolatry is not damnable; and even the more hopeful issues of controversy with the vacillating or the ignorant were not faithfully reported. The Clergy maintained, that conversion by argument was impossible; and, at their instance, the Bull, hitherto kept in reserve, was at length published in 1480.

The question of humanity was ended; but another question of policy remained. The King and Queen remembered that they, as well as the Pope, had an interest in Spain; but they scarcely knew how that interest could be guarded, if the Inquisitors were allowed absolute power over the persons and the property of their subjects. To have demanded, like Venice, lay-assessors and open inquest, might have been reasonable;—supposing that an Inquisition were, in any shape, compatible with reason and religion;—but to have made such a demand to the See of Rome, then more powerful than it had been for ages, would only provoke a quarrel, and enable that court to arm the rest of Europe against the newly united, but not yet consolidated, monarchy of the

Spanish peninsula. A milder proposal was therefore made, and one which involved nothing that could offend the Pope; and this was, that some Priests nominated by the King should be associated with some Priests nominated by the Pope, or that the King should name all, and the Pope confirm his nomination. The "Catholic Sovereigns" calculated, that nominees of Rome would, of course, prefer the rights of the Church to those of the Crown, for such men could only represent an alien power; but they fancied, or they wished to fancy, that Priests of their own choice would prefer their interests to those of strangers. This was an illusion, and therefore Rome made little difficulty; and after correspondence, and some changes, the Supreme Council of the Spanish Inquisition was constituted thus:—

Friar Tomás de Torquemada, *Inquisitor-General*, of whom Llorente says that it was hardly possible that there could have been another equally able to fulfil the intentions of King Ferdinand, in multiplying confiscations; those of the Court of Rome, in propagating their jurisdictional and pecuniary maxims; and those of the projectors of the Inquisition, to infuse terror into the people, by means of acts of faith:—two Jurisconsults, Juan Gutierrez de Chabes and Tristan de Medina, *Assessors*:—Don Alonso Carrillo, a Bishop elect, with Sancho Velasquez de Cuellar and Poncio de Valencia, Doctors of Civil Law, were the King's *Counsellors*. In matters relating to royal power they were to have a definitive vote; but in affairs of spiritual jurisdiction, they could only be suffered to offer an opinion, inasmuch as all spiritual power resided in the chief Inquisitor alone. Within the jurisdiction of the Supreme Council were four subaltern tribunals, and eventually others were added, as we have stated from Mariana; some Inquisitors, holding special powers from the Pope, being stripped of their independence, that the one court might have a uniform and universal action throughout Spain. As the tribunal advanced in labour and experience, the Supreme Council was enlarged; and, in the middle of the last century, consisted, according to Miravel, of a President, (Inquisitor-General for the time being,) six Counsellors with the title of Apostolic, a Fiscal, a Secretary of the Chamber, two Secretaries of the Council, an Alguazil in Chief, or Sheriff, one Receiver, two Reporters, four Apparitors, one Solicitor, and as many Consulters as circumstances might require. Of course they were maintained in a style worthy of their office. The Inquisitor-General exerted an absolute power over every one of His Catholic Majesty's subjects, so that he almost ceased to be himself a subject. He alone consulted with the King concerning the appointment of Inquisitors to preside over the provincial tribunals which have been enumerated above. Each of those inferior Inquisitions was managed by three Inquisitors, two Secretaries, one under-Sheriff, one Receiver, and a certain number of Triers and Consulters. Their functions were considerably restricted, leaving all capital cases and ultimate decisions in the hands of the Madrid "Supreme."

CHAPTER VIII.

SPAIN—TRIUMPHS OF THE INQUISITORS.

But while Ferdinand, Isabella, Torquemada, and the Nuncio were adjusting their plans, and preparing death for heretics, what said Spain? Neither Clergy nor laity were content. After the Bull of Sixtus IV., empowering the King to name Inquisitors furnished with absolute authority, and to remove them at pleasure, had arrived, but lay unpublished, in consequence of the Queen's repugnance, a provincial Synod assembled at Seville, where the Court then was (A.D. 1478). Had Castile desired the Inquisition, the Deputies would have said so; but so far were they from approving of the new tribunal, to which every Bishop would be subject, but where no Bishop would any longer have a voice, that they passed over the affair of heresy in silence, not consenting to accept the Inquisition, yet not presuming to remonstrate. Then would have been their time to add their power to that of the Sovereign, for the suppression of adverse doctrine; and so they would most probably have done, if Inquisitor and Bishop, as in the first Inquisition of Toulouse, were to exercise a co-ordinate jurisdiction; but they saw, with alarm, that the Episcopate was, at a stroke, despoiled of its authority. A few months before the publication of the Bull, but long after every person in Spain knew the purport of its contents, and the certainty that it would be carried into execution, the Cortes of Toledo met; but, instead of avoiding any act that would interfere with the jurisdiction then to be introduced, they made several provisions for separating Jews and Christians, by the enclosure of Jewries in the towns, and for compelling the former to wear a peculiar garb, and abstain from exercising, among Christians, the vocations of physician, surgeon, innkeeper, barber, or apothecary. The Parliament plainly ignored the Inquisition in making this enactment.

And what said the magistracy and the people? Seville represented the general state of feeling at the time. There, when a company of Inquisitors presented themselves, conducted by men and horses, which had been impressed for the purpose by royal order, the civil authorities refused to help them, notwithstanding the injunctions of the Bull, the obligations of canon-law, and a mandate from the Crown. The new Inquisitors found themselves unable to act for want of help; the objects of their mission forsook the city, and found shelter in the neighbouring districts; and Ferdinand had to issue specific orders, to counteract the hostility of all classes, and to compel the Magistrates to assist the new Inquisitors.

Thus fortified, they took up their abode in the Dominican convent of St. Paul, and issued their first mandate (January 2d, 1481). They said that they were aware of the flight of the New Christians; and commanded the Marquis of Cadiz, the Count of Arcos, and all the Dukes, Marquises, Counts, Gentlemen, Rich-men (*ricos-homes*), and others, of the kingdom of Castile, to arrest the fugitives, and send them to Seville within a fortnight, sequestrating their property. All who failed to do this were to be excommunicated as abettors of heresy, deposed from their dignities, and deprived of their estates; and their subjects were to be absolved from homage and obedience. Crowds of fugitives were driven back into Seville, bound like felons; the dungeons and apartments of the convent overflowed with prisoners; and the King assigned to the "new and holy tribunal" the castle of Triana, on the opposite bank of the Guadalquivir, to be a place of custody. And the Inquisitors, elate with triumph over the reluctant Magistrates and panic-stricken people, shortly afterwards erected a tablet, with an inscription, to commemorate the first establishment of the modern Inquisition in western

Europe. The concluding sentences of this inscription were: "May God grant that, for the protection and augmentation of the faith, it may abide unto the end of time!—Arise, O Lord, judge Thy cause!—Catch ye the foxes!"

Their second edict was one of "grace." It summoned all who had apostatised, to present themselves to the Inquisitors within a term appointed, promising that all who did so, with true contrition and purpose of amendment, should be exempted from confiscation of their property,—it was understood that they should be punished in some other way,—but threatening that if they allowed that term to pass over without repentance, they should be dealt with according to the utmost rigour of the law. Many ran to that convent of St. Paul, hoping to merit some small measure of indulgence. But the Inquisitors would not absolve them until they had disclosed the names, calling, residence, and description of all others whom they had seen, heard, or understood to have apostatised in like manner. And, after all, they bound them to secrecy. This first object being accomplished, they sent out a third monition, requiring all who knew any that had apostatised into the Jewish heresy, to inform against them within six days, under the usual penalties. But they had already marked the men; and those suspected converts suddenly saw the Apparitors within their houses, and were dragged away to the dungeons. New Christians who had preserved any of the familiar usages of their forefathers, such as putting on clean clothes on Saturdays, who stripped the fat from beef or mutton, who killed poultry with a sharp knife, covered the blood, and muttered a few Hebrew words, who had eaten flesh in Lent, blessed their children, laying hands upon their heads, who observed any peculiarity of diet, or distinction of feast or fast, mourned for the dead after their ancient manner, or even presumed to turn the face towards a wall, when in the agony of death; all such were suspected of apostasy, and to be punished accordingly. Thirty-six elaborate articles were furnished, whereby every one was instructed how to ensnare his neighbour. But what shall we say of a faith that could only be preserved by the extinction of charity, of honour, of pity, and of humanity? Llorente shall describe the issue.

"Such opportune measures for multiplying victims could not but produce the desired effect. Hence, on the 6th of

January, 1481, there were burnt six unhappy persons, sixteen on the 26th of March, many on the 21st of April, and by the 4th of November two hundred and ninety-eight. Besides these, the Inquisitors condemned seventy-nine to perpetual imprisonment. And all this in the city of Seville only, since, as regards the territories of this archbishopric, and of the bishopric of Cadiz, Juan de Mariana says, that in the single year of 1481, two thousand Judaisers were burnt in person, and very many in effigy, of whom the number is not known, besides seventeen thousand subjected to penance. Among those burnt were many principal persons and rich inhabitants, whose property went into the treasury.

"As so many persons were to be put to death by fire, the Governor of Seville caused a permanent raised pavement, or platform of masonry, to be constructed outside the city, which has lasted to our time," (until the French invasion, if not later,) "retaining its name of *Quemadero*, or 'Burning-place,' and at the four corners four large hollow statues of limestone, within which they used to place the impenitent alive, that they might die by slow fires. I leave my readers to consider whether this punishment of an error of the understanding was agreeable, or not, to the doctrine of the Gospel.

"The fear of others of the same class caused an innumerable multitude of New Christians to emigrate to France, Portugal, and even Africa. But many others, whose effigies had been burnt, appealed to Rome, complaining of the injustice of those proceedings; in consequence of which appeals the Pope wrote, on the 29th of January, 1482, to Ferdinand and Isabella, saying that there were innumerable complaints against the Inquisitors, Fray Miguel Morillo and Fray Juan de San Martin especially, because they had not confined themselves to canon-law, but declared many to be heretics that were not. His Holiness said that, but for the royal nomination, he would have deprived them of their office, but that he revoked the power he had given to the Sovereign to nominate others, supposing that fit persons would be found among those nominated by the General, or the Provincial, of the Dominicans, to whom the privilege belonged, and in prejudice of whose privilege the former nomination by Ferdinand and Isabella had been allowed." So adroitly did the Pope take the absolute control of the

Inquisition into his own hands, and leave the cheated tyrant to eat the fruit of his doings. But, since that time, King and Pontiff have been again united in the management of the Holy Office, the latter, however, in subservience to the former.

Neither in the Appeal nor in the Brief was there anything to divert Torquemada from his purposes; and therefore he hastened to add Aragon to his jurisdiction. Ferdinand convened the Cortes of that kingdom in the city of Tarazona (April, 1484), therein appointed a *Junta* to prepare measures for the establishment of a modern tribunal; and then Torquemada, in pursuance of the latest Pontifical decision, created Friar Gaspar Inglar, a regular Preacher of the Dominican community, and Doctor Pedro Arbues de Epila, a Canon of the metropolitan church, Inquisitors. The King gave a mandate to the civil authorities, a firman compelling them to lend aid to the new officials; and, on the 13th of September following, the Grand Justice of Aragon, with his five Lieutenants of the long robe, and various other Magistrates, swore upon the Holy Gospels that they would give men and arms to defend and to enforce the authority of the Holy Inquisition. And as they swore thus, the chief Secretary of the King for Aragon, the Protonotary, the Vice-Chancellor, the royal Treasurer, whose father and grandfathers had been Jews, and persecuted by the old Inquisitors, together with a multitude of persons of high rank and office, in whose veins flowed Jewish blood, and whose descendants are now among the first families in Spain, looked on with dismay, and sent a deputation to Rome, bearing remonstrance against the newly-created Inquisition, and deputed others to present their appeal at the court of the "Catholic Sovereigns." All these deputies were afterwards proceeded against as "hinderers of the Holy Office;" and the Inquisitors, heedless of the general opposition, set themselves to work without delay. In the months of May and June, 1485, two Acts of Faith were celebrated in Zaragoza, and a large number of "New Christians" burnt alive. The public was enraged, although helpless; and many thought that since the Inquisition had resorted to terror for the conservation of the faith, terror ought also to restrain them in their turn.

In the night of September 14th, 1485, one of the Inquisitors, Pedro Arbues, covered with a coat-of-mail under his robes, and wearing a steel helmet under his hat, (for he was conscious of guilt, and apprehensive of retribution,) took a lantern in one hand and a bludgeon in the other, and, like a brave soldier of the Church, walked from his house to the cathedral, to join in matins. He knelt down by one of the pillars, laying his lantern on the pavement. His right hand grasped the weapon of defence, but stealthily, and half covered with the cloak. The Canons, in their places, were chanting the hymns. Two men came, and knelt down near him. They understood, as do most Spaniards, how most effectually to attack, and how quickest to kill, a man. Therefore one of them suddenly disabled him on one side by a blow on the left arm. The other swung his cudgel at the back of the head, just below the edge of the helmet, and laid him prone. He never spoke again, but expired in a few hours. The murder, however, was made use of to prove the necessity of an Inquisition to repress violence; and the inhabitants of Zaragoza were suddenly overawed by a display of judicial authority, which they were not in a condition to resist. Queen Isabella, horrified at the murder of her Confessor,—for "Confessor of the Kings" was an honorary dignity conferred on each Inquisitor,—caused a monument to be erected to his memory at her own expense; and when the murders perpetrated by Arbues himself had somewhat faded out of memory, he was beatified at Rome, and a chapel was constructed for his veneration in the church where he had fallen. Therein his remains were laid, and over the spot where he received the mortal blows a stone was placed, with an inscription that may serve to end the story. "*Siste, viator*, &c. Stay, traveller! Thou adorest the place (*locum adoras*) where the blessed Pedro de Arbues was levelled by two missiles. Epila gave him birth. This city gave him a canonry. The Apostolic See elected him to be the first Father-Inquisitor of the Faith. Because of his zeal he became hateful to the Jews, by whom slain, he fell a martyr here in the year 1485. The most serene Ferdinand and Isabella reared a marble mausoleum, where he became famous for miracles. Alexander VII., *Pontifex Maximus*, wrote him into the number of holy and blessed martyrs on the 17th day of April, in the year 1664. The tomb having been opened, the sacred ashes were translated, and placed under the altar of the chapel, (built by the Chapter, with the material of the tomb, in the space of sixty-five days,) with solemn rite and veneration, on the 23d day of September, in the year 1664."*

The intelligence of this murder threw all Aragon into commotion. The powers, ecclesiastical and royal, panted for vengeance, and put the murderers to a most painful death. The Jews and New Christians trembled with rage and terror. The inhabitants of many towns, Ternel, Valencia, Lerida, and Barcelona included, compelled the Inquisitors to cease from inquisition; and it was only by means of Edicts and Bulls, followed by military force, that the King and the Pope could overcome resistance after a labour of two years. In Zaragoza, where the murder had been contrived by a party of the chief inhabitants, a consciousness of guilt weakened their hands, and they endeavoured to save themselves by flight. Thousands of people fled, although they had no direct participation in the deed, and were everywhere pursued as rebels; and in that migration incidents occurred which might throw a colour of romance on our history. We briefly mention two. An inhabitant of Zaragoza found his way to Tudela, and there begged for shelter and concealment in the house of Don Jaime, Infante of Navarre, legitimate son of the Queen of Navarre, and nephew of Ferdinand himself. The Infante could not refuse asylum and hospitality to an unoffending fugitive. He allowed the man to hide himself for a few days, and then pass on to France; and for that act of humanity was arrested by the Inquisitors, thrown into prison as an impeder of the Holy Office, brought thence to Zaragoza, a city beyond the jurisdiction of Navarre, and there made to do open penance in the cathedral, in presence of a great congregation at high mass. The Archbishop who presided was an illegitimate son of King Ferdinand, a boy of seventeen; and, to crown the ceremony, two Priests whipped the royal penitent through the church with rods. The other

* If they beatify their martyrs, what should prevent us from declaring ours—as we trust—to be blessed? More than a century before this adoration of Pedro de Arbues, John Foxe had published his Calendar of Martyrs, and been accused by the Papists of the very sin charged upon themselves. But, in his defence, he wrote thus:—"To canonise or to authorise any saints, for man it is presumptuous; to prescribe anything here to be worshipped, beside God alone, it is idolatrous; to set up any mediators but Christ only, it is blasphemous. And whatever the Pope doth, or hath done, in his Calendar, my purpose, in my Calendar, was neither to deface any old saint, nor to solemnise any new."

case was yet more shameful. One Gaspar de Santa Cruz escaped to Toulouse, where he died, and was buried, after his effigy had been burnt at Zaragoza. In this place remained a son of his, who, as in duty bound, had helped him to make good his retreat. This son was delated as an impeder of the Holy Office, arrested, brought out at an Act of Faith, made to read a condemnation of his deceased father, and then sent to the Inquisitors at Toulouse, who took him to his father's grave, and compelled him to dig up the corpse, and burn it with his own hands. Llorente shudders as he relates the fact, not knowing whether the barbarity of the Inquisitors, or the vileness of the young man, is the more worthy of abhorrence. But it is a chief glory of the Inquisition, that it can vanquish natural affection.

The Arch-Inquisitor, shortly after his accession to the office, summoned the subalterns from their provinces to meet him at Seville, and framed, with them, a set of instructions for uniform administration. These were published, twenty-eight in number, on the 29th of October, 1484. On January 9th, 1485, eleven more were added. The former chiefly related to the manner of making inquisition, and giving judgment. The latter were, for the most part, provisions for managing and guarding the jurisdiction and the revenue of the institution. The spirit of those instructions pervades the Directory of Eymeric, into which they were incorporated by his commentator; and they have already passed under review. It is only important to mention here, that an agent was appointed to represent the Inquisition at Rome, and there to defend the Inquisitors on occasions of appeal from subjects of inquisitorial violence, or their friends, or survivers. And this was in spite of a Bull sent into Spain two years before, which had appointed the Archbishop of Seville sole Judge of such appeals. But that Bull was never acted on at Rome.

We mark this point in the history, forasmuch as here began the practically juridical relation between the Court of Rome, as absolutely supreme, and the provinces of the Romish Church, in relation to the Inquisition. More, *much* more, of this hereafter; but, passing over particulars that are foreign from our present object, let it suffice to say that, during thirty years after the establishment of the modern Inquisition in Spain, every one who could effect an appeal to Rome, either by memorial or in person, and who paid for the despatch of Briefs, obtained the indulgence, or the exemption, he desired, until an opposite party came after him, and purchased a contrary decision. In this way the King, the Inquisitors, and the New Christians, all bought, and all were cheated; but money flowed into the Roman Datary, and that was enough to satisfy the Fathers of the faithful.

CHAPTER IX.

SPAIN—GRANADA—EXPULSION OF THE JEWS.

The first resistance to the horrible tribunal having been overcome in Aragon, and its discipline fully organized in that kingdom, it assumed a position of unexampled influence over the general government of Spain, and impressed a singular character on the future history of the nation. We will survey its dealings with the Jews.

The "Catholic Sovereigns" have conquered the Moors everywhere, Granada alone excepted. Their army is laying siege to that noble city. The inhabitants know resistance to be hopeless, and send out a flag of truce. Hostilities are to be suspended for sixty days. The chief men of Granada come into the royal camp, and are encouraged to propose terms of capitulation. Their demands are large, for a vanquished people to make at the close of a hard campaign; but the Spaniards are tired of battle, and resolve to grant almost any terms, trusting to the chance of events for what cannot be now obtained without wearisome negotiation, or continued war. They agree to give this brave remnant of the Saracens a tract of country towards the sea-board, known as the Alpujarra, to be occupied by them as crown-land, on very easy conditions,—a handsome weight of gold, a general amnesty, and special privileges to the Moorish King, Abdilehi, and his family. As many as choose are to quit the city, with all their property, fire-arms and ammunition alone excepted; and further articles, to be hereafter settled, are to be ratified on delivery of the Alhambra, and other fortifications, to Ferdinand and his garrison.

These articles are prepared, during a period of forty days, with careful deliberation, and every possible appearance of good faith. If they are fulfilled, the Moors will be a free people, dwelling unmolested in the hilly tract assigned to them, and its twelve towns; and, in Granada and the suburbs, they will cultivate the lands in their own inimitable manner, and suffer no badge of infamy, nor even the least mark of disrespect. They will have their own laws, customs, and religion. But on this last point an historian of the Inquisition must be explicit, and recite the two articles which seem, most of all, to guarantee them shelter from persecution. We translate them closely from the very words of the treaty, as recorded by Marmol.

"That it shall not be permitted that any person, either by word or deed, ill-treat Christian men, or Christian women, who shall have turned Moors before these capitulations. And that, if any Moor shall have married any renegade woman, she shall not be forced to be a Christian against her will; but that she shall be interrogated in presence of Christians and of Moors, and shall follow her own pleasure. And the same shall be observed as to boys and girls born of a Christian woman and a Moorish husband.

"That no Moor, either man or woman, shall be forced to become a Christian; and if any young woman, or wife, or widow, shall wish to turn Christian, for the sake of any attachment she may have, she shall not be received until she has been questioned; and if she has taken any property, or jewelry, from the house of her parents, or from any other place, it shall be restored to its owner, and the guilty parties shall be punished."

On the day appointed (January 2d, 1492), the Cardinal Archbishop of Toledo, Don Pedro Gonzalez de Mendoza, puts himself at the head of a strong force, with some pieces of artillery, and marches into Granada, to take possession of the Alhambra. Ferdinand and Isabella follow afar off, leading the main body of the army. The vanquished Abdilehi meets him, bids him take possession of those fortifications for the mighty Sovereigns to whom God has given them for the sins of the Moors; and then, turning his back upon them, goes away, sorrowful and unarmed, to deliver himself to his conquerors. Isabella has halted at a distance; but within view of the citadel, where she cannot yet see the Spanish flag. The Kings meet, and she fears some treason or some reverse, and trembles with suspense amidst her

Priests, who are not much more courageous than their mistress. At length she sees the army move towards the gates, covering the hill-side as they march up. When they enter, the crescent falls, and the standard of Castilla and Leon, surmounted by a silver cross, is hoisted. Granada is theirs.—The war is over.—The "Pagans" are under foot. Dissimulation is no longer needed. The whole chapel strikes up a loud chant, and one *Te Deum* suffices for thanksgiving. Notwithstanding their treaty above-cited, they instantly appoint one Fray Hernando de Talavera to be Archbishop of Granada, although, the garrison excepted, there are not yet any persons there bearing the name of Christian; and this Archbishop, without a province, applies himself to the work of converting the Moors. His first measure is to make himself agreeable; and, in a very short time, not yet mentioning doctrine to the inhabitants, his charities and affability have so won their good opinion, that they pay him great reverence, and salute him as the chief Alfaqui of the Christians. By this time, indeed, the said Christians have crowded into Granada, and mass is sung with high magnificence. Still we must do Fray Hernando the justice of saying, that he is a humane and reasonable man.

Now begins the action of the Inquisition on a great scale indeed, yet not towards the Moors first.

It is very remarkable that, by one article of the Moorish capitulation, every Jew found in Granada on its occupation by the Spaniards, was to be shipped away to Barbary, if he did not become a Christian within three years. This shows that an idea of expelling the Jews must have been entertained at that time, although none of them appear to have entertained the least suspicion of any design to ruin them, beyond the measures of ordinary persecution.

Jewish armourers were, at that very moment, working in the camp. Jewish victuallers provided the daily rations. Jewish brokers advanced money to pay the troops. And it is by no means unlikely, that they were Jews who raised the gold which Ferdinand and his Queen had bargained to pay the Moorish King. And it is indisputable that, but for the assistance of that people, in the absence of any efficient system of national finance in Christian Spain, Granada could never have been conquered. But Torquemada followed the court, and, as royal Confessor, might have heard the King's aspirations after wealth, and understood his unwillingness, and perhaps inability, to liquidate his debts. The zeal of the Inquisitor and the dishonesty of the King most seasonably met and harmonised; and it only remained for them to contrive some scheme whereby both passions might be satisfied. Some Monks quickly collected a report that some Jews had stolen a consecrated host, with intention to kill a Christian child, make the host into paste with his warm blood, and poison the Inquisitors. But some particles of the crumbled wafer had got between the leaves of a Hebrew Prayer-Book in a synagogue. Some one present saw the divine substance emit a bright light, and, conjecturing by that signal that the crime of sacrilege had been perpetrated, made it known to a Priest. The Jews' guilt being thus miraculously discovered, the Priests and Monks remembered that those wealthy and serviceable Israelites had been wont to commit sacrilege and murder from spite to the Christians, and endless tales of the kind resounded in the palace of the Alhambra, where the victorious, but scarcely solvent, Sovereigns resided. Torquemada gave judgment that they ought to cleanse the soil of Spain from so vile a race; and they accordingly issued an edict from Granada, dated less than three months after the day of occupation (March 30th, 1492), to banish the entire people, excepting only such as might choose to surrender their faith, and retain their homes in compensation for apostasy.*

The document is long, but its contents may be shortly stated. Their Highnesses had been informed that the Jews had been perverting Christians into their superstition; and seeing that neither separation of them from the population in the Jewries, nor even examples of death by fire, by sentence after inquisition,—nor yet impaling others alive, they might have added,—had restrained them from their attempts to overturn the Christianity of Spain, they resolved on a final and effectual remedy. They did not imagine that all the Jews were guilty; but they conceived that when any detest-

* If Romanism were Christianity, and not idolatry, and if the transition to it from the synagogue were voluntary, through faith in our Lord Jesus Christ, that change would be *conversion*, causing joy in the presence of the angels of God. But in the contrary case before us the renunciation of Judaism deserves no better name than that given to it in the text.

able crime was committed by some members of a college or university, that college or university should be dissolved and annihilated. Therefore they commanded all Jews and Jewesses to quit their kingdoms, and never to return, not even for a passing visit, under penalty of death. The last day of July was to be the last of their dwelling in the country; and, after that day, any person, of what rank soever, who should presume to receive, shelter, protect, or defend a Jew or Jewess, was to forfeit all his property and be discharged from his office, dignity, or calling. During those four months, the Jews might sell their estates, or barter them for heavy goods; but they were not to take away "gold, silver, money, or other articles prohibited by the laws of the kingdom."

The decree of Ahasuerus was not more terrible, and scarcely could the mourning, and weeping, and wailing, which resounded throughout Persia and Media, have surpassed those of the Spanish Jews. They cried aloud for mercy, and offered to submit to any law, however oppressive, if they might remain in their beloved country. Rabbi Abarbanel, whose name is familiar to every Hebrew scholar, a reputed descendant of the family of Judah, a man who had enjoyed the confidence of successive Sovereigns, whom Ferdinand and Isabella had summoned to their court eight years before, and whose services they made large use of while he farmed the royal revenue;—this aged Hebrew found his way into their presence, in the Alhambra, knelt before them, weeping, implored pity on his nation, and offered to lay down as ransom six hundred thousand crowns of gold. Again he returned, and, to use his own words,* "I wearied myself to distraction in imploring compassion. Thrice on my knees I besought the King: 'Regard us, O King, use not thy subjects so cruelly. Why do thus to thy servants? Rather exact from us our gold and silver, even all that the house of Israel possesses, if he may remain in his country.' I likewise entreated my friends, the King's officers, to allay his anger against my people. I implored the Councillors to advise the King to repeal the decree. But as the adder closes its ear with dust against the voice of the charmer, so the King hardened his heart against the entreaties of his supplicants, and declared that he would

* Translated by Mr. Lindo, in his most valuable "History of the Jews of Spain and Portugal."

not revoke his edict for all the wealth of the Jews. *The Queen at his right hand opposed it*, and urged him to continue what he had begun. We exhausted all our power for the repeal of the King's sentence; but there was neither wisdom nor help remaining." The truth is, that those intercessions had nearly prevailed. The King was calculating whether he had not better accept the ready money, instead of trusting to get his share in the profits of the other scheme, which would be squandered among many claimants, when the first Inquisitor ended his hesitation at a stroke.

Torquemada rushed into a room where the King and Queen were sitting, holding up a crucifix, and shouting at the top of his voice: "Judas sold the Son of God once for thirty pieces of silver: Your Highnesses are going to sell Him the second time for thirty thousand. Here He is; here you have Him: sell Him if you will." And then the audacious bigot flung the crucifix before them on the table, and retired in fury. The full weight of Papal indignation seemed to overhang them, and Abarbanel and his friends were put to silence. Here, indeed, the tribunal did not act, but only its head and its members, who engaged their Sovereigns to act instead of them. The expulsion of the Jews, therefore, must not be overlooked, as if it were not a deed of the Inquisition.

Having gained so much, Torquemada made the most of his opportunity. He sent Preachers through the country to convert the Jews, and published an edict, offering baptism and reconciliation; but very few indeed submitted. He forbade Christians to hold any intercourse with them after the month of April, or to supply them with food, shelter, or any necessary, thus annulling a promise given in the royal decree, that during the period of four months no wrong or injury should be done to them. "A contemporary and eye-witness," cited by Lindo,* shall describe their condition at this time. "Within the term fixed by the edict, the Jews sold and disposed of their property for a mere nothing. They went about begging Christians to buy, but found no purchasers. Fine houses and estates were sold for trifles. A house was exchanged for an ass, and a vineyard given for a little cloth or linen. Although prohibited carrying away gold and silver, they secretly took large quantities in their saddles, and in the halters and harness of their loaded

* Bernaldez, MS. Chron. de los Reyes Catholicos.

beasts. Some swallowed as many as thirty ducats to avoid the rigorous search made at the frontier-towns and seaports, by the officers appointed for the purpose. The rich Jews defrayed the expenses of the departure of the poor, practising towards each other the greatest charity, so that, except very few of the most necessitous, they would not become converts. In the first week of July they took the route for quitting their native land, great and small, old and young; on foot, on horses, or asses, and in carts; each continuing his journey to his destined port. They experienced great trouble and suffered indescribable misfortunes on the roads and country they travelled; some falling, others rising; some dying, others coming into the world; some fainting, others being attacked with illness; so that there was not a Christian but what felt for them, and persuaded them to be baptized. Some, from misery, were converted; but they were very few. The Rabbies encouraged them, and made the young people and women sing, and play on pipes and tabors, to enliven them and keep up their spirits." All their synagogues were left unpurchased, to be converted, without compensation, into mass-houses.

An emigration of fifteen hundred wealthy families first embarked. Ships were provided at Carthagena, Valencia, Barcelona, Cadiz, Gibraltar, and other ports, to convey them to Africa, Italy, and the Levant; and they carried with them that dialect of the Spanish language which to this day serves the Jews of those countries as a medium of common intercourse. Some perished at sea by wreck, disease, violence, or fire; and some by famine, exhaustion, or murder on inhospitable shores. Many were sold for slaves; many were thrown overboard by the savage Captains. Parents sold their children for money to buy food. On board one vessel full of exiles, a pestilential disease broke out: the Captain landed all on a desert island, where they wandered about in quest of assistance. Heart-rending tales were told by the survivers. A mother carrying two infants, walking with her husband, expired on the road. The father, overcome with fatigue, fell fainting near his two children: on recovering his consciousness, he found them dead with hunger. He covered them with sand. "My God," exclaimed he, "my misfortunes seem to drive me to abandon Thy law; but I am a Jew, and will ever remain so." The crowded vessels carried disease into the port of Naples, where the inhabitants caught it, and about twenty thousand were carried off. When another famishing division reached Genoa, they found the city also suffering from famine, and were met, on landing, by a procession of Priests, of whom the foremost carried a crucifix in one hand and a loaf in the other, to signify that they who would adore the image might have the bread. It pleased the Pope, Alexander VI., to give them a better reception in his states, leaving it to his more distant servants to do the heavier inquisitorial drudgery, and to suffer the more flagrant scandal. Spain had impoverished herself, in his service, by the loss of eight hundred thousand persons, besides many more who had already fled from the Inquisition during ten or twelve years of terror, and the whole had carried away an incalculable amount of wealth.

Having expelled the Jews, Torquemada and his royal servants next turned their attention to the Moors and Moriscoes. But as this Prince of Spanish Inquisitors did not live to see the accomplishment of his desire in regard to the Moors, of whom we have now to speak, we anticipate the close of his administration of the Inquisition of Castile, not to interrupt the sketch following, and here note the number of his victims, according to the calculation of Llorente, which is quite exclusive of the Jews, and appears to be very moderate, notwithstanding a charge of exaggeration laid against him by modern admirers or apologists of the Holy Office.

Burnt at the stake........................	10,220
Burnt in effigy, the persons having died in prison or fled the country ..	6,860
Punished with infamy, confiscation, perpetual imprisonment, or loss of civil rights......................	97,321
Total	114,401

An equal number of families, at least, must have been ruined; and there must be yet an unrecorded number of persons whose lives were shortened by indigence and grief. Considering the number of his enemies, and the badness of his conscience, we do not wonder that, in his latter years, he was preyed upon by terror; and, to preserve himself from assassination, never travelled without a body-guard of fifty familiars of the Inquisition mounted as dragoons, and two hundred more marching as foot-soldiers.

CHAPTER X.

SPAIN—MOORS AND MORISCOES.

THE persecution and expulsion of the Moors and Moriscoes from the kingdom of Granada was entirely the work of the Inquisition. But the action of the tribunal began gently, and its method was so adapted to the peculiar circumstances of the new province, that a hasty reader might attribute that to Spanish intolerance which in truth belongs to the Inquisitors alone; and although we carefully avoid the general history of persecutions, we cannot exclude this from our pages.

The Catholic Sovereigns had taken possession of Granada, and, after banishing the Jews, rewarded the vassals to whose arms they were chiefly indebted for the conquest with grants of lands, and with offices of trust. They invited to their court persons of high repute for piety, such as it was, and for wisdom. Among the "religious" whom they summoned from their cells to render counsel in affairs of state, the court being then a sort of promiscuous and irresponsible cabinet, was Don Fray Hernando de Talavera, whom we have already mentioned, a Friar Professed of the order of St. Jerome, a man of ready wit and extensive information, an eminent preacher, learned in sacred literature and moral philosophy, and reputed to be unblamable in life. For twenty years he had been Prior of a monastery near Valladolid, whence Ferdinand and Isabella, induced by the fame of his virtues and talents, called him to their presence, made him their Confessor, gave him the bishopric of Avila, and took him into their counsels. We mark this man the more carefully, because he appears in favourable contrast with other Ecclesiastics of the court. After a large number of Christians had come to live in Granada, he begged to resign the see of Avila, in order to devote himself to the interests of the new Church. His desire was honoured, and Pope Alexander VI.

sent him a pallium, with the title of Archbishop of Granada. With a revenue much inferior to that of the diocese resigned, he displayed little or no prelatic pomp, and applied himself diligently to the duties of a new charge, and to the conversion of the Moors.

A gentle spirit and a spotless life won the veneration of the Moors, from whom he appears to have prudently concealed his purpose of attempting their conversion. Nor did he, so far as we can judge, propose to employ any sort of coercion, but endeavoured to teach them Christianity by the word of God. He caused the holy Scriptures to be translated into Arabic for their use; and although the translation was never printed, it is not improbable that parts of it, at least, were copied for distribution. The Mohammedans heard him willingly, meeting him by companies in private houses, where he addressed them through interpreters. Several Ecclesiastics applied themselves closely to the study of Arabic, encouraged by the example of their Diocesan, who also became a learner in his old age; and Moors, emulating their industry, committed to memory the Decalogue, the Apostles' Creed, and several prayers. But the zeal that threw him into those labours at Granada, withdrew him from the court of Ferdinand and Isabella, whom counsellors of another kind entirely governed in all things relating to religion. Torquemada, chiefly, held their conscience at his disposal.

A first stroke of treachery was levelled at the last King of Granada, Zogoybi, who was retired on the estates allotted to him in the Alpujarra. After living there peaceably for two years, he was surprised by the sudden appearance of a servant whom he had appointed to represent him in the train of the Catholic Sovereigns in Aragon. The man came into his presence, bringing mules laden with eighty thousand ducats, and told him that he had sold his lands for that money, wherewith he had better go to Barbary, and there buy him a resting-place, and avoid the danger which would surround him if the Moors, encouraged by his presence, should disturb the tranquillity of Spain. The slave had been corrupted. Zogoybi submitted to a breach of faith which it was not in his power to redress, and embarked for Barbary, overwhelmed with grief and shame.

Now came an effort to convert or banish all the Moors.

The Inquisitors, headed by Don Diego Deza, successor of Torquemada, and their adherents, plied Ferdinand and Isabella with incessant entreaty to banish all who would not be converted and baptized. They affirmed "that by this measure the articles of capitulation granted on the surrender of Granada would not be broken, but that rather their condition would be bettered by an arrangement of so great advantage to their souls;" and they further argued that, as Mohammedans and Christians could not possibly live in peace together, the public good required that the former should either be converted or expelled. The King and Queen hesitated to attempt the proposed expulsion, as they had hesitated, a few years before, to receive a severer form of Inquisition, and as they had more lately hesitated to expel the Jews. "Although these considerations were holy and very just,"—we quote the words of Marmol,—"their Highnesses did not determine that such rigour should be used with their new vassals, because the land was not yet made sure, nor had the Moors altogether laid aside their weapons; and if, haply, they should be driven to rebellion by oppression in a thing on which they would feel so keenly, it might be necessary to resume the war." Their Highnesses thought the measure inexpedient rather than immoral; they were also unwilling to be diverted from other projects; and they hoped that the Moors, like other vanquished nations, would gradually adopt the religion of their conquerors; "and, that this might be effected by love and benevolence, they commanded the Governors, Alcaydes, and Justices of all their kingdoms to favour the Moors, and not allow them to suffer any grievance or ill-treatment, and bade the Prelates and the religious, gently and with demonstration of love, endeavour to teach concerning the faith those who might freely choose to hear them, without oppressing them, in the least, on that account."

It is not for us to inquire too severely how far this expresses the real intentions of the Sovereigns: we know that it is not the language of the Church. After six or seven years of conciliation, under the good care of Fray Hernando, a far different personage, Francisco Ximenez de Cisneros, Archbishop of Toledo, Primate of Spain, followed the court to Granada, saw the unusual charity displayed by the Archbishop of that province towards the inhabitants, and received a royal injunction to remain in the city and promote the great object of conversion, still exercising forbearance, and guarding against every occasion of tumult. But Ferdinand and Isabella rendered conciliation impossible, by allowing Granada to be taken under the jurisdiction of the Inquisition of Cordova. Hernando laid open his plans to his new colleague and ecclesiastical superior. He showed him a manuscript translation of the holy Scriptures into Arabic, ready for the press, with a version, in the same language, of the Missal, some rituals and other books used in worship. Ximenez objected to such an innovation. Hernando thought that nothing better could be done for New Christians, than to put the sacred volume into their hands in an intelligible form, and he desired that prayers should be read in the vernacular language. He sustained his argument by citing the text of St. Paul; and justified his proposal by the example of the Greek Church, whose Liturgies he imagined to be still intelligible to the congregations, and by that of the Latin Church for many ages, until her language had ceased to be vernacular. Ximenez, on the contrary, was persuaded that the Moors would despise his Christianity if they understood it; and, rejecting the sentences of inspired writers as inapplicable to the condition of society in later times, and declaring that prayer in a known tongue would be an insufferable innovation, he forbade the publication of the versions.

Ximenez was not yet Cardinal, nor yet Inquisitor-General; but he must have been in communication with the "Holy Office" at Cordova. In the last year of the fifteenth century he began his mission by holding some apparently amicable conferences with their learned men, presenting to them articles of belief and theological arguments, mingled with offers of civil freedom, rewards, and offices, if they would accept the first elements of Christianity, and teach them to their people. The bargain being struck, Moorish Doctors were heard in the mosques declaiming against the superstitions and errors of Islâm, and exhorting their congregations to embrace the faith of Christ. The reasons for conversion were not gathered out of the Bible, which no one thought of, but were entirely suggested by the Primate, who had power to dispense the favours of the Crown. Such preaching could not but work wonders, and the Doctors led three thousand of their brethren as candidates for baptism into the presence of Ximenez. They were baptized at once. The Archbishop of Toledo sprinkled them "with hyssop" as they walked past him. Hernando would have taught them first; but Ximenez feared that if they were not received then, they might not come again. On the festival of Our Lady of the O,* the mosque of the Albaycin, a quarter of the city privileged with independent jurisdiction, was consecrated to be a collegiate church, under the advocacy of the Holy Saviour. The selection of time, place, and persons, indicated a deep scheme; and the contriver would suffer nothing to hinder its prosecution.

Zegri, a Moorish Prince, was said to have objected to the desertion of so many from his religion; and Ximenez, thinking to put Granada to silence by an effort of authority, had him arrested secretly, and imprisoned in the Alhambra, with a Monk named Leon in the same cell, whose "lion-like" impetuosity, with threats of perpetual imprisonment if he would not be baptized, overcame his obstinacy; and he not only submitted to baptism, but, having gone so far, endeavoured to make the best of the change, by courting the favour of the superior powers. Proselytes continued to flock into the Church,—their number is said to have risen to fifty thousand; and the Archbishop of Toledo resolved to accelerate the work by a new measure, an attempt to force the Elches, or renegades from Christianity, to return to the bosom of the Church. Any renegade who refused on the first summons was usually regarded as guilty of disrespect of authority, and arrested. These arrests became very numerous, and recusants filled the prisons. At length, as an Alguacil was leading away a woman of the Albaycin to prison, the people became infuriated, released the woman, and killed the Alguacil. The general discontent then broke out in an insurrection of the city. A hundred thousand men, capable of bearing arms, were terrible by multitude and unity; the small garrison in the Alhambra could not attempt to act, and, during ten days, Ximenez was besieged in the citadel, which must have surrendered, if the Archbishop of Granada, whose gentleness the zealot had despised, had not calmly walked into the midst of the multitude, imploring them

* "'Our Lady of the O:' The Feast of the Expectation of the Birth of most Holy Mary, so called from the exclamations of the Holy Fathers, who hoped for the coming of the Messiah." (Moreri.)

to cease their violence. Having kissed his garments, as usual, they complained of the breach of the articles of capitulation, respectfully remonstrated against the arrests which Ximenez had committed, the public burning of their Koran, and the indignities, of daily occurrence, which had become insupportable. The Captain of the garrison then dared to come forth, joined in the parley, and promised an amnesty if they would desist from insurrection. The intelligence of these proceedings alarmed Ferdinand and Isabella. Ximenez, justly accused of mad precipitancy, found himself on the verge of disgrace, and hurried away to Seville, to justify his doings to his Sovereigns. With great adroitness he not only appeased their anger, but, after some persuasion, succeeded in engaging them to treat Granada as a revolted city, and to regard the compact with its inhabitants as made void by their rebellion.

The Sovereigns had hesitated; but, as they gave way before Torquemada and banished the Jews, so now they yielded to his successor as their spiritual guide, and gave up the Moors. The Sultan, who had been appealed to from Granada, sent an embassy to demand that his brethren should not be forced into Christianity; but Ferdinand and his Queen assured the Ambassador that there was no compulsion in the matter, but said that, as it was evident that Moors could not be loyal to a Christian King, those who did not freely change religion should be taken to Barbary and allowed every facility for transit, with opportunity to sell their property previously to departure. Great multitudes chose to be baptized. Hernando de Talavera performed the ceremony in the gross; for ceremony it was, assuredly not a Christian sacrament. Those who preferred to leave the country found passage in the royal ships, were treated with the utmost care, and the Captains who conveyed them to the shores of Barbary delivered them to the Governors of the several towns, and received certificates of humanity to exhibit on return. The Jews had not been so treated, because there was no earthly power sufficiently interested to avenge their cause. The Church, although she feared not the God of Abraham, was afraid of the Sultan. But no foreign Moor was thenceforth allowed to enter Spain.

The inhabitants of the Alpujarra, aroused by these outrages, broke into open revolt; and a civil war continued, with intervals, through a period of seventy years. Our business, however, is only to observe the part taken in it by the Inquisition. The Moriscoes, or baptized Moors, had nothing of Christianity but the name, and that name they hated, and were consequently exposed to the utmost severity of the tribunal. Royal mandates were issued to compel them to learn Spanish, to dress like the Spaniards, and to put aside the garb, the language, and the customs of their nation. But it was so evidently impossible to enforce the mandate, that it was again and again withdrawn. By command of the Emperor Charles V., of whom we here speak as Charles I. of Spain, a board of consultation was holden at Granada (A.D. 1526), and presided over by Alonso Manrique, Archbishop of Seville, and Inquisitor-General. It consisted of Prelates and other dignitaries, with members of the Council of Castile and of the Inquisition. They repeated the obnoxious mandates, and devised methods of enforcement, under the direction of a distinct tribunal then first established in Granada for the whole province. Great numbers fled from that city and from the towns, and betook themselves to the highways and to the mountains, everywhere pursued as rebels, or tracked by Inquisitors as heretics. For the consideration, however, of eighty thousand ducats, the Emperor promised them that the severity of the Inquisition should be mitigated as to confiscations; and Clement VII. confirmed the exemptions by a Bull.

To teach the Moriscoes what they were to expect, in spite of any indulgence that the Emperor might grant, or of any remission of pecuniary penalties that the Pope might sanction, in regard to a people who were now extremely impoverished, and had very few among them possessing property enough to be an object of cupidity, the Inquisitors burnt alive, in Granada, a few Judaising heretics. This "Act of Faith" took place the year after Clement granted his Bull forbidding confiscations.

And the severity of Inquisitorial government may be estimated from a single instance. Until the year 1529 the Moriscoes had lived in separate quarters of the city, known by the general name of *Morerias;* but they were then compelled to change their habitations, and live among the "Old Christians," so that no two Morisco families might be in communication. Their most trifling actions were marked, and reported to the Inquisitors at Valladolid, whose dealings with them are exemplified in a case related by Llorente from the original records. On the 8th day of December, 1528, one Catalina, a woman of bad character, delated Juan, a Morisco seventy-one years of age, by trade a coppersmith, native of Segovia, and inhabitant of Benevente. She told the Inquisitors that, *eighteen years before*, she had lived in the same house with him, and seen that neither he nor his children ate pork or drank wine, and that, on Saturday nights and Sunday mornings, they used to wash their feet, which custom, as well as abstinence from wine and pork, was peculiar to the Moors. The Inquisitors summoned the old man into their presence, and questioned him, as usual, at three several interviews. All that he could tell them was, that he received baptism when forty-five years old; that, never having eaten pork or drunk wine until that time, he had then no taste for them; and that, being coppersmiths, he and his sons found it necessary to wash themselves thoroughly once a week. After some other examinations, they sent him back to Benevente, with prohibition to go beyond three leagues' distance from the town; but, two years afterwards, the Inquisition determined that he should be threatened with torture, in order, of course, to obtain some information that might help them to criminate others. He was, accordingly, taken to Valladolid, and, in a subterranean chamber, called "the dungeon of torment," stripped naked, and bound to the "ladder." This might have extorted something like confession from an old man of seventy-three; but he told the Inquisitors that whatever he might say when under torture, would be merely extorted by the anguish, and therefore unworthy of belief; and that he would not, through fear of pain, confess what never had taken place. Having threatened, which was all that they intended to do, they kept him in close prison until the next "Act of Faith," when he walked among the penitents with a lighted candle in his hand, and, after he had seen others burnt to death, paid the Holy Office a fee of four ducats, and went home, not acquitted, but released. It does not appear that he was again summoned, but probably he died soon afterwards.

At length Don Pedro Guerrero, Archbishop of Granada, having to go to the Council of Trent, laid the case of the still unsubdued Moriscoes before Paul III., who charged him to engage Philip II. to take such measures as would prevent the perdition of those souls. The Inquisition was the favourite institution of the Spanish Nero; but, as it could not act alone in the troubled kingdom of Granada, he convened a special assembly at Madrid, constituted similarly to that of Granada, and appointed the term of three years for the Moriscoes to divest themselves of the Arabian costume, disuse the language, and renounce even the most innocent customs, of their nation. Pedro de Deza, Auditor of the Inquisition, went to Granada with the articles then enacted (A.D. 1566), and caused them to be proclaimed; but the proclamation produced little more than a remonstrance and appeal to Philip, who had not wisdom enough to give ear to the complaints of his subjects; and his refusal to hear them precipitated the final struggle. Rebellion followed. A fierce warfare spread havoc over all the province; but the Inquisitors assured the King that his only remedy was to extirpate the Moriscoes; and, after the last of their strongholds was taken, the remnant then scattered over the country was sentenced to expatriation. The bands of the Church military occupied all the kingdom of Granada, now marked out into districts. A troop of licentious soldiery drove the weeping Moriscoes from their houses into the neighbouring churches, and thence carried them away, in such vehicles as could be found, to towns beyond the frontiers; and from those towns they were distributed all over the Spanish peninsula, and mingled with the general population. Thenceforth the hated race has had no visible existence.

Valencia, being a city and province of the kingdom of Aragon, although included in the same decree of Ferdinand and Isabella, in 1502, for the expulsion of the Moors from their dominions, enjoyed a measure of constitutional rights by which the inhabitants could present a determined, although brief, resistance. But the power of the Moors rapidly diminished; and when, in the year 1523, a seditious faction forcibly baptized sixteen thousand of them, merely in order to deprive the noble proprietors of land of the tribute they had received from them as Mohammedans, at least an equal number emigrated to Africa, leaving five thousand houses unoccupied. From that time their strength declined in Aragon. Charles V. obtained a Bull, absolving him from an oath which he had taken, in the Cortes of Zaragoza, not to interfere with their religion. In an ecclesiastical assembly at

Madrid it was determined that the sixteen thousand forcibly baptized were really Christians, and therefore subject to the Holy Office. The Inquisitors were enjoined to convert the rest, and spared no pains in fulfilling the commission. Flight on the one hand, and a mockery of baptism on the other, emptied Valencia of the followers of Mohammed. Those who desperately betook themselves to the mountains were beaten into submission. The vacated mosques became mass-houses. A wholesale baptism was the sequel of each *guerrilla*. Inquisitors waited in the cathedral of Valencia to give absolution, with remission of penance, to all who chose to accept it. In the year 1526, a civil war having terminated in a pragmatic between the insurgents and the Sovereign, they were all baptized; and, after wearing their old garb and speaking Arabic for a few years, these New Christians melted away, under the management of the Inquisition, into the general mass of Spaniards, and, without attaining to any knowledge of their Saviour, utterly forgot the Prophet of Mecca.

We cannot relate—for there is not, so far as we know, any record extant—the particulars of the inquisitorial persecution; but it is certain that, aided by the regal power, the Inquisitors crowded the dungeons and fed the hearths. The Sovereigns, indeed, purchased Bulls at Rome to authorise mitigation of severities; but the Inquisitors set at nought the Bulls, and kept their fires burning, until, in the year 1609, their savage joy was crowned by a final expulsion from Spain of the few Moriscoes that survived. The loss to the population, by successive expulsions of Jews, Moors, and Moriscoes, in obedience to the Inquisition, is estimated at no fewer than three millions.

Having followed the story of the Moriscoes to its close, we must resume our narrative from the point at which we digressed, and survey the progress of the Inquisition, and of inquisitorial legislation, in Spain, from the accession of the next Inquisitor-General until the present time.

CHAPTER XI.

SPAIN—DEZA AND XIMENEZ DE CISNEROS, INQUISITORS.

Pontifical charioteers rein in their steeds, or they apply the goad, as may be the more expedient. Torquemada had no more than obeyed the impulse given at Rome; but he dashed into the field so furiously, as to occasion scandal, and alarm his masters. Towards the end of his career the Pope expressed some disapprobation of his excessive zeal; but a zealot of equal impetuosity was appointed to succeed him. Moderation, or humanity, or honesty, would have disqualified the possessor of such virtues for the rough work that has to be done by an Inquisitor. The Papacy, itself, is gentle. That power, triply crowned, enthroned as if in heaven, serene, impassive, aspiring upward, shutting its eyes to the wretchedness of men, and closing its ears against the crying of the oppressed, holds the Church in its firm grasp, pours the glare of ecclesiastical doctrine on the book of God, and launches vengeful bolts on every opponent. Angels ministrant—not the Papacy itself—direct the fulminations, and smite the heretics. The Papacy, according to this ideal, hurts no man, but commits the scourge to inferior hands, and, like the god of Epicurus, knows no anger, inflicts no pain, and feels no pity.* But we must return to the Spanish Inquisition.

Don Diego de Deza, a Dominican, a Bishop, Professor of Theology in the University of Salamanca, Tutor of the Infant of Spain, and Confessor of the Catholic Sovereigns, deserved the superior dignity of Inquisitor-General of Castile. He understood the theology and the canons of his Church, and he knew the mind of his masters. In the last year of the fifteenth century, a Bull of Alexander VI. established him. Being with the court in Seville, he began his work by decreeing a Constitution in seven articles (June 17th, 1500), which ordained, 1. That there should be a general inquisition

* The vignette on our title-page, which is borrowed from a similar position in a sumptuous edition of the Roman Catechism, exhibits this conception of the Papacy, the intermediate agencies of the Church, and heretics. It pictures the *rationale* of the Inquisition, under an emblem conceived and exhibited in Spain in honour of that supreme authority.

made in every place that had not yet been so visited. 2. That the edict requiring all persons to delate, should be again proclaimed. 3. That the subaltern Inquisitors should search their books, and prosecute all persons noted therein. 4. That no one should be troubled for such trifles as blasphemy, which indicated ill-temper, rather than heresy. 5. That in cases of canonical compurgation, two witnesses should be sworn as responsible for the orthodoxy of each one compurgated. 6. That every one who abjured after vehement suspicion, should promise to hold no more intercourse with heretics, but to delate them. And, 7. That those who abjured after formal conviction of heresy, should do the same. The solemnity of this beginning showed that the new Inquisitor-General meant to be in earnest. His labours to extend the regulations of the Spanish tribunal to Sicily and Naples, we shall notice when speaking of Italy. It was he who instigated Charles V. to break his oath with the Cortes of Aragon; and we have already seen how the Moors and Moriscoes suffered under his administration. In order to illustrate the character of this administration, we may note the persecution of the first Archbishop of Granada, and the crusade on the inhabitants of Cordova.

The Archbishop, Hernando de Talavera, when the Italian Inquisitor proposed to revive the Inquisition in Spain, was the Queen's Confessor, and influenced Her Highness to resist the proposal, and endeavour to subdue Judaism by Christian instruction. It was known that by the channel of his maternal ancestry he had a slight infusion of Jewish blood. When appointed to the new see of Granada, he won the respect of the Moorish population; and afterwards, when the city was insurgent against the tyranny of Ximenez, good Fray Hernando quelled the insurrection by his presence and exhortations, which subdued the infuriated multitude. He caused the Bible to be translated into Arabic. He even dared to argue with Ximenez for making the sacred volume intelligible to the people. He could sway the city by moral influence, whereas the Inquisition steadily purposed to crush by force and to extirpate all whom they could not compel into entire submission to the Church. Deza hated the principles, and Ximenez was jealous of the influence, of Hernando. Deza, as Inquisitor-General, called on Ximenez, while associated with him in endeavouring to convert

Granada, to take information concerning the purity of his religion. Ximenez, not yet brought over to the policy of the Inquisition, although actuated by its spirit, wrote the Pope, Julius II., whom he desired to take the case in hand, lest the archiepiscopal dignity should suffer by the Primate of Spain acting as familiar upon the Archbishop of a province. The Pope commanded his Nuncio to inhibit the Inquisitors from further action, but to send him the reports which they had taken of the religious character of Hernando. The Pontiff assembled several Cardinals and Prelates to hear those reports read, and, with their concurrence, absolved the suspected Archbishop, but not until after he had suffered three years of anxiety and reproach, and seen many of his relatives arrested and imprisoned by the Inquisitor Lucero. And notwithstanding his acquittal, his name figures in the Spanish Expurgatory Index, of which a copy now lies before me, with the rubric of Don Joaquin Castellot, Reviser-General of the Council, in 1789.

This Lucero, whom some called *Tenebrero*, presided over the tribunal in Cordova. No sooner was he installed in that office, than he made a general attack on the most respectable inhabitants of the city, whom he arrested, examined, set down as imperfect "confitents,"—we must borrow a word from the inquisitorial vocabulary,—and condemned as feigned penitents. Some of them, in terror, added to their confession statements utterly at variance with the truth. Informers crowded Lucero's chamber, bringing monstrous tales of a grand conspiracy of Monks, Nuns, and other persons, whom they represented as traversing the country, and holding private meetings to establish Judaism and annihilate the Church. Lucero received them gladly, his Notaries recorded the fables, familiars dragged innocent persons from their beds, the prisons of Cordova overflowed, and the inhabitants would have demolished the Inquisition at a stroke, if the municipality, the Bishop, the Chapter, and the nobility had not appeased them by appealing to Deza, and praying for the removal of Lucero. But Deza turned furiously on the complainants, and by name pronounced a long train of Nobles, Monks, Nuns, Canons, and men of civil authority, abettors of Judaism. At this juncture Philip I. assumed the government of Castile; and the Bishop, with a multitude of persons whose relatives were in dungeons, implored him to transfer their cause to some other court. Philip heard their petition, suspended both Deza and Lucero from the exercise of their functions, and directed that the whole affair should be submitted to the Supreme Council of Castile; but, like many other Princes, when brought into a similar position of resistance to ecclesiastical powers, he died before his order could be obeyed. For Deza that death was opportune; and, during an interregnum, the zealot vaulted into his inquisitorial throne again, and renewed the assault on Cordova. The Marquis of Priego, who had formerly sought redress by petition, now resolved to take it by force; headed the willing inhabitants, broke open the House of the Inquisition (October 6th, 1506), liberated a crowd of prisoners, imprisoned several officers of the Holy Office in their stead, but missed Lucero, who had betaken himself to timely flight on the back of a swift mule. Deza, not more brave, resigned his office of Inquisitor-General; and Cordova, satisfied with deliverance, instantly became tranquil.

No class of persons had escaped this persecution. Antonio de Lebrija, one of the few learned men who shone as lights amidst the darkness of that age, suffered vexatious interruption of his studies, which were purely literary and biblical. He describes the intellectual bondage endured under the reign of Deza in the following impassioned sentences:—"Is it not enough to yield my understanding up to Christ when religion so requires? Must I also be compelled to deny what I have learned on points that are clear to me, evident, notorious, manifest, more brilliant than the light of day, and true as truth itself? Must it be thus with me when I affirm, on serious conviction, not uttering opinion or conjecture, but bringing proof with invincible reasons, irrefragable arguments, and mathematical demonstrations? O, misery! Alas, what slavery is this! What iniquitous domination is this, that by dint of violence prevents one from speaking as he feels, even without interfering with religion in the least! But what is it not to *speak?* It is not even permitted for one to *write* when he is alone, within four walls. It is not even permitted to investigate the true sense of anything, if he happens to suffer a whisper to escape him. It is not permitted to reflect, no, not even in intention. Then what may we think of, if it be not lawful to spend our thoughts on those books which contain the Christian religion? Did not the Psalmist say that this is the occupation of the righteous man? 'His delight,' he says, 'is in the law of the Lord, and in His law doth he meditate day and night.'"* This forcibly recalls a sentence that I remember to have heard, a few years ago, from the lips of the Padre de la Canal, one of the most accomplished scholars and historians of Spain, in his library in the Augustinian monastery in Madrid: "*The Inquisition has ruined Spain.*" And Spain must be colonised, peopled anew, and made Christian, before these traces of ruin, more general and more lasting than the vestiges of Roman, Goth, or Saracen, will disappear from the social condition of that fine people.

Llorente calculates the victims of Deza thus:—

Burnt alive	2,592
Burnt in effigy	896
Penitents	34,952
Total	38,440

The distribution of these numbers is conjectural, and the entire calculation is involved in that of the time of Torquemada; but the aggregates are gathered by our author from sources of indisputable authenticity, and the proportions are suggested by his experience and profound historical information. Lesser men sometimes endeavour to discredit Llorente; but their attempts are vain.

Brute ferocity could no longer revel with impunity. The insurrection of Cordova, and the steady resistance of the kingdom of Aragon, taught the heads of Popedom and of Spain that the Inquisition would fail unless its affairs were conducted with prudence as well as vigour. In this exigency Fernando V., King-Governor of Spain, nominated Francisco Ximenez de Cisneros, Archbishop of Toledo, to be Inquisitor-General of Castile, and raised Juan Engueza, Bishop of Vique, to the same dignity in Aragon. The Pope confirmed the nomination; and the Bull to Cisneros came addressed to him as Cardinal, the Consistory having awarded him the purple as a reward for past services, and as an incentive to zeal for the future. He had to contend not only with the men of Cordova, but with a strongly pronounced disaffection

* Biblioth. Hispanica, A. art. *Antonius*.

in every quarter of the kingdom, and therefore bespoke forbearance by encouraging an inquiry into the conduct of his fallen predecessor. Several persons had approached "the threshold of the Apostles," complaining that relatives were imprisoned without cause, or that their houses had been rased to the ground wantonly, after false rumours that they had been used for synagogues. The Pope had appointed delegates to investigate those cases, and now empowered Ximenez to take cognisance of the whole affair. Entering on the duty with extreme caution, he formed, in conjunction with the King, a "Catholic Congregation," or special board of inquiry, chiefly consisting of Inquisitors; and, after due deliberation, pronounced a sentence of acquittal in favour of the sufferers, restored the dead to honour and fame, rebuilt the ruined houses, and ordered all records to the prejudice of the living to be cancelled. The sentence was published at Valladolid with great solemnity and rejoicing, in presence of King, Grandees, and Prelates; but Lucero, the chief criminal, the man who had wasted so much life, and ruined so many families, was liberated from prison, and sent, unpunished, to live at Almeria, and enjoy the dignity and revenue of *Maestrescuela*, or "Teacher of the Clergy," in the cathedral there. No penalty was inflicted on him or on Deza.

While only a looker-on, Ximenez had favoured the prevalent wish for a reformation of the Inquisition; but no sooner did he find himself intrusted with its control, than he resolved to make the most of it as an engine of government, and led the way for that political application of its agencies which is now so general and effective. He resisted the acceptance of the very proposals which he had formerly encouraged, and had even proffered to Don Carlos of Austria, afterwards Charles V. He directed all his energies to confirm and to extend the institution, without any diminution of even the least of its enormities. He divided the realm of Castile into inquisitorial provinces, placing an Inquisitor at the head of each,—in Sevilla, Jaen, Toledo, Estremadura, Murcia, Valladolid, and Calahorra. His brother of Aragon followed the example, and partitioned his territory under Zaragoza, Barcelona, Valencia, Majorca, Pamplona, Sardinia, and Sicily.

It was by means of his influence and management that Ferdinand received the crown of Spain. He therefore enjoyed unbounded confidence and favour. He was Cardinal of Spain,—a title rarely conferred,—and Governor, under Ferdinand, of all his dominions. As Archbishop of Toledo, he was head of the Clergy; as Inquisitor-General of Castile, he was the terror of every Priest and of every layman within the bounds of his jurisdiction. And, having improved the organization of the Holy Office, he proposed to extirpate the enemies of the Church who occupied the small state of Oran, on the coast of Africa, where every refugee from Spain and the Inquisition could, until that time, find shelter. At the head of fourteen thousand men, fitted out and paid from his own purse, he embarked for Africa, in February, 1509, and soon achieved the conquest. During his absence, Ferdinand curtailed, for a time, the power of the Popes over the Inquisitor, by forbidding the reception of Briefs or Bulls concerning it without his *regium placet*, or permission. But this exercise of royal independence never yielded any measure of mercy to those whom the Inquisitors chose to persecute.

Presiding, in 1510, over the Cortes of Aragon, Ferdinand heard bitter complaints against the Inquisitors in that kingdom. The representatives of the cities and towns declared that those men not only made inquisition concerning faith, but usurped civil authority; threw persons into their dungeons for civil offences, multiplied familiars, all of whom were exempted from paying taxes, until the country was brought to the verge of ruin, and made themselves insufferable by meddling, under pretexts of religion or of privilege, in every court. Whoever attempted to resist those usurpations, whether he were Viceroy, Captain-General, or Grandee, was instantly subjected to insult, and even to excommunication. They, therefore, prayed the King to keep the Inquisitors within their proper bounds, and cause the laws and rights of Aragon to be respected. The King hesitated, promised, equivocated, and delayed; but, after two years' reluctance, was compelled to yield, in part, to their demands. Yet, after solemnly binding himself by oath in open Cortes to enforce the concordat between the Inquisition and the kingdom, he was soon induced to apply to Rome for a consecration of perfidy, and obtained from Pope Leo X. a dispensation from the oath.

Returned from his African campaign, Ximenez resumed the management of the Inquisition, which had been conducted by a substitute during his absence, and gave clearest evidence that, amidst the cares of state, he had no care for the kingdom of our Lord Jesus Christ. A clever impostor, known as the devotee of Piedrahita, filled Spain with wonder, by professing to be favoured with a constant vision of the Saviour and of the holy Virgin, uttering blasphemies that the pen refuses to repeat. Ximenez sent for her to court. He and the King conversed with her. The Inquisitors noted her sayings, and admired her miracles. The Pope and his Nuncio acknowledged that they dreaded scandal; but the Inquisition pronounced her blessed. Scandal there was, indeed; but it came from another quarter. The Inquisitors were known to be accustomed to violate the females whom they had caused to be brought into the "holy houses;" and Ximenez, with due ostentation, decreed that all convicted of that crime should be put to death: but none died, because none were convicted. Nor could any be convicted, for none were prosecuted. Neither did the abomination cease.

The New Christians, on whom the severest persecution fell, offered Ferdinand six hundred thousand ducats of gold, if he would protect them from the horrible secret of the Tribunal, and allow the names of witnesses to be published; and they very nearly succeeded in obtaining the object of their prayer. But Ximenez, with his wonted munificence, or, perhaps, with his usual calculation as to ultimate advantage, laid down a sum, if not equal, at least sufficient to induce the King to reject their overture, and to maintain the secret.* Indulgent to a wretched woman who brought derision on the name of the adorable Redeemer, he had no indulgence for a "penitent;" and, resolving that no penitent should henceforth be spared a blush, he despoiled all the provincial Inquisitors of their accustomed privilege of diminishing the more ignominious part of penance, by forbidding them to allow the *sambenito* to be laid aside.

Meanwhile, the kingdoms of Castile and Aragon were struggling against the regal and pontifical authorities. Fer-

* Here note, and, on every like occasion, recollect, that this class of the population was chiefly persecuted for the sake of the confiscations. To accept even 600,000 ducats, once for all, instead of a constant and unlimited exaction, would have been a loss to the Inquisitors. It is not to be imagined that the money disbursed by Ximenez came from his private purse.

dinand, although Leo X. sanctioned his perfidy, saw that, if he persisted in violating his engagement with the Cortes of Monzon, all Aragon would be up in arms, and therefore prayed the Pope to recall his obnoxious Bull, and restore its jurisdiction to the civil power. And in the same year, 1515, the Cortes of Toledo, in Castile, extorted a similar concession, and forced the King to confine the Inquisitors within their province, and restrain them from interfering with the business of secular Judges. Ximenez bowed, perforce, before the representatives of the nation; but quietly pursued his course of internal advance in discipline, and not only placed Inquisitors, with their establishment, in Cuenca, but set up the Tribunal in the newly-conquered territory of Oran. And, having thus extended it to Africa, he sent it across the Atlantic, to awe the converts of the New World into submission to the "righteousness and mercy" of his Church. Ferdinand V. commanded the "holy Tribunal" to be erected in "the kingdom of *Terra Firma;*" and Ximenez named (A.D. 1516) Juan Quevedo, Bishop of Cuba, as first Inquisitor-General in those regions. But we will not follow him in the present chapter.

Unlike other powers, which usually begin by conciliating the confidence of their subjects, the Inquisition was generally careful to make a first impression of terror. In the new district of Cuenca, one of the first acts of the Inquisitors was to proceed against the memory and estate of Juan Henriquez de Medina, saying that, although he died in peace with the Church, having received the sacraments of confession, eucharist, and extreme unction, he was, in reality, an impenitent heretic, and a feigned Christian. They declared him infamous, commanded his remains to be exhumed and burnt, his effigy, covered with a *sambenito*, to be exhibited at the same time, and his property to be confiscated. The heirs of Medina appealed to Ximenez, who appointed Commissioners to examine the case; but the Commissioners proceeded in entire agreement with the Inquisitors themselves. The aggrieved family appealed from Ximenez to the Pope, who commanded the Commissioners to exercise impartiality, and these were induced to give sentence in favour of the deceased. A similar case occurred at Burgos, where a dead man was arraigned, absolved, and then accused of heresy again. The family appealed to Leo X. on behalf of the deceased, Juan de Covarrubias, whom Leo recognised as a friend of his youth, and the more earnestly, on that account, interposed his authority to quash a project of spoliation and infamy. But the Cardinal of Spain, and Regent of Castile,* elate with power, resisted the Pope, rallied the inquisitorial host into revolt against their supreme Pastor, and was in the height of the quarrel when death silenced him. But disgrace came first. His new Sovereign, Charles V., had commanded him to retire to his archbishopric; and there, at war with the world, and scarcely in agreement with the Church, he expired, eighty years of age, on the 8th of November, 1517. His victims were:—

Burnt at the stake	3,564
Burnt in effigy	1,232
Penitents	48,059
Total	52,855

Nearly fifty-three thousand witnesses, whose testimony would contradict the praises lavished by many credulous reciters of other men's praises on that *learned, liberal, munificent Cardinal Ximenez de Cisneros.*

CHAPTER XII.

SPAIN—THE INQUISITION UNDER CHARLES I. AND PHILIP II.

HAVING traced the history of the modern Inquisition in Spain under the government of four Inquisitors-General, we will very briefly note its condition during the reign of Charles V., or Charles I., as the Spaniards count, under the administration of the Cardinals Adriano, Tabera, and Loaisa, who successively presided, and the former part of that of the Archbishop Valdés.

Charles did not come to Spain until two years after the death of his predecessor. He was a German by birth,

* Appointed by Ferdinand to be Regent after his death, in consequence of the insanity of his second wife, Juana, until the arrival of his grandson, Charles, afterwards the Emperor Charles V.

education, and language. His education chiefly consisted in historical reading; and by this he had learned the evil of Papal interference with the rights of Kings, and resolved to abolish the Inquisition in his new kingdom, or, at least, to change its character. Some Universities and Colleges, both in the Netherlands and Spain, had given sentences confirmatory of his own opinion; and in the fervour of youthful purpose,—for he was only eighteen years of age,—he resolved to confer this benefit on Spain. After a magnificent entry into Valladolid, he there met the Cortes of Castile (February, 1518), who laid a petition before him, containing this prayer:—"We supplicate Your Highness to command provision to be made, that in the Office of the Holy Inquisition the proceedings be so conducted, that entire justice be observed; that the wicked be punished, and that good men, being innocent, suffer not; that they observe the Sacred Canons *and the Common Right*, which speak on this point; and that the Judges who may be appointed to this end be generous,* of good character and conscience, and of the age which the law requires, such persons as may be expected to do justice; and that the Ordinaries be righteous judges." † So intent were the Deputies of Castile on their object, that they made a present of ten thousand ducats of gold to the King's Chancellor, a man of extreme venality, to engage him to promote their suit. The King, who needed no persuasion, answered the petition by a pragmatic sanction, or decree, having force of law until the next Cortes. The paper reads beautifully. Almost every sentence is in direct contradiction to the laws and customs of the Inquisition, and the whole system would have been overturned had it come into effect. But there are critical moments when the angel of death seems to wait upon the pleasure of Inquisitors, and with wondrous opportunity he wafts away their adversaries. Whether that angel be sent from above or evoked from beneath, no man can say. The Chancellor Sauvage died, and the pragmatic was never published.

From Valladolid Charles went to Zaragoza, where he met the Deputies of Aragon, and swore to maintain the rights and laws of their kingdom, wherein were included restric-

* *Generosos*, "noble by descent."

† Llorente, xi., 1, gives the press-mark (D. 153) of his manuscript authority in the Royal Library of Madrid.

tions on the Holy Office. But by this time the Inquisitor-General, Adriano, had gained the young King's ear, and, by reasons of state, soon converted him into an ardent patron of the very institution he had intended to destroy. The Cortes of Aragon met a second time (close of 1518), represented to His Highness that the existing restraints on inquisitorial power were insufficient, and prayed for the addition of articles like those promised to Castile. In reply, he told them that they must confine their requests within the limits of the Sacred Canons and Pontifical Decrees, attempting nothing against the Inquisition; that if they had any complaint to make against an Inquisitor, they must carry it to the Inquisitor-General; and that, in case of doubt, it must remain with the Pope to arbitrate. But this refusal was conveyed so artfully, that they imagined his words to bear a favourable meaning; and, like many others of their own communion, fancied that in "the Sacred Canons" they might find abundant authority on the right side. Nothing can be more fallacious than such an expectation.

A similar discussion arose between the King and the Cortes of the principality of Catalonia, and closed with equal ambiguity. The Inquisitors, on the other hand, revenged themselves by seizing the Secretary of the Cortes at Zaragoza, and throwing him into prison as a heretic. But this provoked the Aragonese to refuse a grant which they had agreed to give the King, on the understanding that he would redress their grievances; and His Highness, after making a slight concession, merely to secure the money, prosecuted the cause of the Inquisition with the utmost zeal. Leo X. gladly heard appeals from Spain against the wickedness and cruelty of the Inquisitors; and Cardinals, richly bribed, espoused the cause of the complainants. Favourable Briefs were issued to meet some particular cases, and a Bull of reform was actually despatched. Still Charles and the Inquisitors remonstrated. The Bull was not published. The Pope, having made a good market of his supremacy as the only Judge in this controversy, suffered himself to be persuaded, that a reform of the Inquisition would be prejudicial to the Holy See, and intimated to his son Charles, that if the document were returned to him, unpublished, he would cause the lead to be broken; and thus, without submitting to the shame of recalling what the world ought to think irrevocable, he would make it useless. Whether or not the seal was broken, the Bull never saw the light; and just as its suppression was agreed to, Leo died.

Let it not be imagined, that either the jealousy of civil authorities, or the dissatisfaction of the public, restrained the tormentors in the least. One example will show the contrary. A physician, Juan de Salas, was accused of having used a profane expression, twelve months before, in the heat of a dispute. He denied the accusation, and produced several witnesses in his defence. But the Inquisitor Moriz, at Valladolid, where the charge was laid, caused De Salas to be brought again into his presence in the torture-chamber, stripped to his shirt, and laid on the *ladder*, or *donkey*, an instrument resembling a wooden trough, just large enough to receive the body, with no bottom, but having a bar or bars so placed that the body bent, by its own weight, into an exquisitely painful position. His head was lower than his heels, and the breathing, in consequence, became exceedingly difficult. The poor man, so laid, was bound round the arms and legs with hempen cords, each of them encircling the limb eleven times. During this part of the operation they admonished him to confess the blasphemy; but he only answered, that he had never spoken a sentence of such a kind, and then, resigning himself to suffer, repeated the Athanasian Creed, and prayed "to God and Our Lady many times." Being still bound, they raised his head, covered his face with a piece of fine linen, and, forcing open the mouth, caused water to drip into it from an earthen jar, slightly perforated at the bottom, producing, in addition to his sufferings from distension, a horrid sensation of choking. But again, when they removed the jar for a moment, he declared that he had never uttered such a sentence; and this was repeated often. They then pulled the cords on his right leg, cutting into the flesh, replaced the linen on his face, dropped the water as before, and tightened the cords on his right leg the second time; but still he maintained that he had never spoken such a thing; and, in answer to the questions of his tormentors, constantly reiterated that he had never spoken such a thing. Moriz then pronounced that the said torture should be regarded as begun, but not finished; and Salas was released, to live, if he could survive, in the incessant apprehension that if he gave the slightest umbrage to a familiar or to an informer, he would be carried again into the same chamber, and be racked in every limb. Llorente transcribes the original record of this deed, with the signature of the Notary affixed. Let it be carefully noted that the sufferer was not a Jew, Turk, or heretic, but a child of the Holy Roman Catholic Apostolic Church, against whom no suspicion lay of any greater offence than a word spoken hastily; and even one of the accusers, himself suffering moral torment at the time,—for they were both imprisoned in the Inquisition, and under examination, when they criminated Salas,—affirmed that he had afterwards, with an air of repentance, confessed the sin, and taxed himself with folly. But the truth is, that Protestants have suffered less than others from the Inquisition, which spends its fury chiefly on the children of the Church, giving little encouragement to those whom that Church would entice into her bosom.

Popular dissatisfaction, not only represented in Cortes, but made manifest in tumults, and threatening civil war, together with disputes between the King and the Pontiffs, rose to such a height that, at length, Charles withdrew the sanction of royal jurisdiction from the acts of the Tribunal (A.D. 1535); and the Spanish Inquisition suffered a humiliation of ten years.* But we must refrain from narrating the history of those disputes, and pass on to a period of mournful interest to every Protestant.

About the year 1541, the guardians of Romish faith in Spain began to proceed formally against Lutherans, as they were called who gathered their knowledge of Christianity from the Bible. During eighteen years, cases of Lutheran heresy frequently occurred; but they were single, and the Inquisition did not think it necessary to put forth its utmost energies until the year 1559, when a chapter of surpassing importance opens in our history.†

Judaism was dislodged from Spain, after having flourished there from times anterior to the Christian era. The religion of the Koran had been driven from the shore; and there was

* It has been hastily inferred, from this act of the King, that the Inquisition was suspended; and so some of the Deputies in the Cortes of Cadiz, in 1812—13, stated. But we find the Inquisitors active in that interval. Had it been suspended, it could hardly have been revived by Philip.

† The leading examples of persecution during those eighteen years, may be found in "Martyrs of the Reformation," chapter v.

neither mosque nor muezzin remaining. The Jews had formerly enjoyed legal protection, and the Mohammedans had almost occupied the Peninsula as their own territory; yet both the one and the other gave way before the united power of the King and the Inquisitor. Evangelical Christianity was never acknowledged, nor even known to the laws but as an offence. Without any ostensible communion, or even a single edifice erected for Divine worship, small companies of brethren had peacefully and silently resisted forces that to all others had been resistless. Without any charm of antiquity, or any appeal to human motive, those disciples of our Lord Jesus Christ braved the peril of death for twenty years; and for eighteen of those twenty were, doubtless, yielding themselves to imprisonment, to torments, and to death, far beyond the scanty records that have come to our knowledge; and were thus proving the superior power of that faith which can persevere at all hazards, and in the absence of every earthly succour or incitement. At length, as the obnoxious races had been swept away by two great efforts, so Lutheranism, as it was called, was marked for annihilation by a third.

In the years 1557 and 1558, a large number of persons were imprisoned as Lutherans. Many of them were of illustrious descent, and eminent for learning and official rank. From the usual examinations, it became evident that an evangelical reformation was extending rapidly; and Philip II., with the Inquisitor-General Valdés, resolved to employ some extraordinary means to crush it, if possible, for ever. The King laid the whole case before the Pope, Paul IV., who addressed a Brief to Valdés (January 4th, 1559), authorising him, notwithstanding anything to the contrary that might be found in the general rules of the Inquisition, to deliver over to the secular arm, for punishment of death, all dogmatizing * Lutheran heretics, even although they had not relapsed, as well as those who professed penitence, but were still subject to suspicion. This was an excess of cruelty beyond that of Ferdinand and Torquemada, who never put penitents to death, even if the recantation were evidently extorted by fear, unless they had afterwards relapsed. And on the day following the Pope gave another Brief, revoking all licences to read prohibited books, authorising the prosecution of all who read such books, and instructing all

* *Teachers.*

Confessors to examine their penitents, and to require them to declare at the Holy Office the names of all whom they knew to possess such books, under penalty of the greater excommunication. The Confessor who omitted this examination and injunction was to be laid under equal condemnation. Bishop, Archbishop, King, or Emperor, every one was included under the terrible obligation, to go to the Holy Office, and give information of the slightest shade of heresy that they might have detected or imagined in another. The Jesuits were, by this time, very numerous in Spain, and exerted themselves, beyond all others, in the delation of heretics.*

The particular heresy that it pleased the keepers of the faith to mark, at this time, for visitation with capital punishment, cannot be so well described as in the words of the Cardinal Inquisitor-General Manrique, who commanded, in agreement with the Council of the "Supreme Inquisition," that to the articles recited in the annual edict requiring all persons to inform against heretics, the following should be added :—

"If they know, or have heard, that any one has said, defended, or believed, that the sect of Luther or his followers is good, or that he has believed and approved any of its condemned propositions; to wit,—

"That it is not necessary to confess sins to the Priest, since it is sufficient to confess them before God;

"That neither Pope nor Priests have power to absolve from sins;

"That the true body of our Lord Jesus Christ is not in the consecrated host;

"That we ought not to pray to saints, nor ought there to be images in the churches;

"That there is no purgatory, nor any necessity to pray for the deceased;

"That faith, with baptism, is sufficient for salvation, without any need of works;

* Popular dislike already pursued the Jesuits. It was rumoured that they, like Ignacio Loyola himself, were prosecuted for heresy, and that the cells were full of Jesuits. So confidently was the rumour spread, that Valdés found it necessary to send private instructions to the Inquisitors of the several tribunals, to assure the Lords, Prelates, and others, that the contrary was the case. De Castro copies this letter from a Spanish authority.

"That any one, although not a Priest, may hear another in confession, and give him the communion under the two kinds of bread and wine;

"That the Pope has no power to grant indulgences and pardons;

"That Clerks, Friars, and Nuns may marry;

"That there ought not to be Friars, Nuns, nor monasteries;

"That God did not institute the regular religious orders;

"That the state of marriage is better and more perfect than that of unmarried Clerks and Friars;

"That there should be no more feast-days than the Sunday;

"That it is not a sin to eat flesh on Fridays, in Lent, and on other days of abstinence.

"If they know, or have heard say, that any one has held, believed, or defended various other opinions of Luther and his followers, or that any one has left the kingdom to be a Lutheran in other countries."

When the Inquisitor-General prescribed these additions to the edict, he told the provincial Inquisitors that they might also insert something to direct information against the *Alumbrados* (Enlightened), or *Dejados* (Careless), as they were also called, a sect of Antinomians, a folk who are too numerous at all times, but especially abound when a once-dominant religion, whether true or false, has decayed, and while the masses of the people are untaught. In such a condition of society, truth and error are wildly mingled and confounded. But even the speculations of the Spanish *illuminati* would be rather exaggerated by the Inquisitors than stated fairly. The Council of "the Supreme" afterwards took up the suggestion; and in *cartas-acordadas*, or "letters of instruction," issued on the 28th of January, 1568, and 4th of December, 1574, prescribed the following questions, which we may take as characteristic of the times:—

"Do you know, or have you heard, that any person, living or dead, has said or affirmed that the sect of the *Alumbrados*, or *Dejados*, is good?

"That mental prayer is of Divine command, and that by it is fulfilled all that remains of the Christian religion?

"That prayer is a sacrament hidden under accidents?

"That this sacrament is only verified in mental prayer, since vocal prayer is of little value?

"That servants of God should not busy themselves in bodily exercises?

"That a parent, or other superior, ought not to be obeyed, when he commands things that would hinder the exercise of mental prayer and contemplation?

"Have you heard that any one has spoken evil of the sacrament of matrimony, or said that no one can attain to the secret of virtue, without learning from those who teach this doctrine following?—

"That no one can be saved without the prayer that they practise and teach, and without making a general confession.

"That the heats, tremblings, and faintings, which usually appear in the said teachers, and their good disciples, are indications of the love of God.

"That, by these signs, they are known to be in grace, and to possess the Holy Spirit.

"That they who are perfect need not perform virtuous works.

"That on reaching the state of one perfect, the essence of the most Holy Trinity is made visible in this world.

"That such perfect persons are directly governed by the Holy Spirit.

"That for doing, or for not doing, anything, these perfect ones are not subject to any other rule than that of inspirations directly received from the Holy Spirit.

"That people ought to shut their eyes when the Priest elevates the host.

"That any one has said that, on arriving at a certain degree of perfection, the perfect can no longer see images of saints, nor hear sermons, nor other discourses that treat of God?

"Have you seen or heard any other piece of bad doctrine of the said sect of *Alumbrados*, or *Dejados*?"

To receive the crowds of informers who rushed to the Tribunal of the Faith, and discovered entire congregations of Lutherans assembled in private houses, and to conduct the procedure of inquisition, Don Pedro de la Gasca was appointed by Valdés his sub-Delegate in Valladolid; and in Seville, Don Juan Gonzales de Munebrega. For in those two cities, and in their neighbourhood, the Gospel was making extraordinary progress. Valdés also appointed a set of ambulatory officers, who dispersed themselves all over the country, and, gaining information of persons who were leaving their homes to avoid prosecution, mounted on post-horses, pursued them from stage to stage, and, flight being held equivalent with confession of heresy, brought them back, and threw them into dungeons. The revenue of the Holy Office, rich as it was, was said to be insufficient to defray the cost of the crusade; and therefore the Pope, at request of the Inquisitor-General, required the revenue of a canonry in each metropolitan cathedral and collegiate church to be transferred to this new service; and, by another Brief, he alienated, from the ordinary ecclesiastical revenue of Spain, the sum of one hundred thousand ducats of gold. Many Chapters demurred at the impost, and one, at least,—that of Majorca,—refused to pay so much as a maravedí; but they generally submitted in the end; and never was army better equipped for a campaign, than were those Inquisitors for theirs. Public expectation ran high. The Priests and the populace demanded spectacles answerable to the rank and number of the heretics, and they were not disappointed.

CHAPTER XIII.

SPAIN—PREPARATIONS FOR AN AUTO DE FE.

Here, once for all, we may describe the preparations for a Spanish *Auto de Fé*, for the public execution of heretics.

When an Inquisitor had determined to pronounce sentence on a company of prisoners, he appointed, as we observed when describing the "Sermons" of Toulouse, a Sunday or feast-day for the solemnity; avoiding, however, a Sunday in Advent or Lent, or Easter-day, or Christmas-day, or any great festival, because, for such days, special entertainment is provided in the churches, and must not be interrupted. The day being fixed, general notice was given by the Curates from their pulpits that, at the time and place appointed, there would be "a general Sermon of the Faith" delivered by the Inquisitor; and that, in honour thereunto, all other Preachers would be silent. A living picture of the Last Judgment, said they, would be represented for the instruction of the faithful.

If any were to be delivered over to the secular arm, due notice was given to the chief civil authority, that he might be present, with all his subalterns, to receive the culprits. On the day before the *Auto* it was usual, in Spain, to carry a bush to the *Quemadero*, or place of burning, in procession, thereby to signify many things to the people, which are scarcely worth the trouble of narration here. A Secretary and Ministers, with a crier, came forth in a body from the palace of the Inquisition, and, in the squares and public places, unfurled a banner, on which was displayed an order that no person, of whatever station or quality, from that hour, until the day after the execution of the *Auto*, should carry arms, offensive or defensive, under pain of the greater excommunication, and the loss of such arms; and that this same day, until two in the afternoon, no person should proceed in coach or sedan, or on horseback, through the streets where the procession was to pass, nor enter the square in which the scaffold was erected. In the evening came the procession of the Green Cross. All the communities of Friars of the city and neighbourhood, having assembled at the Inquisition, together with the Commissaries, the scribes, and the familiars of that district, sallied forth in long array. After them walked the Consultors and the Triers (*Qualificatores*), with all the officials of the Tribunal, each carrying a large white taper, lighted. Between the officials went men burdened with a bier that was covered with a pall. A numerous band, vocal and instrumental, followed last, performing the hymn, *Vexilla regis prodeunt.** In this order the procession reached the square in which the platform and galleries were erected, for the exhibition of the morrow. On that scaffold was an altar, and, the pall being removed from the bier, a large green cross, covered with a black veil, was taken off it, carried to the platform, unveiled, erected on the altar, and illuminated with twelve large white tapers. Some Friars of St. Dominic, and a strong body of lancers, took their station round the cross, to watch there during the night, and the procession dispersed. Meanwhile, preparations began in the "Holy House," where the prisoners had their beards shaven, and

* The hymn so beginning may be found in the Breviary, *infra Hebd. quartam quadragesimæ.* It contains the often-quoted passage: "Hail to thee, O cross, our only hope! In this time of passion, increase grace to the pious, and blot out their crimes for the guilty!"

their heads shorn close, that they might present an appearance of humiliation and nakedness, suitable to wretches who had forfeited baptismal grace.

On the morning of the fatal day, by sunrise, or earlier, the culprits were brought out of their cells into the chapel, or hall, already attired for the spectacle. Penitents of the lowest class were merely dressed in a coarse black coat and pantaloons, bareheaded, and without shoes or stockings. The more guilty wore a *sambenito*, or penitential habit, as represented in the plate. It was yellow, and the St. Andrew's cross which appears on it was red. Sometimes a rope was put round the neck, as an additional mark of ignominy. They who were to be burnt were distinguished by a habit of the same form, called *zamarra*,* and a conical paper cap, slightly resembling a mitre, about three feet high. They called it *coroza*.† On the zamarra there was no cross, but painted flames and devils, and sometimes an ugly portrait of the heretic himself,—a head, with flames under it. The coroza was painted in like manner. Any who had been sentenced to the stake, but indulged with commutation of the penalty, had inverted flames painted on the livery; and this was called, *fuego revuelto*, "inverted fire." The penitents of all degrees were permitted to sit upon the ground in profound silence, not moving a limb, thus to await the hour. Those condemned to burn were taken into a separate apartment, where the Inquisitors beset them with importunate exhortations to repent, and be reconciled to the Church. The inducement offered was, that they should be put to death by strangulation, not by flames, leaving only lifeless bodies to be consumed, and that they should be spared from hell.

They who came to take part in the *Auto* assembled in the palace of the Inquisitor, crowding the apartments, and partook of an abundant breakfast, to fortify them for the labours of the day. The penitents, the impenitent, and the relapsed, also had a meal prepared for them; and sometimes, as if in mockery, the breakfast set before the condemned to fire was ostentatiously sumptuous.

* An old Spanish word, denoting the material, and derived, according to the Academy, from the Hebrew צֶמֶר "wool."

† Peggiorative of *corona*, "crown."

The great bell of the cathedral had been tolling from early dawn, and now the city was in motion. All preparations being complete, the chief Inquisitor proceeded to the palace-door, attended by his Notary, who read the roll, beginning with the names of those who had offended least, and closing with them on whom the Holy Office poured its bitterest curses. Each person came to call, with all his marks upon him,—marks of starvation, torture, terror, shame, or oftentimes with a smile of conquest on his countenance, and words of triumphant faith bursting from his lips. But criminals of that class known as dogmatizers were generally gagged,—the mouth being filled with a piece of wood, kept in by a strong leather band fastened behind the head, and the arms tied together behind the back. In Goa, as each came, or was brought, the Notary read another name, that of a guard, or sponsor, who was to perform the meritorious duty of walking beside him in the procession. In Spain, however, there were two guards to each.

The Dominicans, honoured with everlasting precedence on all such occasions, led the way, in Goa and in Spain; singing-boys also preceded, chanting a litany. The banner of the Inquisition was intrusted to their hands. The Spanish banner was a rude green cross, on a black ground, with an olive-branch on one side, and a sword on the other, showing the alternative of reconciliation or death offered by the Holy Office. The motto was, *Exsurge, Domine, et judica causam Tuam :* " Arise, O Lord, and judge Thy cause." The Inquisition of Goa displayed a portrait of St. Dominic, holding the olive-branch and sword, standing on a cloud, with a dog—of which his mother dreamt*—having a brand in its mouth, to set the globe on fire. By his motto, *Misericordia et justitia*, he seemed to offer the choice of mercy or justice. We pause here, to note that the rules of the Inquisition preclude the exercise of mercy, and set at nought even the common forms of justice. After the banner walked the penitents; a penitent and a sponsor, two and two. In Goa, a cross-bearer brought up the train, carrying a crucifix aloft, turned towards them, in signal of pity; and, on looking along the line, you might have seen another Priest going before the penitents with his crucifix turned backwards, inviting their devotions. In Spain, the banner which pre-

* See above, page 7.

ceded was itself a cross, and answered the same purpose. They to whom the Inquisition no longer offered mercy, walked behind the penitents, and could only see an averted crucifix. Two armed familiars walked, or rode, beside each of these, who was mounted on an ass, and two Ecclesiastics, probably Theatines, or some other clerks regulars, also attended. After these, the images of heretics who had escaped were carried aloft, to be thrown into the flames; and porters came last, tugging under the weight of boxes containing disinterred bodies, on which the execration of the Church had fallen, and which were also to be burnt.

To do honour and service on that occasion, the whole body of civic authorities, high and low, walked in order after that miserable train; then the secular Clergy; then the regular Clergy. The staff inquisitorial, not to be confounded with any others on that triumphal day, had gone before; a long space intervening between them and the general procession. They were attended by a strong body of armed familiars, all mounted on horseback; and, overshadowed by the banners of the Pope and of the King, they entered first into the Grand Theatre, and ceremoniously took their places. This theatre was a temporary wooden erection, but very spacious. It was, in fact, a large amphitheatre, resembling those which are used for bull-fights, except that it was not an unbroken circle, but consisted of separate galleries, facing each other, on two or three sides of a square, with stages for the chief officers of Church and State, and one magnificent altar, at least; the fourth side being left open for entrance and egress. On one side of the altar was a pulpit for the delivery of the sermon, and the publication of the sentences; and sometimes there were more pulpits than one. The members of the procession ascended the galleries in order, and the open area was left free for the ceremonies that were to take place. Outside the city—as in the valley of Gehinnom, for the fires of Tophet and for the sacrifices to Moloch—was a hearth, or place of burning. As our own language is too poor to provide a name for such a thing, we consent to borrow from Spanish its peculiar designation, and call it the *Quemadero*. This Quemadero was a piece of pavement devoted to the single use of burning human bodies; and, besides other sufficient reasons why it should lie without the walls, there was this, that the act of killing might be done

Engraved by G. Stodart.

SAMBENITO.

Published by J. Mason, 14, City Road; & 66, Paternoster Row.

Engraved by G. Stodart.

FUEGO REVUELTO.

Published by J. Mason, 14 City Road; & 66, Paternoster Row.

Engraved by G. Stodart.

ZAMARRA.

Published by J. Mason, 14, City Road; & 66, Paternoster Row.

apart, and so made, the more formally, that of the civil power; and that the smoke of those horrid sacrifices might not offend the nostrils of the higher Clergy, they, only, going to witness the execution of their own sentence, to whom the sight would be agreeable, or who might, in superior devotion, wish to attend at the performance of the meritorious deed. Sometimes the Quemadero was a raised platform of stone, and sometimes adorned with pillars, or other bits of masonry, to distinguish and beautify the spot. Some were surrounded with statues. Our attention shall now be chiefly given to the four most famous *Autos de Fé* that were celebrated in Spain in the reign of Philip II. Never were heretics baited and consumed with greater pomp; and, therefore, although these most savage spectacles were very numerous and long continued, fuller examples cannot be found of inquisitorial splendour than these following.

CHAPTER XIV.

SPAIN—AUTOS DE FE.

On Trinity Sunday, May 21st, 1559, was the first royal *Auto de Fé* at Valladolid, in the great Square. The King himself was not able to be there; but the Princess, Doña Juana, Governess of the kingdom in his absence, and the Prince, Don Carlos, were on the stage. They were surrounded by the Councillors of all the Councils that attended the court, many Grandees of Spain, a large number of titled Marquises, Counts, Viscounts, Barons, and gentlemen; ladies of all classes; and on the ground a vast concourse of spectators. The platform, stages, chairs of state, galleries, altars, and pulpits, were fitted up with unsparing sumptuousness. When the procession entered the arena, this courtly audience counted sixteen persons wearing penitential badges, brought to be reconciled to the Church, and then doomed to life-long dishonour; fourteen to suffer death by fire; and a box, with the mortal remains of a lady who was reported to have died under the taint of Lutheranism; and this lady's effigy was also carried as a mark of special shame.

We note the highest class of sufferers more particularly.

Doña Leonor de Víbero, wife of Pedro Cazalla, King's Comptroller, daughter of one who had held the same office, was proprietress of a chapel and burial-place in the church of the monastery of St. Benedict in Valladolid. Doña Leonor died in communion with the Romish Church,—communion signified by the ceremonies of confession, eucharist, and extreme unction. Some prisoners of the Inquisition, when on the rack, or threatened with it, declared that she had entertained and acknowledged Lutheran opinions at the time of her decease; and, on inquiry, it was found that religious meetings were wont to be holden in her house. Sentence was therefore given that she had died in heresy. Her children and grandchildren were declared infamous. Their property was confiscated. Her exhumed body was carried in the procession to the Auto, and thence to the Quemadero, and burnt openly. Her effigy was paraded through the streets, with *coroza*, *zamarra*, flames and devils, amidst the yells of zealots. The house where she had lived, and where the "Lutherans" had met for prayer, was razed to the ground; and a pillar was erected on the spot, with an inscription setting forth the offence, the sentence, and the execution. "I have seen the site, the pillar, and the inscription," says Llorente; "but they tell me that it is no longer to be found, a French General, in the year 1809, having caused this evidence of ferocity towards the dead to be taken down."

The following were burnt:—

1. *Doctor Agustin Cazalla*, Presbyter, a Canon of Salamanca, Chaplain of Honour and Preacher to the King and to the Emperor, son of Pedro Cazalla, King's Comptroller, and of Doña Leonor just mentioned. They say that he was, in common with many of the first people in Spain, of Jewish extraction. He was accused of being "chief dogmatizing Lutheran heretic of the conventicle of Valladolid, and correspondent of that of Seville." At first he denied the facts, and even swore to the denial. But when condemned to suffer torture, and taken to the chamber, he confessed, and signed his confession and a promise to be "a good Catholic," if they would allow him to be reconciled under penance. The Inquisitors thought it impossible to remit capital punishment to one who had been accused of dogmatizing; but they encouraged him to hope for mercy, and to reveal the history of his life, and many particulars relating to other

persons, which might serve their purpose. On the day before this Auto, one Fray Antonio de Carrera, a Jeromite Monk, went to him, by order of the Inquisitors, and told him that they were not yet satisfied with his declarations, which did not disclose all the truth; and that it would be for the good of his soul to confess all that he could remember of himself, or that he knew of others. He answered, that, without bearing false witness, he could confess no more, for he knew no more. Then, after much conversation, the Friar bade him to prepare to die the next day. Astounded at this intelligence, he asked if there were no hope left for a mitigation of the sentence; and hearing that there was none, unless he would make a larger confession, he seemed to look to Him, at length, from whom alone mercy could be had. "If it be so," said he, "let me prepare to die in the grace of God; for, without falsehood, I cannot say more than I have said already." But he obtained exemption from the stake by confessing with the Friar, and was therefore strangled before the burning of his body.

2. *Francisco de Víbero Cazalla*, brother of the Doctor, was a Presbyter, Curate of the town of Hormigos. At first he denied the charge of Lutheranism, but confessed when under torture, and ratified the confession; and it is said that he implored reconciliation to the Church with penance. Him they would not pity, because, although not a dogmatizer, they thought that his "repentance" only rose from fear of death. But it does not appear that he did repent. On the contrary, he persevered in confessing Christ; and when his brother, at the Quemadero, was speaking to the spectators under the character of a penitent, he manifested grief and indignation at his unfaithfulness, and gave himself calmly to the flames. Both he and his brother were degraded in the Square, before being led away to the place of execution.

3. *Doña Beatriz de Víbero Cazalla*, sister of the two preceding, denied, confessed when on the rack, implored reconciliation and pity, failed to obtain either, was strangled, and then burnt.

4. *Alfonso Perez*, Presbyter, Master in Theology, denied, confessed on being tortured, was degraded, strangled, and consumed.

5. *Don Cristóbal de Ocampo*, from Zamora, Knight of the order of St. John, Almoner of the Grand Prior of Castile and

Leon of the same order, was strangled, and thrown into the fire.

6. *Cristóbal de Padilla*, a private gentleman, strangled and burnt.

7. *The Licentiate Antonio Herrezuelo*, Advocate, from the city of Toro, condemned as an impenitent Lutheran, died with a good confession. Agustin Cazalla exhorted him, as they were going to the Quemadero, to follow his example, and by confession, so called, avoid the flames, and at the spot continued the exhortation; but Herrezuelo was unmoved: he sang psalms and recited passages of Scripture as they went through the streets, and smiled when they bound him to the stake. He could not then speak, for they had gagged him; and a soldier of the guard, to signalise his zeal, stabbed him with his halberd; but the wound was not mortal; and, bleeding and burning at the same time, he silently endured the last suffering, and expired.

8. *Juan García*, silversmith. It was his wife who first told the Inquisitor where meetings were held for prayer. García, who frequented the house, died, of course. He confessed, and was strangled at the stake; but she was rewarded for betraying her husband with an annual pension from the treasury of the Holy Office.

9. *The Licentiate Perez de Herrera*, a Magistrate of the city of Logroño, was condemned, confessed, strangled, and his body burnt.

10. *Gonzalo Baez*, a Portuguese, condemned as a Judaizing heretic, confessed, and suffered in the same manner.

11. *Doña Catalina de Ortega*, a lady of rank in Valladolid, condemned as a Lutheran, confessed, and died as the others.

12. *Catalina Roman*, a woman from Pedrosa;

13. *Isabel de Estrada*, a *beata*, or devout woman, of the same town; and,

14. *Juana Blasquez*, servant of the Marchioness of Alcanices, were all conducted to the burning, and, with the exception of the Portuguese, who was probably a descendant of Jews, they all suffered for Lutheranism: and it is worthy of special remembrance that, of this promiscuous company, two refused to make the perilous concession of an external reconciliation with the Church of Rome, but, by confessing the Lord Jesus Christ, triumphed over Antichrist.

The sixteen sack-bearers were led back from the parade of that doleful day to the cells of the Inquisition, there to spend one other night. If the rules were kept, the work of persecution was resumed, next morning, with accelerated vigour. For every one who had taken any part in the Auto, even but as a spectator, and contributing nothing to it beyond his presence, or perhaps one passing execration on the heretics, forty days' indulgence had been proclaimed. Every one who had rendered any active aid was bidden to rejoice in three years' respite from the pains of purgatory. And every one who would help to make up another burning by information of another lurking heretic, was incited by an offer of the same indulgence. The Inquisitors, refreshed by a night's repose, met in their palace, and had the sixteen culprits brought once more into their presence. The sentence given against each was read; and one of the fathers instructed him concerning the manner, the degree, and the duration of his penance. This monition ended, each was sent to his proper place. Some, destined to the galleys, were taken to the civil prison, thence to be transferred to the chain, the oar, and the lash. Some, stripped and flogged, went bleeding through the streets and market-places. Some, covered with *sambenitos* and dragging ropes, were made to show themselves in squares and in churches, there to be tormented by the ribald mob, who heaped on them every sort of insolence. And all were sworn to seal up in everlasting silence all that they had seen, heard, or suffered, under peril of a repeated prosecution. The *sambenitos*, or *zamarras*, worn by the persons burnt, were hung up in the church of the Dominicans, with the name of each, and the word *combustus*, "burnt."

And, meanwhile, the gracious providence of God did not slumber. The Princess Juana, and the young Prince of Asturias, Carlos, in their places on the platform, had been required to swear fidelity to the Holy Office; binding themselves, by that oath, to give notice of everything that they should ever know to be spoken or done against it. The royal persons reluctantly submitted; but the Prince, then but fourteen years of age, writhing under the indignity, eyed every part of the ceremony with horror. The hatred of the Inquisition, and compassion for the Protestants, which then sprang up within him, cost him his life eventually; but not until he had contributed to create that jealousy of the

Tribunal which soon took deep root in the court of Spain, and never left it until the Inquisition was abolished.

The managers of the next Auto in Seville, on Sunday, September 24th, 1559, could not boast of royal presence; but the church of God acknowledges a noble band of martyrs who suffered on that day. In the Square of St. Francis was the usual apparatus at the service of the Church. Four Bishops, all experienced in the service, the Inquisitors of the faith in Seville, the Chapter of the cathedral, some Grandees, many titles, Knights, the Duchess of Bejar, and a train of ladies, with the usual concourse, were actors, abettors, and witnesses. Twenty-one came to be burnt, followed by one effigy, and eighteen penitents. We must notice some of them.

The effigy represented the Licentiate Francisco de Zafra, a beneficed Presbyter of the parish church of St. Vincent, of Seville, condemned as an absent contumacious Lutheran heretic. Reynaldo Gonzalez de Montes * says, that he was very learned in the holy Scriptures; but so skilful in concealing his opinions, that the Inquisitors did not suspect him, but employed him frequently as a Trier of doubtful propositions, and that, in this capacity, he served many of his friends, by giving a favourable judgment of their writings and speeches. A weak-minded *beata*, whom he supported in his house, and who had become acquainted with his connexions, ran mad, was placed under the severe discipline then thought necessary for maniacs, and confined to her chamber. But she escaped; and, in revenge, went straightway to the Inquisition, asked an audience, and informed against as many as she could think of, Zafra included. By her good help, the Inquisitors made out a list of more than three hundred persons. At first he succeeded in persuading the Inquisitors that he could not be suspected of heretical taint on the testimony of an insane woman; but they had caught the clue: a multitude of persons were soon in durance, and their prisons in the Castle of Triana, and all available places of confinement in Seville, were crowded. Zafra was arrested also; but the suddenness of the procedure

* Better known as Reginaldus Gonsalvus Montanus, author of a small volume intituled, "Sanctæ Inquisitionis Hispaniæ Artes aliquot detectæ," containing the fruits of his own experience when a prisoner in the Holy House at Seville.

made it impossible to provide secure prisons, and he, with several others, effected his escape. His effigy was burnt.

First of those given over to the secular arm was *Doña Isabel de Baena*, a rich lady of Seville, in whose house a congregation had met. She was burnt, and her house razed to the ground, like that of her sister in Valladolid.

Don Juan Gonzalez, Presbyter, of Seville, an eminent preacher. With admirable constancy he refused to make any declaration, in spite of extremely severe torture, saying that he had not followed any erroneous opinions, but that he had drawn his faith from holy Scripture; and for this faith he pleaded to his tormentors in the words of inspiration. He maintained that he was not a heretic, but a Christian; and absolutely refused to divulge anything that would bring his brethren into trouble. Two sisters of his were also brought out to this Auto, and displayed equal faith. They would confess Christ, they said, and suffer with their brother, whom they revered as a wise and holy man. They were all tied to stakes on the Quemadero. Just as the fire was lit, the gag which had silenced Don Juan was removed, and, as the flames burst from the faggots, he said to his sisters, "Let us sing *Deus laudem meam ne tacueris*." And they sang together, while burning, "Hold not thy peace, O God of my praise; for the mouth of the wicked and the mouth of the deceitful are opened against me: they have spoken against me with a lying tongue." Thus they died in the faith of Christ, and of His holy Gospel.

Fray García de Arias, called "the white Doctor," from his snow-white hair, an aged Monk of the monastery of St. Isidore of Seville. For many years he had entertained evangelical opinions in secret, but few of the more eminent converts being aware of them. He was universally revered, and thought to be a thorough Romanist, except by the few who knew him. Indeed, he had been among the most zealous opponents of the Reformation, and persecutors of the Reformed. The Inquisitors constantly consulted him on questions of doctrine; he was notorious as a favoured Consulter and partisan of the Holy Office; and when his change of views aroused suspicion, and the Inquisitors began to receive accusations against him, they imagined that Lutherans were endeavouring to revenge themselves, and advised him to be more cautious, for the future, when in the presence of suspicious persons. As yet his opinions were changed, but not his heart; and he concealed his convictions in an extraordinary manner. Then it was that Gregorio Ruiz, a Preacher in the cathedral of Seville, gave great offence by evangelical expositions of holy Scripture; and when he was delated, the Inquisitors resolved to test him by a formal disputation. Ruiz applied to his friend for counsel, who concerted with him a course of argument that seemed cogent enough to reduce the divines to silence, whoever they might be; but he was amazed to find his friend among the Inquisitors, arguing against him, and demolishing the very arguments which he had suggested. Ruiz yielded,—for the mysterious contradiction deprived him of self-possession, —and, by yielding, escaped the vengeance of the Inquisition. And, afterwards, Arias told him and other brethren, that he had by that contrivance averted from the whole party the death that he now saw imminent. But this dissimulation could not continue. He became increasingly earnest, and laboured incessantly in communicating his growing knowledge of the truth to some who subsequently bore a conspicuous part in the labours of the Reformation. The light could not be covered. Delations were renewed; and the Inquisitors, enraged to find that they had been deceived, threw him into a secret dungeon. His companions had taken timely warning and fled, leaving him in the very jaws of death. He then resolved, in the strength of God, not to dissimulate any more; and made a bold and most explicit confession of his faith, defended his belief concerning justification, the sacraments, good works, purgatory, images, and all the points in controversy; and declared the Romish doctrine to be grossly erroneous. In short, he turned the attack upon the Inquisitors, who were utterly unable to contend with him. He taxed them with ignorance, and put them to silence with his learning. But such a contest was unequal. They could hide their shame under the veil of secrecy; and he was brought forth with the coroza on his reverend head, and with the cope of infamy. He died, as they would say, impenitent, having entered into the pyre rejoicing that, by the grace of God, he could bear witness in a good confession.

Fray Cristóbal de Arellano, a member of the same convent, a truly Christian community, was, even by confession of the

Inquisitors, profoundly learned in the holy Scriptures. And he was no less bold in his confession. They condemned him as a contumacious Lutheran. When, in the Square of St. Francis, the "merits" of his cause were read, one of the propositions imputed to him was, that the Mother of our Lord was no more a virgin than he himself. Unable to suffer so shameful an accusation, he rose, and cried aloud: "That is false! Never have I uttered such a blasphemy. Always have I believed the contrary; and now, and in this place, will I prove out of the Gospel the virginity of Mary." Such were the *merits* published at those times, to stir up the multitude against the followers of our blessed Saviour. When they reached the Quemadero he was intensely earnest in exhorting two of his brother Monks, Crisóstomo and Casiodoro, to stand firm in Gospel truth. Nor was his exhortation lost. They all suffered a triumphant martyrdom.

Fray Juan de Leon, another inmate of the same monastery, was among those who, after consultation with brethren, absconded, in hope of saving their lives. Unable to bear separation from Christian society, he secretly returned, but found that they also had fled, and were at Frankfort. Thither he followed them, and thence they proceeded in one company to Geneva. At Geneva, hearing that Queen Elizabeth was on the throne of England, instead of Mary, they resolved to seek a refuge here, and set out on the journey. From the time, however, that the Christians were known to be fleeing from Seville, the Inquisition employed spies in Milan, Frankfort, Antwerp, and other towns of Italy, Flanders, and Germany, giving handsome rewards to all who could bring back fugitives. Fray Juan was among those who fell into their hands. They caught him in Zealand, just as he was about to embark for England, together with Juan Sanchez, who was burnt in Valladolid. They loaded Fray Juan de Leon with irons on his arms and legs, put a cap of iron over his head and shoulders, with a sort of iron tongue passing into his mouth, and pressing down, as Llorente words it, "the natural tongue of flesh," and brought him to Seville. When thrown into prison he confessed his faith, and maintained it too. Condemned to be delivered to the secular arm, he was brought to the Auto with a gag in his mouth, thrust in so cruelly that it caused excessive torture, and gave him a most pitiable appearance. Contrary to custom, he was not shaven; and his haggard, attenuated figure presented an appearance scarcely human. They removed the gag when he was at the stake, that he might say the Creed, profess the Catholic faith, and be confessed, in order to avoid the death by fire. An old schoolmate, and Priest of the same monastery, implored him to take pity on himself; but he would not hazard the loss of God's mercy, and steadfastly persevered in confessing Christ his Saviour, that he might enter, even through fire, into rest.

The Doctor Cristóbal de Losada, who had practised as a physician in Seville, and was regarded as Minister in a congregation of the Reformed, in that city, resisted every persuasion to recant, directly or indirectly, and was burnt alive.

Fernando de San Juan, a schoolmaster, at first showed some signs of instability, but recovered strength, confessed boldly, and was burnt alive. *Morcillo*, a Monk of St. Isidore, and his fellow-prisoner, who had encouraged him to this effort of constancy, wavered at the last moment, and was strangled by the inquisitorial grace, usually granted to those who make a "sacramental confession."

Doña María de Bohorques, illegitimate daughter of a gentleman of Seville, not quite twenty-one years of age. She had been instructed by Doctor Juan Gil, Canon Magistral of Seville, and Bishop elect of Tortosa. She knew Latin well, had some knowledge of Greek, possessed a good library with many Lutheran books, knew much of the sacred text by memory, and was well taught in evangelical doctrine. When confined in a secret dungeon, she made bold confession, and argued calmly with her persecutors. She acknowledged all that was true in the charges laid against her, and denied what was false or misapprehended; but maintained an impenetrable silence on whatever would lead to discovery of others. The Inquisitors put her to the torture, and made her say that her sister Juana had not reproved her for the opinions she entertained. Beyond this they could extract nothing. During the intervening days incessant attempts were made to subdue her constancy: but she overcame them all; and when a company of Priests came, the night before her death, to make a last effort, she thanked them for their pains, but assured them that she was infinitely more interested in her own salvation than it was possible for them to be. When the iron was on her neck at the stake, they bade her recite the Creed, which she did most readily, but began to expound it in such a manner as to allow no doubt of her consistency. To prevent this, they strangled her, and her ashes were mingled with those of the martyrs of Seville, than whom there never was a nobler company. But there was another victim, who did not appear in the procession, nor at the Quemadero,—*Doña Juana Bohorques*, the sister of María. The single word that had escaped from María, when in the anguish of torture, was enough for the Inquisitors. She had not reproved her: there had not been any breach of sisterly affection: therefore, Juana was to be suspected of heresy. To be suspected, in the logic of the Holy Office, is to be guilty; and this lady was instantly seized, and thrown into the Castle of Triana. As they found that she was soon to become a mother, they allowed her to remain in an upper apartment until the birth of a male child, which was taken from her at the end of eight days, and, after the lapse of seven more, she was thrown into a dungeon. Then began the trial. Charges were made which she could not acknowledge with truth, and they were not slow in applying torture. But how could they be expected to pity this young mother? To bind her arms and legs with cords, and to gash the limbs with successive strainings by the levers, or to dislocate her joints by swinging her from pulleys, yet sparing vital parts, would have been the usual course of torment; but from that she might have recovered. The savage tormentors, in their fury, passed a cord over her breast, thinking to add new pangs, and, by an additional outrage of decency, as well as humanity, extort some cry that might serve to criminate husband or friend. But when the tormentor weighed down the bar, her frame gave way, the ribs crushed inwards, blood flowed from her mouth and nostrils, and she was carried to her cell, where life just lingered for another week, and then the God of pity took her to Himself. The murderers had not committed the least inquisitorial irregularity; for she did not expire when in their hands. They needed no absolution, they showed no compunction; but they strove to smother the report, for fear of scandal; and over her dead body they pronounced a sentence,—not that she was innocent, as some say,—but that the accusation of heresy had not been proved. If hell can be upon earth, it must be in an Inquisition.

CHAPTER XV.

SPAIN—MORE AUTOS DE FE.

HAPPILY for England, Philip II. missed the crown by the death of his wife, Mary. He had gone over to his hereditary dominions before her decease, and was in Brussels, anxiously negotiating a peace with France, when the first Auto took place at Valladolid. His return to Spain was by sea. Having embarked at Flushing, he found his way into the Bay of Biscay, and was within sight of Laredo, when, between rough weather and bad seamanship, his fleet began to founder. In that extremity he made a vow that, if God would permit him to set foot on firm ground again, he would take signal vengeance on the heretics of Spain. He landed, and it was resolved that the vow should be fulfilled without delay in Valladolid.

On Sunday, October 8th, 1559, in the grand Square, as before, an Auto was celebrated with unprecedented pomp. The "heretics," with their guards, occupied a gallery so contrived, that from all parts the culprits might be seen. Independently of the King's oath, it had been predetermined that he should be recreated by the spectacle now exhibited; and several prisoners were reserved to supply the entertainment. *His Majesty*, the young Prince of Asturias, for the second time, his sister, also for the second time, his cousin, the Prince of Parma, three Ambassadors from France, the Archbishop of Seville, the Bishops of Palencia and Zamora, several Bishops elect, the Constable and Admiral, the Dukes of Nagera and Arcos, the Marquises of Denia and Astorga, the Counts of Ureña, Benavente, and Buendía, the Grand Master of the military order of Montesa, the brother of the Duke of Gandia, the Grand Prior of the order of St. John of Jerusalem, a brother of the Duke of Alva, other Grandees not named, many men of title, the Countess of Ribadavia, and other grand ladies of Spain, with all the councils, tribunals, and constituted authorities of the city, in their seats of state, represented every power and hierarchy, and made that "Act of Faith" as truly national as any act could be. France was represented by Ambassadors, and so was Rome. All southern Europe assented to the deed, and another sin to be retributed was registered on high.

The Bishop of Cuenca preached "the Sermon." The "most illustrious" Prelates of Palencia and Zamora went to the spot appointed, and performed the ceremony of degradation on the Clerks brought to undergo that last act of canonical authority. Then Valdés, the Inquisitor-General, Archbishop of Seville, advanced to the King, and demanded of him the oath prescribed. The King rose, drew his sword, and brandished it bravely. Valdés read the form: "It having been, by Apostolical Decrees and Sacred Canons, ordered that Kings should swear to favour the holy Catholic faith and Christian religion, does Your Majesty swear by the Holy Cross, with your royal right hand upon your sword, that you will give all favour that is necessary to the Holy Office of the Inquisition, and to its Ministers, against heretics and apostates, and against those who defend and favour them, and against whatsoever person, directly or indirectly, may impede the efforts and affairs of the Holy Office, and that you will force all your subjects and people to obey and observe the Constitutions and Apostolical Letters given and published in defence of the holy Catholic faith against heretics, and against those who believe them, receive them, or favour them?"* Philip answered, *Así lo juro:* "Thus I swear."

We now turn to the victims.

Don Carlo di Sesso, native of Verona, *son* of the Bishop of Piacenza, of noble family, forty-three years of age, a scholar, long in the service of the Emperor, chief Magistrate of Toro, married into a Spanish family that boasted descent from Peter the Cruel, had come to reside in Spain, in consequence of his marriage, at Villa Mediana, near Logroño. He was reputed to be the principal teacher of Lutheranism in Valladolid, Palencia, Zamora, and their respective districts. They arrested him in Logroño, and took him to the secret prisons in Valladolid, where he answered to the accusation of the Fiscal on the 18th of June, 1558. On the day before this Auto, they told him that he must prepare to die, and exhorted him to confess whatever he had not yet disclosed,

* Given by De Castro, in his "Spanish Protestants," from a MS. by the Bishop of Zamora, above-mentioned, who recorded the oath as written by himself on the day preceding.

either respecting himself or others. In reply to those exhortations, he asked for paper and ink, and deliberately wrote a full confession of his faith, adding that the true doctrine of the Gospel was not that which the Church of Rome taught, and had taught through several ages of corruption, but that which he had then written; and affirmed that he wished to die in the same faith, and to offer his body up to God, through living faith in His Son our Lord Jesus Christ. With indescribable vigour and energy, he wrote full two sheets of paper without a pause. Through the whole night the Friars laboured to extort some word of submission, and again on the morning of the day, but without a shadow of success. He therefore appeared at the Sermon with a gag in his mouth, sat gagged during the whole ceremony, and was thus taken to the hearth, lest he should speak heresy in hearing of the people. Then they bound him to the stake, removed the gag, and again exhorted him to confess. But with great seriousness, and in a loud voice, he answered, "If I had time, I would make you clearly see that you, who do not follow my example, condemn yourselves. But light up the fire as soon as possible, that I may die in it." They did so immediately, and he died unmoved.

Pedro de Cazalla, brother of Doctor Agustin Cazalla. He had asked to be reconciled to the Church; but they refused him, because he had dogmatized, or taught. When bound to the stake, and while they were lighting the faggots, he begged permission to be confessed. They confessed him, strangled him, and burnt the body. *Domingo Sanchez*, a Presbyter, underwent the same penalty.

Fray Domingo de Rojas, Dominican and Priest, a son of the Marquis of Poza, had shown some irresolution, but was undoubtedly a believer in the Gospel. When leaving his seat to go to the place of execution, he attempted to appeal to the King, who drove him from his presence, and he went gagged to the stake. More than a hundred of his order followed him, entreating him to recant; but he persisted in an earnest, although inarticulate, refusal. Some of them chose to understand him differently; and, perhaps to boast that he had made concession, the Inquisitors allowed him to be strangled.

Juan Sanchez, an inhabitant of Valladolid, had fled into Flanders, but was discovered, arrested by order of the King, and was now condemned to die. When the cords that had confined him snapped in the flames, he *bounded* in the air with agony: the Priests offered him mercy if he would be confessed; but he called for more fire, which was given, and thus he "kept the faith."

Besides these five, nine others perished. One, at least, would have recanted, if thereby she could have saved her life; but it was determined that she should die. Another, in despair, committed suicide, and her body was burnt. The King, be it noted, went from the scaffold to the hearth, witnessed all the executions, and made his guard assist. There were sixteen sentenced to the *sambenito*, and still there were forty-five prosecutions pending. One case occurred in connexion with this Auto which deserves especial notice, as illustrating the inexorable spirit of the Inquisition, even prevailing over the considerations of personal regard which sometimes find place among the thoughts even of an Inquisitor.

When Doña María Miranda, a Nun of the Cistertian convent of Bethlehem, in Valladolid, was in the hands of tormentors, it escaped her that one of the sisterhood, *Doña Marina de Guevara*, a lady of high family connexions, partook of her opinions. Marina, perhaps apprehensive of such a disclosure, and not prepared by the grace of God to suffer martyrdom, went to an Inquisitor on that very day (May 15th, 1558), and laid what is called a spontaneous information against herself. The Inquisition invited such delations, promised indulgence to all who would bring them, and, in its own code, laid down a general rule that, in every such case, the Inquisitor receiving the informant should deal gently with him (*semper mitius se habendo erga eum, quia venit per se, non vocatus*); and the Council of Beziers had determined that a spontaneous self-accuser should not suffer death, imprisonment, exile, nor confiscation of goods, if the confession were true and full (*pœnitentes et dicentes plenam de se ac de aliis veritatem, habeant impunitatem mortis, immurationis, exilii, et confiscationis bonorum*). Trusting in the letter of the law, and unwilling to suffer for a merely intellectual faith, Doña Marina threw herself at the feet of the Inquisitor Guillelmo, and told him that she had admitted some Lutheran opinions as probable, but had never given them full assent, and desired to renounce them altogether. He proceeded, according to the rigour of law, to exact a judicial confession, which she made, saw it reduced to writing by a Notary, and again, on the 16th, 26th, and 31st of the August following, returned to him with confidence to make voluntary additions, as her memory recalled the most trifling words that she had ever spoken on the points in controversy. But Guillelmo and his colleagues were secretly weaving a net wherein to take their prey. All whom she mentioned were arrested and examined; and her Lutheranism being made out to the satisfaction of the Inquisitors, they removed her from the convent to their secret prisons (February 11th, 1559), and subjected her to three more examinations; but without finding anything to be added to her voluntary declarations. The Fiscal then (March 3d) read her twenty-three articles of accusation, most of which she acknowledged to be true; but pleaded that the propositions of those articles expressed her doubts rather than convictions, and, by a petition duly signed by an advocate allowed her, she prayed for absolution. Again (May 8th) she applied for another hearing; and afterwards made some slight additions to her confession, which were duly ratified according to a judicial decree. A summary was then shown to her, with requisition to confess *the whole truth*, and to confirm what others had witnessed, but she had neglected to confess. Yet again she asked for an audience (July 5th), and declared, "that she had seen the 'publication of witnesses,' and thought that it must have been given to her rather that she might learn errors than be delivered from them; and that, therefore, she did not dare to read it, lest some of them should remain in her memory. For the love of God she prayed them to believe her statement; for, in His sight, and on oath, she had told them the whole truth, and could neither say nor remember any more." And she repeated her former declarations in a distinct paper, following it up (July 14th) with a petition to be absolved; or, if that were too much to ask, to be reconciled with penance. The Abbess and five Nuns of her convent certified, on oath, her "good religious conduct." Even the Inquisitor-General, who knew several of her friends, interested himself in her behalf, and, knowing the unfavourable temper of the Inquisitors of Valladolid, sent (July 28th) her cousin, Don Alfonso Tellez Giron, Lord of the town of Montalban, and cousin of the Duke of Osuna, to entreat her to confess what the witnesses had deposed against her, and to tell her that by that means only could she escape death. Perhaps dreading the living death of one branded with heresy, she replied, that it was impossible, without falsehood, to add anything to the confession already made. The Judges were inexorable, and being assembled with the Consulters (July 29th), all voted that she should be put to death, one only dissenting, who advised that she should be laid upon the rack. The Council of the Supreme confirmed their sentence.

Of this, however, she was not informed until the eve of the Auto, when the Inquisitor-General, still hoping to save her, sent Don Alfonso once more to advise her to confess all, and save herself from death. The provincial Inquisitors refused him admission, complaining that it was scandalous to display so much anxiety to save that single Nun, when many others had been killed for lesser faults. Valdés appealed to the "Supreme," who resolved that their President might be gratified; but that the Inquisitors, or one of them, should be present at the conference, together with her advocate. This was done; but Marina still refused to make a false confession, even to save her life, and she therefore suffered the *garrote*, and her body was burnt. The sentence read at the Auto was remarkable, for all in it that is definite may be summed up in few words:—That she had heard some one constantly repeat this sentence, *Being justified by faith, we have peace with God through Jesus Christ our Lord;* she thought that it sounded well, and believed it, although she understood not in what sense. For this only was she put to death; and so unanimous were all others in the sentence, that not even the Inquisitor-General could save her!

The Inquisitors at Seville had hoped for the presence of the King at a second Auto in that city, as well as at Valladolid; but were disappointed; and therefore deferred its celebration until December 22d, 1560, when fourteen persons and three effigies were burnt, and thirty-four condemned to penance.

One of the effigies was of Doctor *Juan Gil*, or Egidius, a Canon-Magistral of the cathedral of Seville. He had been prosecuted for Lutheran opinions, and underwent imprisonment in the Castle of Triana. After that punishment, he renewed his intercourse with the Reformed, and took a journey to Valladolid to see them; but soon died, and was buried at Seville. Among other discoveries in the course of their inquisitions, the Judges of the Holy Office made that of his communion with the persons whom they were labouring to extirpate: they instituted a suit against his body, and caused it to be exhumed and burnt, together with his effigy. They confiscated his property, as usual, and declared his name infamous.

Another effigy represented the Doctor *Constantino Ponce de la Fuente*, also Magistral-Canon of Seville, a fellow-student of Gil in the University of Alcalá de Henares, and his successor in the canonry. With him he had laboured to promote the study of the holy Scriptures, and from the pulpit of the cathedral to raise the standard of popular exposition. Profound learning and extraordinary eloquence brought him the patronage of the Emperor, who made him his honorary Chaplain and Preacher; and for several years he followed the imperial court in Germany. Vast congregations heard him in the cathedral of Seville, and his reputation as a philosopher, a theologian, and a Greek and Hebrew scholar, commanded universal deference. But his sermons abounded in propositions which were marked as Lutheran, and reported to the Inquisition, whence came spies to add their evidence, and contribute to the preparation of a charge. At length some papers, written by his hand, were found in the house of a lady whom they had imprisoned for heresy; and these papers furnished copious evidence that his belief was in utter opposition to the Romish dogma. In a secret dungeon the papers were laid before him; and he not only acknowledged them to be his own, but defended the doctrines therein written, and steadfastly refused to say a word that would betray his brethren. Enraged and mortified, they threw him into a subterranean cell, damp and pestiferous, where he could scarcely shift his position for want of room, and where no relief was allowed him even for the necessities of nature. Oppressed beyond endurance, he is said to have exclaimed, "O my God! were there no Scythians, cannibals, nor beings yet more cruel and more inhuman, in whose power Thou couldest have left me, rather than these barbarians?" But life could not endure in such a place, and, by an attack of dysentery, he was delivered from their power. There was none to tell of him in the hour of death; and all we know is, that he was one of a countless multitude of victims whose only record is in heaven. *Fray Fernando*, a Monk of San Isidro, suffered at the same time, for the same cause, and in the same manner, and was also represented by an effigy. A third figure told of the absence of the Doctor *Juan Perez de Pineda*, who had escaped the clutches of his persecutors by timely flight.

Among the fourteen burnt was *Julian Hernandez*, a Spaniard, Deacon, it is said, of a Lutheran church in Germany. From the remarkable smallness of his person, he was known as Julian *el chico* ("the little"). Dressed as a muleteer, exceedingly active and shrewd, he travelled between France and Spain, concealing books among the goods that he carried; and, traversing the country, not only to Castile, but even to Andalusia, he delivered the principal works of the Reformers to persons of education and rank in several of the chief cities in Spain. His learning, skill in argument, and piety, were not less remarkable than the diligence and courage with which he baffled, for several years, all the vigilance of the Inquisitors, and, in hourly peril of the death which now befell him, had cheerfully hazarded his life for the sake of Christ. Great pains were taken to pervert him during his imprisonment. Relays of Monks tried their skill; but to no effect. When a party of beaten disputants had left his cell, he would exult in their discomfiture, and cheer his fellow-prisoners by singing,—

Vencidos van los Frailes, vencidos van;
Corridos van los lobos, corridos van.

"There go the Friars, there they run!
There go the wolves, the wolves are done!"

The "wolves" tried the virtue of the rack, after argument had failed. But he gave not the slightest clue for the discovery of those who had aided him in his peculiar mission nearly through the length of the Peninsula. Lest he should spoil the decorum of this Auto by unwelcome speech, they brought him gagged. Two Priests, who knew the doctrine of the Gospel, but fought against conviction, came to persuade him to be confessed; but he reproved them sternly for their hypocrisy, drew a faggot of dry wood near his head that it might help to consume him quickly, and, by the grandeur and constancy of his faith, filled the spectators with amazement.

A Nun, *Francisca de Chaves*, of the order of St. Francis

of Asis, in the convent of Santa Isabel, in Seville, gave up herself to martyrdom. She had used great plainness of speech after her imprisonment, telling the Inquisitors, as our Lord told the Pharisees, that they were a generation of vipers. They classed her as pertinacious, and burnt her alive.

The Inquisition, being "supreme and universal," condescended not to heed the rights of nations; but gloried in the sacrifice of three foreigners in this festival of blood. *Nicholas Burton*, a citizen of London, had traded with Spain in a vessel of his own, and, about two years before, being at Cadiz, was arrested by a familiar. His alleged offence was having spoken something contrary to the religion of the country to some persons in Cadiz, and to some others at S. Lucar de Barrameda. What this something was does not appear; but the real cause of his arrest was his being owner of a fine ship, and, as the Inquisitors believed, of all the cargo, and other valuable property. Surprised at finding himself arrested without a word of accusation, he demanded the reason; but was answered only with threatenings, dragged to the common prison, kept in irons fourteen days, and, not imagining himself to be there as a heretic, but on false accusation of another kind, unconsciously supplied his persecutors with material for their purpose, by exhorting the prisoners to repentance, and explaining to them the word of God. Witnesses to his heresy being thus made, they conveyed him to Seville, laden with irons, and threw him into a secret prison in the Triana. There he must have lain for two years, at least; and now he was brought into the theatre in the attire of an obstinate heretic, "his tongue forced out of his mouth with a cloven stick fastened upon it, that he should not utter his conscience and faith to the people;" and whatever were the torments he had suffered, or the confession he made before his tormentors, we know them not. Llorente found records to the effect that he was a "contumacious Lutheran heretic," and that "he remained constant in his sect, and was burnt alive; the Holy Office of Seville taking possession of ship and cargo."

To recover that ship and cargo, a Bristol merchant, in part owner, sent his attorney, *John Frampton*, to demand restoration. Frampton spent four months in Seville in useless legal formalities, when his powers were pronounced insufficient, and he returned to England for a more ample commission. Thus furnished, he landed a second time at Cadiz, where the servants of the Inquisition seized him, set him on a mule, "tied him with a chain that came under the belly of the mule three times about, and, at the end of the chain, a great iron lock, made fast to the saddle-bow." Two armed familiars rode beside him; and thus he went to Seville, alighted within the walls of the old prison, and was thrown into a dungeon, where he found some Spaniards under treatment for heresy. Next day he was interrogated as to his name, travels, calling, and relations, and, lastly, required to say the "Hail, Mary." His recitation did not include the Romish addition, "Holy Mary, mother of God, pray for us sinners;" and this served in proof that he might be detained as an English heretic, that the course of law might be interrupted, and ship and cargo transferred to the Inquisitors. After this he was racked, and, at the end of fourteen months, brought out in a *sambenito*. Burton saw his baffled advocate among the penitents, yet not knowing who he was; and Frampton, having seen Burton burnt alive, was taken back to prison for another fourteen months, and then released under the usual humiliating injunctions, with an obligation to abide in Spain. But a favouring Providence restored him to England, and he divulged the whole. He lost £760 cash, and understood—let this be well noted—that the gains of the Inquisition by that single Auto were above £50,000. He saw *William Brook*, a mariner of Southampton, and *Barthélemi Fabianne*, a Frenchman, burnt on the same hearth with Burton.

Ana de Ribera, widow of the schoolmaster, Hernando de San Juan, who was burnt the year before, now suffered as a Lutheran heretic; as did *Juan Sastre*, a Monk of S. Isidro, and *Francisca Ruiz*, wife of an Alguacil of Seville. The reader may remember that a mad woman had given the first information of the Reformed congregation in Seville. Recovered from insanity, the poor woman regained her enjoyment of religion, and died for it, in this Auto, with *Leonor Gomez*, her sister, wife of a physician, and with *Elvira Nuñez*, *Teresa Gomez*, and *Lucía Gomez*, her unmarried daughters. One of these daughters was imprisoned first, and put to the torture, to declare accomplices, but made no disclosure. The Inquisitor then tried another method. He had her brought into the audience-chamber, sent his subordinates out of the room, and professed that he had fallen in love with her, and was resolved to save her life. Day after day he repeated the declaration, and at length persuaded the poor girl that he was indeed her lover. He then told her that, although she knew it not, her mother and sisters were accused of heresy by many witnesses, and that, for the love he bore to her, he desired to save them, but that, in order to effect his object, he must be fully informed of their case, under secrecy, that he might so proceed as to save them all from death. She fell into the snare, and told him all. His point was gained. Their conversation ended. The very next day he called her to another audience, and made her declare, judicially, what she had revealed to him in the assumed character of lover. That was enough. The mother and her daughters were sent together to the flames. And the fiend-like Inquisitor saw his victims burnt.

Enough of Autos for the present. They became ordinary spectacles, as familiar to the Spaniards as bull-fights are at this day. Each particular Inquisition had its annual celebration, necessary to maintain dread of the Clergy, to fill the pockets of the Inquisitors, and to supply entertainment to the populace. A rumour of heresy, or any sudden impulse of suspicion, cupidity, or even fear, would arouse the Holy Office to special action, and add an extraordinary spectacle to that of the year current. With regard to these Autos, one or two notes of technical information, which ought not to be omitted, are given at the foot of the page.*

* A *general* Act of Faith is such as one of those just now described. A *particular* Act is only different from a general one, in that it has not the apparatus and pomp. The "Holy Office" alone is there, and just one civil officer, if there is any one to be killed. If there be only persons for death by slow degrees, he is not wanted. A *singular* Act is that wherein there is but one culprit for exhibition. An *Autillo*, or "*little* Act," is celebrated within the halls of the Inquisition where the sentence is pronounced. There may be visiters present, by express invitation of the Inquisitor, who brings them in. The doors may be shut, for greater convenience; or they may be open, yet none admitted but by authority of the Inquisitor. Or it may be performed in presence of a class of persons called "Ministers of the Secret," and of these only.

CHAPTER XVI.

SPAIN—THE CASE OF CARRANZA, ARCHBISHOP OF TOLEDO.

So swiftly did the providence of God retribute, that while Philip II. was presiding at the murder of Christian men and women at Valladolid, one of his chief assistants in persecution, and no less a person than the Archbishop of Toledo, Primate of Spain, lay in a prison of the Inquisition.

Bartolomé Carranza was born at Miranda, a town of Navarre, in the year 1503, of noble parents. In the year 1520, after good advance in studies, he entered a Dominican monastery in Alcarría, now called Guadalajara. As soon as he had professed, he was sent to Salamanca to study theology, and, in the year 1525, became Fellow of the College of St. Gregory, in Valladolid. But during this honourable career he allowed himself a greater freedom of thought than consisted with submission to his Church; and, in 1530, a Lecturer of his College delated him to the Inquisitor Moriz, who already suspected him of unsound opinions. Another Friar also complained of him. He was examined, and censured for having defended some propositions of Erasmus, and spoken lightly of some vulgar superstitions; but his reputation was so well established, that the Inquisitors did no more than record their examination, and dismiss the case, which probably remained unknown to all except the persons concerned, and certainly was not remembered to his prejudice. Yet it eventually became evident that there was a germ of "Lutheranism" in him. Not suspecting him of heterodoxy, the Rector and Councillors of St. Gregory recommended him, in that same year, to the chair of Philosophy, in 1533 they named him Regent of Neology, and in 1534 they made him Regent-Major. Then he became Theologian "Qualificator," or Examiner, of the Holy Office of the Inquisition of Valladolid, and in that capacity often acted. In 1539 he was raised to the General Chapter of his order in Rome, and with great credit assumed the dignity, passing through his inauguration with applause. Amongst other honours was that of permission to read prohibited books, conferred on him by Paul III.

In 1540 he was again at Valladolid, shining as Doctor of Theology in the professorial chair, generally esteemed for good qualities which ought to adorn the clerical office, and so splendidly charitable that, on the failure of a harvest, he sold all his books—except the Bible and the Sum of St. Thomas—to feed the poor; and yet he had not charity for heretics. He now laboured incessantly in the Holy Office, examining processes, and, in his own house, censuring books that were sent to him from the Council of the Supreme. In the public "place" of the city he preached the Sermon at the first burning of a Lutheran, Francisco San-Roman, in 1544, witnessed his patience, triumphant over fear of death, and heard his last remonstrance: "Do you envy me my happiness?" He became an eminent preacher of those bitter Sermons. The bishopric of Cuzco, in America, was offered to him, but he refused it; and in 1545 we find him at the Council of Trent, as Theologian of the Emperor, foremost among those who declaimed against the non-residence of Bishops, and exalted the Episcopate at the expense of the Pontificate. Yet he was one of the stoutest pillars of his Church. He spent three years in Trent, and at that time enlarged his reputation, by appearing as an author. On his return to Spain in 1548, he was appointed Confessor of Philip II., to accompany His Highness in Flanders and Germany, but declined that honour also, and, in 1549, refused the bishopric of the Canaries. He accepted, however, the priorate of the Dominican convent of Palencia; and there expounded St. Paul's Epistle to the Galatians, unconsciously to himself, perhaps, treading in the steps of Luther. In 1550 he was elected Provincial of Castile, and rigorously enforced discipline in his visitation of the monasteries of that province. In 1551, when the Council of Trent was opened a second time, Carranza was there again by order of the Emperor, and as proxy of the Archbishop of Toledo; and he perseveringly took part in all the sessions and congregations.

To him was first entrusted the formation of an Index of Prohibited Books, for which purpose large numbers were put into his hands. He examined the volumes, destroyed such as it pleased him to condemn, and gave the "good ones" to the Dominican convent of San Lorenzo of Trent; and, on returning to Valladolid, devoted himself, with eminent zeal and application, to similar toils in the service of the Inquisition. Little did he think that his own name would soon be registered on the same pages with the names of men whom he was burning.

When marriage was agreed on between his King, Philip, and Mary of England, he came over to prepare, in conjunction with Cardinal Pole, for the reconciliation of this country to the See of Rome, and obedience to the Pope. "The King followed, and words cannot describe the labour of Carranza in favour of the Catholic religion. He preached continually, he convinced and converted heretics without number, and confirmed many waverers, answering their arguments verbally and in writing. In 1555 Philip went from London to Brussels, and Carranza remained with the Queen, to assist her in settling the Catholic doctrine in the Universities, and attending to other important objects. By order of Cardinal Pole, the Pope's Legate, he drew up the Canons that were to be passed in a national Council. He was zealous for the punishment of several pertinacious heretics, particularly Thomas Cranmer, Archbishop of Canterbury, Primate of England, and Martin Bucer, a famous dogmatizer of the errors of Luther; which several times brought him within a little of death.* In 1557 he went over to Flanders, to inform King Philip of what had taken place in England; and, with the greatest earnestness, he collected and burnt books containing Lutheran doctrine. In Frankfort he did the same, by means of Fray Lorenzo de Villavicencio, an Augustinian religious, whom he sent for that purpose dressed as a man of the world, and in Spain also, telling the King that they were introduced by way of Aragon, which His Majesty communicated to the Inquisitor-General, that he might have them seized. With the same intent he formed a list of the Spanish fugitives from Seville and other places, who were living in Germany and Flanders, and who sent heretical books to Spain, which list was found among his papers, when they were all taken from him at the time of his arrest." Thus does Llorente set forth his merits.

On the death of the Archbishop of Toledo, he was offered that see, the highest ecclesiastical dignity of Spain, but

* We shall not digress to examine the truth of this statement. If he was *thought* to have hazarded his life in labouring to suppress heresy, his claim on the Inquisition, for favourable consideration, ought to have been the more readily acknowledged.

manifested such reluctance, that it became necessary for Philip to command him, by his "obedience and fealty as vassal," to accept it; and that injunction was also found among his papers. On the 16th of December, 1557, his preconisation took place in a consistory of Cardinals at Rome, the Pope, Paul IV., having dispensed with the usual precaution of taking information from persons in his diocese, saying that such information was not necessary for Carranza de Miranda, whom he had intimately known in Trent, and of whose services in England, Germany, and Flanders he had such abundant intelligence. Carranza, therefore, was one of the last persons to be a prisoner in the Inquisition, and one of the most likely to wear a red hat or the triple crown. But, all this time, there were secret agencies at work to effect his ruin.

Many Prelates had been offended by his insisting, in the Council of Trent, on the residence of Bishops in their dioceses, and by his publishing a treatise on the subject. Many aspirants after honour were jealous of his advancement. On his nomination to the archbishopric, a Monk of his own order, Melchor Cano, broke out into declared enmity, and so did Juan de Regla, Confessor of Charles V. The Inquisitor-General, Valdés, partook of the same feeling, as did Pedro de Castro, Bishop of Cuenca, and several others. They concealed their malice, but sought, in secret, how to humble him, and did not despair of finding some heresy in his writings or discourses that might serve their purpose. For some time past the Archbishop had been composing "Commentaries on the Christian Catechism."* It was printed at Antwerp, in 1558, the sheets were sent to Valladolid as they were printed off, and read with avidity both by friends and foes. Among the latter, Melchor Cano gave his utmost diligence to detect heresy, and declared, in all companies, that it was full of propositions, ill-sounding, dangerous, and smelling strongly of Lutheranism. The Inquisitor, Valdés, bought several copies, and put them into the hands of examiners, charging them to make notes privately, and keep silence for the present. To Castro, Bishop

* That is to say, on the Apostles' Creed, the Decalogue, the Lord's Prayer, and the Sacraments. *Catechisms*, properly so called, had been only known among the Waldenses and Protestants, until, a very few years before this time, some were written by Jesuits.

of Cuenca, it would seem that Valdés had made a special request for a prompt report, and Castro wrote that there were Lutheran propositions under the title of *Justification:* that he entertained a very bad opinion of the belief of the author, for he had heard him speak in the same manner in the Council of Trent; and although he had not then believed that Carranza admitted error in his heart, he did now believe it: that Lutheran propositions were many, and very frequent, betraying an inward sentiment; and that other circumstances, already explained to Doctor Antonio Perez, Councillor of the Supreme Inquisition, concurred to induce this judgment.

The industry of the chief Inquisitor and his coadjutors quickly collected a mass of evidence to inculpate Carranza. De Castro said that he had heard him preach in London, three years before, in the King's presence, when, in an apostrophe to the Saviour enthroned in glory, he spoke of justification by living faith in such terms as a Lutheran might have used. In other sermons preached in England, Carranza was said to have spoken heretically of sin, and not respectfully enough of indulgences of the Bull of the Crusade, which he had imprudently stated were on sale in Spain for two reals each,—"perilous language" in England, and before heretics! Some one had even whispered, after one of those London sermons, "Carranza has preached just as Philip Melancthon might have done." But if Carranza had continued a plain Friar, no one would have given those things a second thought. Several persons were interrogated in the Inquisition concerning what they had heard, seen, said, or thought of the Archbishop; but not much could be gathered from their answers. Some one, however, had heard some one say, that he had said, that "he saw no clear proofs in Scripture of the existence of a purgatory;" yet the same person thought that he must himself believe in such a place, because he had strongly recommended foundations to pay for masses for the dead. Many witnesses were questioned on this point; but their testimony showed that Carranza really believed and taught the purgatorial fable. Some, who had been in his confidence, stated that, having licence to read prohibited books, he had borrowed some things from them, and inserted them in his own writings; but was accustomed to observe that heretics mingled good and bad so artfully together, that even their good sayings were not to be trusted. A Franciscan Monk deposed that he had heard Carranza say, in a sermon, many things that coincided with other things that Lutherans were wont to say; that he had affirmed that "mercy should be shown to converted heretics; and that sometimes persons are reputed to be quietists, *alumbrados*, and so on, if they be only seen on their knees, beating their breasts with a stone before a crucifix." This very sermon was afterwards found among his papers, tested, and reported sound in Romish faith. One said, when on the rack, that he had heard Carranza say, that if a Notary were to come to his bed-side when he was dying, he would bid him take his confession "that he renounced all merit of good works, and only desired to avail himself of those of Christ; and that his sins were as if they never had been, since Christ had made atonement for them all." Others confirmed this evidence by stating that they had often heard him use like expressions, but thought them admissible in a Catholic sense.

Fray Juan de Regla ran to tell of the Archbishop of Toledo, that when Carranza was at Yuste, visiting the Emperor Charles V. on his death-bed in the convent, he had used Lutheran expressions concerning the pardon of sins; and that, when arguing in the Council, he had manifested a scandalous indulgence towards the Lutheran heresy. But other witnesses disproved the latter charge. Perhaps the most remarkable saying of Carranza was one that he addressed to Charles when dying, exhorting him to trust in the merits of Christ alone. But everything that malignity could collect from common report, from persons under torture, or in the audience-chamber of the Inquisition, or from unguarded passages in his Commentaries, was thrown together; and as his dignity was higher than that of the Inquisitor, Valdés had a summary of the charges prepared, and sent it to the Pope, with a request that he might be authorised to make the Primate of Spain a prisoner. And Paul IV., by a Brief, surrendered his friend into the clutches of the Inquisition, but without naming him; and his successor, Pius IV., who came to the Papacy before Valdés had accomplished his purpose, confirmed the licence.

On the reception of the latter Brief, Valdés made official record of his acceptance of the powers; and the Fiscal of the Inquisition, soon afterwards, applied to him for permission to proceed, by virtue of that authority, against a personage whom he did not name, but would make known in due time. After some further formalities of office, the Fiscal presented a second petition, saying, "That Don Fray Bartolomé Carranza de Miranda, Archbishop of Toledo, had preached and pronounced, written and dogmatized, many heresies of Luther in conversations and sermons, in his Commentaries and other books and papers, as appeared from witnesses, books, and writings which he presented, and promised to accuse him more in form. Wherefore he prayed that the Archbishop might be taken, shut up in secret prisons, and his property and revenue seized and placed at the disposal of the Inquisitor-General." Valdés consulted the Council, and the Fiscal was required to present the documents, which were presented accordingly. Everything being thus made ready, Valdés consulted the King, who had already agreed to the proceeding, and required that when the *person* of Carranza came into their power, his *dignity* should be respected. Still, there was much correspondence between the King and Carranza, as well as with Valdés; and the object of persecution had sufficient information to expect a severe censure, but not to apprehend any personal suffering. To expedite the matter, some more witnesses were found, and a stronger case made out. The Fiscal then repeated his application to seize Carranza.

In compliance with this formality, the Inquisitor-General decreed (August 1st, 1559) permission to the Fiscal to imprison the Archbishop; and Philip had written to his sister Juana, Governess of the kingdom in his absence, desiring her to call the Primate up to court under some decent pretext, and there let him be taken into custody, to avoid the scandal and trouble of executing an order of the Holy Office at his residence in Alcalá.* A false report was therefore circulated of the King being on his way to Spain; and the Princess Governess wrote a letter to Carranza desiring him to hasten to Valladolid, to await his arrival. Scarcely had the morning of the 9th of August begun to dawn, when Rodrigo de

* Thus far, my chief guide has been Llorente. In relating the circumstances of Carranza's imprisonment, and *there only*, I follow a recent writer, Adolfo de Castro, because, in this passage of his "Spanish Protestants," he evidently brings good authority, and is not warped by vanity or system.

Castro, brother of one of Carranza's capital enemies, bearing the royal letter, alighted in the town of Alcalá de Henares, at the gate of the archiepiscopal palace, and hastened to put the letter into his hands. He read that the Princess wished to see him at Valladolid as soon as possible, desired him not to wait for his usual equipage, but to travel with all speed; and promised that everything necessary for his public appearance should be provided at his lodgings. He instantly made preparation for the journey, and ordered a solemn procession, next day, to pray for the safe arrival of the King. De Castro, however, was so much fatigued with his journey, that he had to remain in bed for some days; and Carranza, not without misgiving, yet unable to believe danger so near at hand, had no heart for speed, and waited for the recovery of the messenger, that they might set out together, and perform the voyage with comfort and decorum. After a delay of eight days they set out from Alcalá, and the Archbishop had arranged to stop at some places on the way, for the purpose of holding confirmations. But just a week after the arrival of De Castro, another messenger came to Alcalá. It was the chief officer of the Inquisition of Toledo, who immediately visited the Archbishop, telling him that Don Diego Ramirez, Inquisitor of that tribunal, would arrive that very night, to publish an Edict of the Faith; and Carranza caused proclamation to be made immediately for celebrating it in the church of San Francisco. The Archbishop himself was to preach the sermon, and a vast congregation assembled in the church. The hour for the sermon being come, the Primate ascended one pulpit, and the person appointed to read the edict occupied another. The person who represented Don Diego, the Inquisitor,—for Ramirez himself had disappeared,—sent a message desiring the reader to wait until after his reverence should have preached. Carranza delivered the sermon with great earnestness, exhorted the people to obey the edict, by informing against all suspected of heresy, and eloquently descanted on the good that from such obedience would redound to their souls. The edict was then read; but it was afterwards remarked that it contained no reference to prohibited books, which silence was thought respectful to the dignity of the Archbishop, whose person was so nearly in their power.

At Fuente el Saz he met with Fray Felipe de Menezes, a

Professor of one of the colleges of Alcalá, who called him aside, told him that a rumour was current in Valladolid that the Holy Office had resolved on arresting the Archbishop of Toledo, and advised him, as Providence had allowed him intimation of the report, either to return to Alcalá or hasten to Valladolid, without delay, where, perhaps, he might find some way of extrication from the peril threatened. To this he is said to have replied, that such a rumour was incredible; that the Princess herself had summoned him, and sent Don Rodrigo de Castro to convey her desires. And he could appeal to God, he said, to witness, whether at any period of his life he had been tempted to fall into any error, the cognisance of which could in any way pertain to the Inquisition. On the contrary, God had made him His instrument to the conversion of more than two millions of heretics. On Sunday, August 20th, in the morning, the Archbishop reached Tordelaguna, and was there met by Father Master Fray Pedro de Soto, who told him that his correspondent Fray Luis de la Cruz had just been arrested in Valladolid. "What do you say, Father Master?" answered Carranza in surprise. "Then, according to this, I suppose they will also wish to make *me* a heretic?" Fray Pedro assured him that, in fact, Inquisitors had already left Valladolid to take him; and he left the Archbishop in much perplexity.

It was too true. And they were on that very spot. During four days the chief Alguacil of the Council of the Inquisition had been concealed in an inn at Tordelaguna, in bed by day; and at night, with two servants on horseback, in disguise, he had gone to visit Rodrigo de Castro at Talamanca. Having returned, he hid himself at the inn again. He had also sent to Alcalá, and informed Diego Ramirez that he was there in readiness; and Diego, in order to complete the plan, instantly left Alcalá, pretending that he had an urgent call to Madrid, and joined him. This caused a great stir in Alcalá, which was increased by the distribution of twenty wands of justice to as many men, who were mounted on horseback, and led out of the town by a Minister of the Inquisition, none of them knowing whither, nor wherefore. He travelled by devious roads, impressing others into the same service as they went; and, on Tuesday, 22d, at day-break, a party of nearly a hundred men were within half a league of Tordelaguna. These men were exhorted to obey the Holy Office, and be constant to it in what they were about to do; but they had not the slightest intimation of what that would be. Tordelaguna was the chief of three towns, all under one jurisdiction; and it would appear that the Archbishop continued there in the discharge of his functions, during the whole week, knowing that imprisonment awaited him in Valladolid, and afraid to seem to flee by turning out of the road, which would cause the Inquisitors to treat him as a fugitive.

On the Sunday night, 27th, Rodrigo supped with the Archbishop, and, under pretence of fatigue, left early, went to his own host, and arranged for impressing a dozen more assistants. De Castro and his host then returned, privately, and bade Salinas, host of the Archbishop, have all the doors of his house open at break of day. About one o'clock, Rodrigo and his servants, with the new assistants, went to the house of the Governor of the three towns, who had married a sister of Carranza, entered, seized the Governor, and left him a prisoner under guards. So did they with all the other civil authorities; and these doings kept them busy until day-break. By that time Ramirez and his people were arrived; and a strong body of men, impressed into the service of the Inquisition, stood ready to earn merits by doing as they might be commanded.

Ramirez, De Castro, the Alguacil, and a few men with wands, went up stairs, and knocked at the door of an antechamber where a lay-Friar, in attendance on the Archbishop, was sleeping. "Who calls?" cried the Friar. "Open to the Holy Office," said they; and instantly the door was open. Leaving guards there, they walked through to the chamber of the Archbishop, knocked at the door, and, when he called, answered again, "The Holy Office." "Is Don Diego Ramirez there?" asked he; and on hearing that he was, he bade a page open the door. Rodrigo entered first, approached the bed, knelt on one knee, and begged his reverence to give him his hand and pardon him. Then he beckoned to the Alguacil, who also came forward, and said, "Most illustrious Señor, I am commanded by the Holy Office to make you its prisoner." "Have you orders to do that which you are now undertaking to do?" "Yes, Señor." And he produced and read an order of the Inquisitor-General, and the Council of the Inquisition. "But these gentlemen are not aware that they cannot be my judges, being, as I am, by my dignity and consecration, immediately subject to the Pope, and to no other person." In answer to this, Don Diego advanced, saying, "On this point your reverence shall have entire satisfaction," and, drawing the Pope's Brief from under his robe, read it. It was unanswerable; and the Archbishop surrendered himself without another word. In obedience to the wish of Philip, they refrained from insolence of language, but made him feel the humiliation and bitterness of his new condition. The remonstrances of a few faithful servants were soon silenced; they kept the Primate under arrest that day, and the next midnight set him upon a mule, and a body of armed familiars conducted him out of the town. On entering Valladolid, he begged, as a favour, that he might be lodged in the house of a friend, a principal inhabitant of the city, and was told by De Castro that his desire should be gratified. He was taken to the house, and, at first, could scarcely believe himself a prisoner. But restraints multiplied; the building had been previously bought by the Inquisition, apparently for this very purpose; and the shadows of an impenetrable secrecy soon closed round the captive.

The Inquisitor-General and his Council proceeded to the usual ceremonies of examination; but he refused to acknowledge their jurisdiction, and appealed to the Pope. They claimed power by virtue of the Brief: but he maintained that when that document was granted, authorising the prosecution of suspected Archbishops or other Prelates in Spain, there was neither Archbishop nor other Prelate in Spain suspected of heresy; that, at that time, he was not in Spain, but in the Netherlands, labouring for the extirpation of heresy and the exaltation of the Church; and that, therefore, the Brief could not possibly have reference to himself. On that plea he refused to answer any question, or by any act, or any submission, to acknowledge the jurisdiction of Valdés. And he further objected to submit to any judgment of Valdés, even as a delegate of the Pope, because he was his enemy; and even the letter of inquisitorial law allowed a prisoner to object to the evidence of a known enemy. The elevation of his rank, the confusion and obscurity of the answers given by witnesses, the favourable judgment of his Commentaries on the Catechism already pronounced by many of the most eminent Spaniards, and a serious division of opinion in the Supreme Council, concurred to deter the Inquisition from proceeding in this case as if it were that of an inferior person. They even feared the effects of popular indignation if they should terminate the cause, without being able to make out a justification of their conduct in beginning it. Nearly a hundred new witnesses were examined, but without any definite result; and Carranza, by his advocate, Azpilcueta, had appealed to the supreme Pontiff. Year after year passed away in litigation and delays, he being still in custody; and, meanwhile, the Council of Trent, in spite of the remonstrances of Philip, had appointed a commission to examine his Commentaries, and received a favourable report. In short, his case became one of relative powers,—the Court of Rome claiming jurisdiction on one side, and the King and Inquisition of Spain claiming it on the other.

At length the Pope superseded Valdés, by appointing a coadjutor to act for him, on pretence that his age rendered him incapable, forbidding him to take any further part in the affair of the Archbishop of Toledo, and revoking the cause to be tried in Rome. Rome could no longer be resisted altogether, and, although the Inquisitors did not obey the Pope by setting him at liberty without requiring any security for his further appearance, they allowed him to go to Rome. Conducted by a strong military escort, he left the prison of Valladolid, after a confinement of six years and a quarter, and embarked at Cartagena on the 27th of April, 1567, after some delay there, in company with several Inquisitors, who went to make the best of their case, and with that notable personage, the Duke of Alva, in the chief cabin, until they reached Genoa. At Civita Vecchia the Archbishop landed amidst great care for his safe-keeping, and such marks of honour as could be rendered to a captive wearer of a pallium, and was conveyed to the Castle of St. Angelo, the state-prison of Rome. There he lay until the 14th of April, 1576, when a persecution and imprisonment of seventeen years was brought to a close by the firmness of Gregory XIII. Carranza abjured Lutheran articles which there was no proof that he had ever held; submitted to a suspension of the functions of Archbishop, to which his constitution, impaired by suffering, and worn by age, was no longer equal; and, after having seen the Spanish Inquisitors mortified by a constant manifestation of disrespect during protracted investigations in secret consistories in the presence of the Pontiff and Cardinals, behind whose benches they were compelled to stand, day after day, and week after week, he solemnly said mass, in token of reconciliation with the Church that ought to have crowned him with honours, if it were only for his zeal against those whom the Church persecutes; and then, almost as soon as he had received the congratulation of his friends, and witnessed, in his own case, a trifling triumph of the Court of Rome over the Court of Madrid, he died. I have marked his persecution the more carefully, as it illustrates the action of private passion, and of political faction, on the theatre of the Inquisition, even in contempt of the dignities and the reputation of the Church herself.

CHAPTER XVII.

SPAIN—PROGRESS AND DECLINE OF THE INQUISITION.

So terrible an institution could not always retain undisputed power. The people could not continually be persuaded to hate Protestants; and the Supreme Council of the Inquisition in Madrid already saw the animosity of Romanists in France so far diminished, that it was impossible to burn heretics as formerly; therefore they concurred in a general purpose, if not in the plot, to destroy the Huguenots by some stroke of state, or secret conspiracy, as was done in the massacre of St. Bartholomew. And in Spain itself so little Lutheranism remained, and, at this time, so feeble were the vestiges of Judaism, that there was no object conspicuous enough to serve as a butt of popular bigotry, and keep up the splendour of periodical processions and burnings. Consequently the Inquisition was driven to new expedients, and people, having time for consideration, became persuaded, although by slow degrees, that the existence of such a tribunal was incompatible with civil rights. Contentions between it and the civil power were frequent; and in the conflict that continued for two centuries and a half after the great Autos of Sevilla and Valladolid, the advantages were sometimes with one party, and sometimes with the other. We hasten rapidly through this period, avoiding consecutive narration, and only marking the more characteristic incidents.

The transatlantic and insular dominions of the Kings of Spain were brought, as we shall observe in the proper place, under the rule of Inquisitors; but, at home, the confusion between civil and ecclesiastical authorities began to appear in the inquisitorial administration. Philip and the Spanish Inquisitors, ill-content that on the high seas there should be any respite from the thraldom,—now extended over both hemispheres,—and fixing their eyes on the great fleets then on the waters, desired a naval Tribunal, one that should float on every sea, and plunge heresy into its depths, as if to prefigure the drowning of their own Babylon. Pius V. lost not a moment in granting the necessary Bull (July 27th, 1571), and up sprang "the Inquisition of the Galleys," or, as it was afterwards called, "of Army and Navy." The Inquisitor-General of Spain saw the broad ocean added to his dominion,—fleet and camp placed under his control. In every seaport a Commissary-Inquisitor visited the ships, took an official declaration from every Captain that there were no prohibited books on board, nor any object that looked heretical; or, if there were, he seized it, being portable, or he carried a note of it on shore. The bales of merchandise also underwent examination and cleansing from every heresy-infected object. This marine Inquisition flourished grandly in Cadiz, chief seaport for commerce with the West. The Visiter-Inquisitorial embarked with Notary, Alguacil, Porter, and a company of servants, to be ready for active service. Soon as his reverend feet touched the deck, a salute proclaimed him present. First of all he and his train descended into the chief cabin, found refreshment of all sorts, a respectable fee ready for certification that the ship was clear of heresy; and oftentimes, when matters were suspicious, handsome presents induced favourable and quick dispatch. The attendant familiars, being generally commercial men, made advantageous purchases, and, having fulfilled their service to the Church, found the boat ready for use in their own, and returned, with their chief, to shore. But the merchants became impatient of the new system, and made a bargain with the Holy Office, through the Custom-house, to be exempted from direct visitation. At length this arrangement fell into disuse. The Captains, too, accustomed to command their crews alone, found the ships' duty interrupted by the meddling of Chaplains. A strange sail hove in sight, or the wind freshened, while able-bodied men were between decks undergoing inquisition. Of course inquisition was cut short at such times, and the Inquisitor-General soon heard that his interference on the high seas hindered navigation. So the marine Tribunal came to nought.

In Galicia, where the Inquisition had been silent for a year, it was renewed (A.D. 1574), to enforce an edict of the Supreme, published two years before, forbidding trade, at the frontiers, in saltpetre, sulphur, or gunpowder, lest those articles should come into the hands of heretics, and be used as ammunition wherewith to fight against the Catholic faith.

Encouraged by the favour of the King, some zealots projected the establishment of a new military order, under the direction of the Inquisitor-General, and with the title of "St. Mary of the White Sword:"—the sword of St. James was *red*, to show blood. To the new dignitary they would give entire possession of the property of all members, and absolute control of their persons. The new legions would fight against all heretics, real or suspected, and be free from royal control. No fewer than eleven provinces accepted the scheme with enthusiasm, and an army was just on the point of starting into array, when a patriotic gentleman, Don Pedro Venegas, of Cordova, represented to the King that the Inquisition had been, as yet, diligent enough in taking care of the Church; that the regular forces were able to defend the State; that if there were any extra service to be performed, the existing military orders would be forthcoming; that so formidable an armament, under control of the Inquisitor, might join the King's enemies, or be in itself strong enough to overturn his throne; and, in short, he brought such a weight of argument against the scheme, that Philip appointed a commission to examine it, in conjunction with the royal Council; and, as they could not agree to recommend its adoption, he was, for once, wise enough to foresee the evil, and refused the royal sanction.

While the Inquisition was enduring these reverses, its officers were persecuting some of the most eminent Ecclesiastics who, some in the Council of Trent, and some in Spain, had given judgment favourable to Carranza, and, of course, were making themselves enemies within the bosom of the

Church. They even threatened, and endeavoured to convict, the most respected lady in Spain, Santa Teresa, who trembled for the consequences of their censure, but, by a witty antiphrasis,—for she called them *angels*,—flattering submission, and some external influence besides, conjured the tempest. They went further still, and waged open war on the Society of Jesus. Several members of that Society, whether disgusted with its evils, or weary of its discipline, delated the Provincial, and some of the more eminent Fathers, to the Holy Office at Valladolid. Their information afforded the Inquisition an opportunity for display of power. The Provincial, Marcenius, was arrested with some others (A.D. 1586). The Society was required to produce their rules, and all documents relating to the internal management of their affairs, to be examined by the Triers. Their discipline, studies, morals, all were subjected to a searching investigation. Aquaviva flew to Rome, and implored the Pope to interpose his supreme authority, and save the Society. Xystus V. heard the prayer, and commanded his Nuncio at Madrid to espouse the cause of Jesuitism. Philip II. inclined to favour them. Xystus revoked the cause to the Apostolic See; and, after hot war between the two chief legions of the Papacy, they were set at peace with each other, so far, at least, that they could again agree to turn their weapons against their common foe, evangelical Christianity.

The reign of Philip III. was remarkable for frequent and loud remonstrances against this enormous oppression. Four times did the Cortes of Castile implore him to lay some restraint on the Inquisitors; but as often did he put them off with empty words, and the persecutors grew reckless in their insolence.

Philip IV. chose to be entertained, on his accession to the throne, with an Auto at Madrid (June 21st, 1621), where no one, indeed, was burnt, because a heretic could not be found for the fire; but a lewd Nun, who had added to licentiousness with her Confessors and others a profession of compact with the devil,—no very dissimilar offence,—appeared in a *sambenito*, and gagged, received two hundred lashes, and was carried away to perpetual imprisonment, furnishing the friends of the Inquisition with a rare instance of its usefulness for purifying the morals of the Clergy.

The Clergy now began to add their complaints to those of the laity, remonstrating against the usurpation of spiritual power by the Inquisitors. The Bishop of Cartagena and Murcia, for example, with his Chapter, appealed to the Council of Castile, who addressed the King in such words as these:—"Will Your Majesty consider if it be not enough to make one weep when he sees this high dignity" (of the episcopate), "so revered by us all, outraged, laid prostrate, and defamed in the pulpits, persecuted and trodden down at the tribunals, and all this by an Inquisitor-General, and a Council of Inquisitors, who, while they should be the very men to maintain the authority of religion, strip that authority from the first fathers of religion, the Bishops?" (October 9th, 1622.) But the King, like his predecessors, paid no regard to Chapter or Council, and, instead of diminishing the power of the Inquisitors, put a new instrument of mischief into their hands, a few years afterwards, by giving them jurisdiction over smugglers, and authorising them to seize all the silver or copper money that they might find on Spaniards leaving the country, and to reserve a fourth part of it for their own treasuries (A.D. 1627). And, if we might digress into the history of Jesuitism, we should find that a spirit of rivalry between the Inquisitors and the Jesuits, both pillars of the Church, both supporters of despotic sovereignty, and both aspirants after ascendency over civil society, often broke the peace of those guardians of the faith, and involved them in positions of difficulty out of which their Tribunal could never more be extricated.

The two bodies, however, tended to coalescence rather than to opposition; and often the astute policy of Jesuitism, guiding inquisitorial operations, rendered them less conspicuous, and therefore more formidable. This union was marked strongly in the appointment of Father Nithard, a Jesuit, and Confessor of the Queen of Philip IV., to the offices of Inquisitor-General and Councillor of State, after the death of that King, and during the minority of his son, Charles II. As Confessor, Councillor, and Inquisitor, Nithard held the reins of both temporal and spiritual government, and encountered the opposition of Don Juan of Austria, an illegitimate son of the deceased King, who resisted the Austrian and Jesuitical policy then dominant at court. He had both spoken and written freely of Nithard, and many of the Clergy supported him by their advice and influence. The Inquisitor directed censors to examine his *propositions*, which, of course, they pronounced heretical; and Don Juan would have been immured, at least, had not public indignation risen so high, that the Jesuit-Inquisitor found it expedient to decamp, and shelter himself under the wing of Clement IX. at Rome (A.D. 1669), where a red hat soon rewarded his ambition.

The Government of Spain, although not overthrown by the resistance of Don Juan and his adherents, was contemptibly feeble, and owed much to the infamous Tribunal for its existence. The successor of Nithard amused Charles, at his attainment to the majority, and marriage with a French Princess, with a grand Auto. For the gratification of the young Queen, a hundred and eighteen culprits were marched into her presence at Madrid, charged with various delinquencies: amongst them were eighteen Judaisers, and one apostate to Mohammedanism, sentenced to be burnt alive, and they were burnt accordingly (A.D. 1680). Then arose the great questions between the courts of Rome and Paris concerning the limits of royal and pontifical authority, and the independence of the national Church from the Roman Pontiff. The Spanish Inquisition, instead of leaving the contending parties to settle their dispute, chose to involve itself in the controversy, by taking a part no less offensive to the good sense of mankind in general, and to all true Christians, than vexatious to the French Clergy. They, in a solemn Assembly, made a declaration containing four articles, which have since been strongly marked in the general history of the seventeenth century; and of those articles the first reads thus:—"At first, to St. Peter and to his successors, Vicars of Christ, and to the Church herself, God gave power in spiritual things, pertaining to eternal salvation, but not in civil things; for the Lord said, 'My kingdom is not of this world;' and again, 'Render therefore to Cæsar the things that are Cæsar's, and to God the things that are God's;' and therefore the apostolic precept must stand, '*Let every soul be subject to the higher powers, for there is no power but of God, for the powers which be are ordained of God; therefore, he who resists the power, resists the ordinance of God.*' Kings, therefore, and Princes, are not subject to any ecclesiastical power in temporals, by the ordination of God; neither, by the authority of the keys of the Church, can they be directly or indirectly deposed, nor their subjects be exempted from fealty and obedience, nor released from the oath of fealty that they have taken. And this sentence is necessary for public tranquillity, is no less useful to the Church than to the empire, and ought to be inviolably retained, as agreeing with the word of God, the tradition of the Fathers, and the examples of the saints." The Spanish Inquisition submitted this article, as well as the others, to the examination of Consulters, and adopted their report, that it was rash, erroneous, and heretical.*

As the seventeenth century advanced, with its growing literature, and earnest controversies, the Inquisition, pretending to rule every question, and to exert a universal censorship, could not but catch a little of the polemical spirit; and its ministers, indulging the dangerous temper, ventured to break through the ancient restraints of silence, and condescended to a public advocacy of principles that were each day controverted more and more. A single example of inquisitorial theology may be admitted here. Many pages might have been filled with such material; but the reader may think himself sufficiently instructed in this branch of exegesis, if he can master the following abstract of a sermon preached in the church of the Franciscan convent in Zaragoza, on Sunday, March 1st, 1671, by Brother Manuel Guerrera y Ribera, a Trinitarian shod, Doctor of Theology, Professor of Philosophy in the University of Salamanca, Preacher to the King, and wearer of many other honours. The occasion was the publication of the annual edict for general inquisition. It is translated closely from the Spanish of Llorente.

"And He was casting out a devil, and it was dumb," &c., &c.—
Luke xi. 14—28.

"On the 1st of March Moses opened the tabernacle, Aaron clothed himself as High Priest, and the Princes of the tribes offered to obey his precepts, because on the 1st of March the temple of St. Francis would be opened, the pontifical mandates to delate heretics to the Inquisitors, Vicars of

* Discusion del Proyecto del Decreto sobre el Tribunal de la Inquisicion. Discurso del Señor Villanueva, en la Sesion del Dia 21 de Enero de 1813.—The speaker cited his authority for the information of the Cortes of Cadiz.

the supreme Pontiff, be published, and the principal citizens of Zaragoza would promise to obey them. Aaron was Inquisitor of the law, and he is this day represented by the Inquisitors of Zaragoza. Jesus Christ is accused of superstition. This is a crime for inquisition. I shall reduce my sermon to two points: first, the obligation to delate; second, the holiness of the office of Judge-Inquisitor.

"*First point.* Religion is a warfare. Every soldier should give notice to his chief if he knows that there are enemies. If he does not, he deserves to be punished as a traitor. The Christian is a soldier; and if he does not denounce the heretics, he is a traitor: justly will the Inquisitors punish him. St. Stephen, when stoned, prayed God not to impute the sin to his persecutors: but they had two sins; one, that of stoning Stephen; another, that of resisting the Holy Ghost, which is a sin for the Inquisition. He asks God to forgive that of killing him, because he could ask it; but not to forgive the other, because it was a sin for the Inquisition, and he delated it to God. Jacob separates himself from the house of Laban, his father-in-law, without saying, 'Good bye.' Why did he not pay respect to his father-in-law? Because Laban was an idolater; and in matters of faith, religion must be above all human considerations. Therefore, the son ought to delate the heretic to the Inquisition, although that heretic be his own father. Moses was Inquisitor against Pharaoh, his foster-grandfather, plunging him into the sea because he was an idolater; and against his brother Aaron, reproving him for having consented to the golden calf. Therefore, in offences of Inquisition, you must not stop to think whether the delinquent be your father or your brother. Joshua was Inquisitor against Achan, commanding them to burn him, because he had stolen property confiscated under the curse of Jericho which ought to have been burnt in fire. Therefore, it is just for heretics to be burnt. Achan was a Prince of the tribe of Judah, and yet they delated him. Therefore, every heretic ought to be delated, though he were a Prince of royal blood.*

"*The second point.* Peter was Inquisitor against Simon

* His hearers would not fail to think of Don Carlos, whom his father, Philip II., with concurrence of the Inquisitors, caused to die in prison, because he thought him tinged with heresy.

Magus. Therefore the representatives of the Vicar of Peter ought to punish magicians. David was Inquisitor against Goliath and Saul: with the first, severe, because Goliath outraged religion wilfully: with the second, merciful, because Saul was not quite his own master, for he acted under the possession of an evil spirit; and therefore Inquisitor David soothed him in his proceedings, by playing on a harp. Therefore the stone and the harp signified the sword and the olive of the inquisitorial office. The book of Revelation was closed with seven seals, because it signified the process of the Inquisition, so secret that it seems to be closed with seven thousand. Only a lion opens it, and then the lion is changed into a lamb. What can be a clearer figure of an Inquisitor? To make inquisition into crimes he is a lion that terrifies; after having sought them out, he is a lamb, that treats all the guilty written in that book with gentleness, kindness, and compassion. Other Elders attended with little vials of pleasant odours at the opening of the book. They were little vials (*redomitas*), and not vials (*redomas*); they had their mouths little. Therefore the Inquisitors and their servants ought to speak little. The odours were aromatic: St. John says that they signified the prayers of the saints. These saints are the Lord's Inquisitors, who offer prayer before they pronounce the sentence. The text says, that the Ministers carried harps (*citáras*) also. Why not lutes or viols (*arpas ó vihuelas*)? Nothing of the kind. The chords of these musical instruments are made of skins of animals, and the Lord's Inquisitors do not skin any one. The harps have chords of metal, and the Inquisitors must use iron, tempering it, and adapting it to the circumstances of the guilty. The viol is played with the hand, symbol of despotic power; the harp with the quill, hieroglyphic of knowledge. Let it be a harp, then, and not a lute or viol, because the Inquisitors decide with knowledge, and not with despotism. The hand depends on the body and its influences; the quill is a separable, independent thing; therefore it must be harp, not lute, because the sentence of an Inquisitor does not depend on influences."

In an age and with a people who could listen to such folly, when Kings had such Preachers, and colleges such Professors, the Inquisition might carry its daring to great length; but those times of ignorance were passing rapidly away. Preachers like the orator of Zaragoza, and Inquisitors like Rocaberti and the royal Confessor Diaz, who could hunt for witchcraft all over Spain, in order to find out by whose fault Charles II. was childless, were not the men to turn back a tide of discontent that flooded higher from year to year. And it was in this reign that the first effectual measures were taken to undermine the strength of the "horrible Tribunal."

Two Councillors of State, two of Castile, two of Aragon, two of Italy, (for the Spanish possessions in Italy,) two of the Indies, two of military orders, and a Secretary of the King, constituted what was called "the Great Junta," summoned by the King to consider the complaints that came from all quarters against the Inquisition. After grave deliberation they reported (May 21st, 1696), that the usurpation of jurisdiction by the Inquisitors was found to be as old as their establishment in His Majesty's dominions. They had assumed power in every kind of case, and over persons of all conditions. Persons of all ranks had been thrown into their prisons, and families covered with disgrace. The slightest disrespect shown to any of their dependents or domestics, who had come into the possession of exorbitant privileges, they punished with relentless severity. The very forms of their judicial proceedings were insolently contemptuous towards the royal courts, and prejudicial to all civil authority. The King's "vassals" had ever been discontented, and the Emperor, Charles V., had been so persuaded of the justice of their complaints, that he suspended the sanctions hitherto given to the Inquisition; but Philip II., being Governor in his absence, (after his abdication of the empire,) restored them after a suspension of ten years, but under some restrictions which never were observed. Spoiled by long indulgence, the insolence of the Inquisitors became insufferable. They exercised jurisdiction over secular persons, and in matters not pertaining to religion, (as is related in this chapter,) but forgot that such jurisdiction belonged to the Sovereign alone, and was only delegated to them by his favour. They even denied this; and, with equal contempt, set aside the restrictions of canon-law and of Bulls which lay in their own archives. The Junta stated that they might justly ask for a revocation of all the privileges which had been thus abused, but would only recommend that the original restrictions should be enforced, and that no one should be confined in prisons of Inquisitions, except for crimes against religion. They further recommended a permission to appeal from the Inquisition to the throne, with a public examination of causes before the royal courts. And they enumerated many evils resulting from privileges of the Inquisition, undefined and unlimited as those privileges were, and extended to all connected with an Inquisitor. His coachman, or his lacquey, demanded reverence of every one; and fancied himself privileged to commit unbounded insult. His servant-girl complained if she were not served quickly or well enough in the market or the shop; and whoever offended one of those menials was liable to be flung into the deepest dungeon. They then described the discontents and tumults which the Inquisition had provoked in various provinces of Spain, and proposed that its jurisdiction should be narrowed, its privileges diminished, and the civil authorities enabled to resist its encroachments. But the King was too feeble to resist the influences which held him in subjection, and the grievances of the nation were not redressed.

The eighteenth century opened somewhat more hopefully for Spain. Philip V., grandson of Louis XIV. of France, was the first who refused to have an Auto at his coronation; but, following the advice of his grandfather, he maintained the Inquisition as an instrument of despotic government, and actually employed it to punish, as heretics, those who had any doubt—for there was a war of succession—concerning his title to the crown. And he not only humbled the Tribunal to this political service, but deprived an Inquisitor-General of his office who had presumed to proceed, for heresy, against some high officers of state. Irritated by the presumption of the Inquisitors, he ordered a decree for the suppression of their office; but, dreading the rebound of his own stroke, dared not to carry the decree into execution. The Cortes of Castile again (A.D. 1714) recorded their condemnation, but without any further effect than that which eventually results from every disclosure of a truth. The same body repeated their complaint a few years afterwards (A.D. 1720). But while Philip V. used the Inquisition for his own service, and the evangelical doctrine which had prevailed two centuries before no longer left a trace of its existence, there were multitudes of persons accused of attempting to revive Judaism, and others offended by their activity in propagating Freemasonry. This gave the Inquisitors abundant pretext for the discharge of their political mission; and when Philip V. died, it was found that there had been, during his reign of forty-six years, seven hundred and eighty-two Autos in Spain alone. Llorente calculates that 1564 were burnt alive, and 782 in effigy, with 11,730 penitents; making a total of 14,076 victims.

There were two incidents of this reign worthy of notice. In the year 1713 Gibraltar was ceded to Great Britain; and, by an article of the treaty of Utrecht, "Her Britannic Majesty, at the instance of the Catholic King, consented and agreed that on no account should Jews or Moors inhabit or have dwelling in the said city of Gibraltar;" but "Her Majesty, the Queen of Great Britain, promised that the inhabitants of the said city of Gibraltar should be allowed the free exercise of the Roman Catholic religion." The very next year, Isaac Martin, an Englishman, was imprisoned and tortured by the Inquisition in Granada, on the very spot where the edict was written for the expulsion of the Jews from Spain; as if to show Great Britain the effect of principles to which she had rendered obeisance in the proscription of the Jews at Gibraltar, and the return she might expect for indulgence towards "the Roman Catholic religion" within her own dominions.

During the reigns of Charles III. and Charles IV. a revival of literature, and an advance in political science, guided the attention of the Clergy and of the Government to the pretensions of the Court of Rome, as well as to the proceedings of the Inquisitors. The former of these Monarchs nearly yielded to the persuasion of his best advisers,—the Marquis of Roda, and the Counts of Aranda, Floridablanca, and Campomanes,—who advised him to suppress the Inquisition, as well as to expel the Jesuits. He banished the Fathers of the Society, but could not summon up courage to extinguish that terrible police. A mysterious dread held back his hand from giving sanction to a decree that would have made his title as Benefactor of Spain complete. Even an Inquisitor-General,—rare instance of humanity!—the Archbishop of Selimbria, proposed a scheme for its reformation; but an intrigue of court unseated him, and confined him to a monastery (A.D. 1794). When the Inquisition had prepared to cast into its dungeons Don Ramon de Salas, whom Charles IV. rescued, and the Prince of the Peace, a decree for suppression was actually drawn up; but the Prince of the Peace himself was induced to dissuade the King from signing it (A.D. 1797). The project of reformation, however, was no more lost sight of; and, at length, the first step was taken, by the exertion of Urquijo, Prime Minister of Charles, who obtained a royal prohibition of interfering with foreign Consuls in Spain (A.D. 1799). From that time those functionaries have been allowed to exercise the Protestant religion in the consulates, and to have in their libraries whatever books they please; and it is gratifying to know that a few of them have made good use of the liberty then conceded. Meanwhile, sentences to death nearly ceased; and when a good man, whose heart the Lord had touched, and who steadfastly refused to compromise his conscience by any concession to Romish idolatry, was sentenced to be delivered over to the secular arm, in compliance with the letter of the law, the Inquisitors themselves connived at a humane fraud, if we may so speak, a certificate of lunacy, resorted to by agreement between all parties, as an evasion of the law. By this contrivance Don Miguel Solano, Priest of Esco, a town in Aragon, walked out of the secret dungeons of the Inquisition of Zaragoza as a maniac, forgiven his heresy, and, as a maniac, exempted from priestly ministration, while every one knew him to be a reasonable man, and treated him accordingly. Nothing, however, could repress his zeal for Christ; and, after bearing open testimony to the truth, and resisting every effort to dissuade him from that confession, he was released from controversy by death, and, refusing the wafer and the unction, departed in the faith (A.D. 1805), and was buried in unconsecrated ground, within the walls of the Inquisition, on the bank of the Ebro, but without any sentence of infamy, or posthumous condemnation. So great a revolution had taken place in the views of Spanish Ecclesiastics.

At this point we may transcribe the summary of the number of sufferers given by Llorente at the close of his "Critical History," only noting that this gives the lowest possible estimate. From the time of Torquemada, until the year 1809, there were, at least,—

Burnt alive	31,912
Burnt in effigy	17,659
Penitents	291,450
Total	341,021

Let us not fail to note that, fifteen years before the death of Solano, the word of God had been translated into the language of the people by Padre Scio, tutor of the Prince of Asturias, and that its universal reading, by persons of all ranks and ages, was advocated by Don Lorenzo Villanueva with a scope of learning, and clearness and warmth of eloquence, that would adorn the literature of the most polished nation, in the most enlightened age. Our page brightens. We approach better times.

CHAPTER XVIII.

SPAIN—INQUISITION ABOLISHED—TRIBUNALS OF THE FAITH.

Napoleon Bonaparte had succeeded in embroiling the royal family and court of Spain. Charles IV. abdicated, and his son, Ferdinand VII., received the crown. This was brought about by the nefarious contrivances of the Emperor and his Frenchmen, and every true Spaniard regarded the foreigners with abhorrence. It so happened that the Pope did not smile on that scourge of Europe; and the Inquisition also, from repugnance to the political principle of the French Revolution, refused to commit itself to the French influence which had become paramount at Madrid. The Inquisitor-General, however, Don Ramon de Arce, choosing rather to bend than break, resigned his office (March 23d, 1808) to the young King Ferdinand, whom Bonaparte induced to retire into France. The Council of the Supreme stood firm, and asserted their power to act without a General, in case of his death or inability; but it is not likely that they ventured to continue an active inquisition of French books, either infidel or revolutionary. Spain was deluged with foreign influences, and they were helpless.

In a few months more the imperial standard crossed the Bidasoa. Bonaparte carried all before him. On the 2d of December, 1808, he entered Chamartin, a village one league from Madrid, established his head-quarters there, and sent troops to take possession of the capital, and demand submission of all the public bodies. The Council of the Inquisition had courage to refuse, and, on receiving information of their passive resistance, he took his pen, and wrote, in few words on a slip of paper (December 4th), an order to arrest the Inquisitors, abolish the Inquisition, and sequestrate its revenue. Some of the Inquisitors escaped, their brethren were carried prisoners to Bayonne; and the invader of Spain did what its worthier Sovereigns, especially Charles III., had often wished to do, but never dared. Probably this is the only act of Bonaparte in Spain that Spaniards could approve, and he thought thereby to acquire popularity; but, as they could not honourably accept deliverance, even from the Inquisition, at the hands of a usurper, so soon as a Council of Regency could be formed, to administer government and conduct war, in the name of the captive King, they instructed one of the fugitive Inquisitors, then in Cadiz (August 1st, 1810), to assemble as many of his colleagues as possible, and to continue the functions which had been interrupted by the violence of the enemy. Constituent Cortes then assembled at Cadiz (September 24th), and, in pursuance of the act of the Regency, enjoined several formalities, from time to time, tending to complete the restoration.

But those acts were no more than formalities. In preparing a fundamental code for future government, the leading statesmen deliberated on the relations that ought to exist between the temporal and spiritual authorities, and, as a first measure, framed an article of the new Constitution, which, although excessively intolerant, was constructed to serve an important purpose. It ran thus: "The religion of the Spanish nation is, and shall be perpetually, the Catholic, Apostolic, Roman, only true. *The nation protects it by wise and just laws*, and prohibits the exercise of any other." The same Cortes, in preparing a coronation-oath, provided that the Sovereign should swear to "defend and preserve the Roman Catholic Apostolic religion, without permitting any other;" and the hottest bigots might, therefore, have thought their cause secure. Meanwhile, both Cortes and Regency took measures for the restoration of the Supreme Council. But there were some, even in those Cortes, who spoke freely on behalf of religious liberty; and a yet larger number of Deputies professed their hope, notwithstanding the enactment of perpetuity to Romanism, that the new code would soon be succeeded by a better, and that Protestants would have permission to erect churches in Spain.

The Inquisition might possibly have been restored, under some restrictions, but for the precipitancy of the Inquisitors, who would not wait to be instructed as to the constitution of their body, and the extent of their jurisdiction, but notified to the Regency (May 16th, 1811) their intention to proceed forthwith. There were, also, reasons for distrust on part of the Government towards some of them, and they were forbidden to act without further authority. The whole affair of the Inquisition was remitted to the consideration of a special Commission; but, instead of preparing a plan for the guidance of the Holy Office, they divided on the question of its compatibility with the Constitution, and, after much delay, the case daily assuming an appearance of greater complication, the Cortes ordered their Committee for the Constitution, which was not yet complete, to entertain that fundamental question, and to report thereupon. They undertook the charge, amidst general anxiety; the laity, on one side, desiring the abolition of the Tribunal, and most of the Clergy trembling lest the main support of Popery should be taken from them. At length (December 8th, 1812) the Commission presented an elaborate and profoundly interesting Report, containing a review of the history of the Spanish Inquisition from its earliest and most authentic records, so far as they were then accessible, and concluding that it could not be re-established consistently with the liberties of Spain. The document is extremely valuable, and is itself a history. On the main question it speaks thus:—

"This is the Tribunal of the Inquisition; that Tribunal which is not dependent upon any in its proceedings; that, in the person of the Inquisitor-General, is sovereign, since he dictates laws for judgments wherein sentence to temporal punishment is pronounced; that Tribunal which, in the darkness of night, drags the husband from the side of his wife, the father from the arms of his children, the children from the sight of their parents, without hope of seeing them again until they be absolved or condemned, without power to contribute to their defence, and that of the family, and with no means of knowing that, in truth and justice, they ought to suffer punishment. And, after all this, besides the loss of husband, parent, child, they must endure the sequestration of their property, the confiscation of their estates, and the dishonour of their family. And can this be compatible with the Constitution, by which order and harmony have been established between the supreme authorities, and in which Spaniards perceive the shield that must preserve them from the attacks of arbitrary power and of despotism?

"*First:* It is not compatible with the sovereignty and independence of the nation. In the judgments of the Inquisition the civil authority has no influence; for Spaniards are imprisoned, tortured, and condemned to civil penalties, without any intervention of the secular power; prosecutions are instituted, trials conducted, proofs admitted, and sentences pronounced, according to laws dictated by the Inquisitor-General. How, then, can the nation exercise its sovereignty in the judgments given by the Inquisition? It cannot. The Inquisitor is a Sovereign in a sovereign nation, and beside a sovereign Prince; for he dictates laws, he applies them in particular cases, and he watches over their execution. The three powers which the Cortes have regulated in the wise Constitution, given for the happiness of Spaniards, are united in the Inquisitor-General, together with his Council, and make him a real Sovereign, without any of the modifications established for the exercise of the national sovereignty; a thing the most monstrous that can be conceived, and that destroys the very first principles of national independence and sovereignty." And after establishing these positions by a comparison of laws and facts, the Commission asks:—"Has not he," Napoleon, "filled France with bastilles, where freeborn men, without number, lie groaning in fetters, having been arrested by a police whose manner of proceeding differs in no respect from that of the Inquisition? There, as here, the accuser is not known, the names of witnesses are not known, the cause of imprisonment is not told, and sentence is executed in outrage of all judgment. This is the liberty and independence of France with the police of Napoleon; and this will be ours too, if Inquisitors may accommodate the liberty and independence of Spain to the Inquisition. What Deputy will then be able to speak against the will of the Prince? Who shall declaim against arbitrary administration, and the unlawful acts of a sagacious and revengeful Secretary of the Home Department, or dare to bring him to his responsibility? Who, like Macanaz, will defend the rights of the nation against the influence of Alberoni? Will he not have reason to fear that envy and hate will load him with calumny, and bury him in the dungeons of the Inquisition? Undoubtedly. Members could not utter their opinions freely in the face of the Inquisition. The Cortes cannot exist together with this establishment; and it cannot be compatible with the sovereignty and independence of the nation, if it annihilates in Cortes the national representation on which that sovereignty and independence rest.

"*Neither* is the Tribunal of the Inquisition compatible with personal liberty, for the assurance of which various maxims have been sanctioned in the Constitution that are opposed to this establishment." The provisions for guarding against arbitrary imprisonment are then enumerated. "But what liberty," asks the Commission, "do Spaniards enjoy in the Tribunals of the Inquisition? They are taken to prison without having seen their Judges; they are immured in dark and narrow cells, and, until the sentence has been pronounced, they are allowed no communication. At such time and manner as may please the Inquisitors, they are asked to make a declaration; they are never told the name of the accuser, if there be any, nor the names of the witnesses that depose against them; scraps of evidence only are read to them, and the depositions themselves are disguised by being written in the third person; in the Tribunal of the Faith of God, who is truth itself, all truth is violated, in order that the prisoner may not come to the knowledge of the enemy by whom he has been slandered and persecuted. The cause is never published, but sealed up in the secret of the Inquisition; so much is extracted from it as seems good to the Inquisitors, and with that only there is made a 'publication of proofs,' and the person treated as a criminal is invited to ground his defence on that, pleading for himself, or through an advocate who has been given to him, or to object to the witnesses. But how can he object to persons whose names he knows not? The unhappy culprit is bewildered with thinking, remembering, suspecting, guessing. He forms rash and hasty and false conjectures. He struggles with his own conscience, with his sense of honour, with his affections of friendship, trying to discover the covetous person who has sold him, the ambitious one who has sacrificed him, the false friend who has betrayed him with a kiss of peace, the lewd one who could not freely satisfy a brutal passion. '*I feel the pain,*' the innocent Fra Luis de Leon cried from the dark dungeons of the Inquisition, '*I feel the pain, but I cannot see the hand, nor is there a place for me to hide or shelter me.*'—At this point the Commission, overwhelmed with horror and amazement, knows not in what language to find utterance.—Priests, Ministers of that God of peace and charity who went about doing good, are they who decree the torture, and are present at its infliction, to hear the piteous cries of innocent victims, or the execrations and blasphemies of the guilty! It is inconceivable, Sir, how far prejudice can fascinate, and false zeal can lead astray."

The Commission added to their Report a project of law that passed the Cortes after a debate protracted from December 8th, to February 5th.* By that law the Tribunal was abolished, it is true; but the murderous principle of the Inquisition was most fully recognised. The civil power partially sustained its own jurisdiction, and but partially, still leaving heretics to suffer. One is ashamed to find such a law enacted in a European Parliament in the year 1813, and sorry to record it as yet in force, and with the aggravation that, by a recent Concordat between the Pope and the Queen of Spain, the clauses that would restrict the ecclesiastical Judges are divested of their force. "The General and Extraordinary Cortes," as we read, "desiring that the provision made in the 12th article of the Constitution," cited above, "be carried out to the fullest effect, and that the faithful observance of so wise a measure be insured for the future, declare and decree:

"Art. 1. The Catholic, Apostolic, Roman religion shall be protected by laws consistent with the Constitution.

"2. The Tribunal of the Inquisition is incompatible with the Constitution.

"3. Therefore the law ii., title xxvi., partida 7, is re-established in its original force, inasmuch as it leaves free the authority of the Bishops and their Vicars to take cognisance

* The whole "Discussion" was reprinted from the Diary of the Cortes, "Cadiz: En la Imprenta Nacional: 1813."

in matters of faith, agreeably to the Sacred Canons and Common Right, and that of the secular Judges to declare and inflict on heretics the penalties which the laws determine, or which shall be determined hereafter. The ecclesiastical and secular Judges shall proceed in their respective cases according to the Constitution and the laws.

"4. Every Spaniard is at liberty to accuse of the crime of heresy at the ecclesiastical Tribunal: in default of accuser, or even if there be one, the ecclesiastical Fiscal shall take the place of accuser."

Articles 5, 6, and 7, regulate the respective action of the secular and ecclesiastical officers. Article 8 makes it "lawful to make appeals to the civil authority in the same manner as in all other ecclesiastical judgments;" and the last article is but a reproduction of an old Inquisitorial regulation.

"9. When the ecclesiastical judgment shall have been given, a statement of the case shall be forwarded to the secular Judge,"—this, however, supersedes the *Auto de Fé*,—"and the criminal shall thenceforth remain at his disposal, in order that he may proceed to inflict on him the penalty which may be allowable according to the laws."

And the partida cited in this "decree for the establishment of tribunals protective of the faith," provides "that heretics be burnt, with exception of those who are such in the lowest degree, who, not being yet formal believers" (in the heresy), "have to suffer perpetual banishment from these kingdoms, or imprisonment until they repent, or turn to the faith." Other penalties, like those in use by the Inquisition, are minutely prescribed.

A second chapter in this decree supplied a substitution for the second department of Inquisitorial jurisdiction; which is, uniformly, the censorship, suppression, and prohibition of books. The King, it was provided, should appoint literary Inquisitors in the frontier custom-houses; a system of censorship, slightly mitigated, was to prevent the publication of heresy in Spain; and the Council of State was directed to perform, in conjunction with ordinary Cortes, and under the royal sanction, the functions of a Spanish Congregation of the Index. By that arrangement, it was intended that a prohibitory Index for Spain should perpetually hide every ray of evangelical intelligence from the public eye.

The Clergy might well have been satisfied with this

enormous power to burn, to banish, to confiscate, and to suppress; but a considerable number of them, headed by the Papal Nuncio, refused to acknowledge the new law, and attempted, even while the enemy was on their borders, to stir up an insurrection on behalf of the suppressed Inquisition. But they failed, and the Nuncio, with several others, was banished from Spain.

Ferdinand VII. returned in the summer of 1814, and was no sooner established in Madrid, than he arrested the member of the Cortes who had come up from Cadiz, although to them and the Spanish people he owed restoration to his throne. He had them taken from their beds to dungeons in perfect Inquisitorial style, declared that they were all infidels and rebels, and issued a decree (July 21st) to restore the Tribunal of the Holy Office. A Council of the Supreme was again assembled; an Inquisitor-General, Francisco Xavier de Mier y Campillo, Bishop of Almería, issued instructions to a new company of Inquisitors throughout Spain and Spanish America; and after a few months had been spent in efforts to repair the shattered fortunes of the establishment, the General revived one of the ancient customs by issuing an Edict of the Faith. Prudence required that the language of this edict should be somewhat subdued. He lamented that licentiousness and infidelity, chiefly in consequence of the presence of foreign soldiers, had overrun Spain; and took credit to himself for greater gentleness than that of the disciples who would have called down fire from heaven to burn the Samaritans. He offered mercy to the guilty, and commanded all who laboured under consciousness of heresy to denounce themselves at the Holy Office before the end of the year, but graciously promised that they who did so should be absolved in secret without any punishment. But he further commanded the people to delate all persons whom they knew to be faulty in doctrine, and required Confessors to exhort all penitents to do the same, lest they should be themselves accused and prosecuted by the Tribunal of the Faith. It does not seem that many persons, if any, thought it advisable to present themselves to the new Inquisitors in Spain; but means were found to sacrifice a political victim in an "Act of Faith" in Mexico, before the year had ended.

And here we must spend a few moments to note an instance of Inquisitorial deception.

An advocate of the Holy Office, in the Cortes at Cadiz, had the effrontery to say that, for a century past, torture had been discontinued; but the contrary was too well known for his assertion to be credited. Three years and a quarter *after* he had said that no one had been tortured for at least a century, a letter from Rome, dated March 31st, 1816, published in the "Gazette de France," No. CV.,* told the French that His Holiness had *then* prohibited torture in the Tribunals of the Inquisition, and commanded this resolution to be communicated to the Ambassadors of Spain and Portugal at Rome. While this rumour was yet on the lips of the Parisians, another letter from Rome, dated April 17th, announced that a reform of the Tribunals of Inquisition was going forward in earnest, and would be extended to all countries where there was a Holy Office. Proceedings were to be thenceforth regulated according to the custom of other courts, and the dictates of humanity. All was to be transacted openly; every presumption was to be in favour of the accused; and even delations were to be discouraged, and made difficult. A new code was to be framed, and then sent to all the courts of Europe. Pius VII. was said to be preaching mercy and charity to the Congregation of the Inquisition most fervently.† Another letter, dated May 9th, described the Pontiff as a mirror of benevolence, and a reformer of the Holy Office.‡ At this rate, with all that had been said of a prohibition of torture, of torture discontinued for a century, and therefore beyond the possibility of prohibition,—and while the courts of Europe were waiting to hear of the abolition of torture, and of all other abominations of the Inquisition,—there must have been some insuperable obstacle at Rome; for no such reformation was announced. At length, nine months more having lingered away, another letter from Rome appeared in the same Gazette, telling of a probability that the reform promised would really take place within another year. And the writer went so far as to say, that the Inquisition might, even then, be regarded as extinct.§ We shall see that the Roman Inquisition is not yet extinct; but, for the present, we are limited to Spain. In Spain, in the years 1812 and 1813, it was said that torture had been out of use for a century. In

* Llorente, tom. ix., p. 105. † Ibid., p. 106.
‡ Ibid., p. 107. § Ibid., p. 108.

Spain it was reported in 1816 and 1817, that the Roman Congregation was going to order it to cease, perhaps, after waiting one year more. In Spain, again, on the night of November 20th, 1817, Colonel Van Halen, charged with belonging to an association of Spanish liberals, and with desiring to subvert the government and religion of the country,—a government and a religion equally obnoxious to the enlightened and humane,—was taken from his bed in a cell of the Inquisition in Madrid, by four men with their faces covered, carried by the dim light of a lantern into the torture-chamber, questioned, raised from the ground on two tall crutches, his right arm bound down to one of them, and his left arm extended horizontally in an iron frame, questioned again, and his arm stretched by machinery until he fainted with anguish. And he was questioned again and again, and variously tormented, in order to extort the disclosure of names to be added to the list of those whom Ferdinand and his friends desired to proscribe or put to death. Van Halen was afterwards delivered from the dungeons, and related the particulars of his torture. Yet, all this time, some said that there was no torture; others, that it would shortly cease to be permitted; and others, that the Inquisition had ceased to act. But the Tribunals of the Faith acted vigorously during the reign of Ferdinand VII., especially after his return to power in 1823. How many deaths there were on account of religion it is impossible to say; but I have evidence of *one.* A schoolmaster of Busafa, a village in the neighbourhood of Valencia, was reputed to be a Quaker. He was accused before the Tribunal of the Faith, condemned, thrown into the prisons of St. Narcissus, as they are called, and there detained for some time, together with the vilest felons. "The Lords of the Tribunal of the Faith," says my informant, a Priest of Valencia, "endeavoured to induce him to make a solemn recantation of his belief as a Quaker; but he said that he could not do anything against his conscience, nor could he lie to God. They condemned him to be hanged; and he was transferred to the condemned cell, and resigned himself fully to the will of God. On July 31st, 1826, he was taken from the prison to the scaffold, displaying the most perfect serenity. The crosses were removed from the scaffold. He was not clothed in the black dress usually put on culprits when brought out to execution, but appeared in a brown jacket and pantaloons. With a serious countenance and unfaltering mien, he ascended the scaffold, conducted by Father Felix, a barefooted Carmelite Friar, who exhorted him to change his views. But he only replied, 'Shall one who has endeavoured to observe God's commandments be condemned?' When the rope was put round his neck, he asked the hangman to wait a moment, and, raising his eyes towards heaven, prayed. In three minutes he ceased to live." I have been shown the spot, and have conversed with some who saw "the Quaker schoolmaster" die.

To follow the alternate suppressions and restorations of the Tribunal until its abolition in 1834, it would be necessary to trace the history of Spain during a long struggle for civil liberty. In general, it may be stated, that a more equitable Constitution in that year, and a better state of public feeling, rendered prosecution for heresy almost impossible; and the Inquisition was again abolished. But Tribunals of Faith might be assembled, if Judges could be found to sit there. The law of the partidas above cited was taught in the Universities as a part of Spanish jurisprudence, as I found in the University of Seville in the year 1838. In 1839, Christina, Queen-Governess of Spain, by a note from her Secretary of State to the British *Chargé d'Affaires*, required me to leave Spain under peril of the extreme penalty prescribed in that law,—*las ultimas penas*,—for having officiated as a Protestant Minister; and if the Inquisition be not now formally revived there, the vigilance of the priesthood, and the concurrence of the civil authorities in acts of persecution, provide a most effective substitute. It is true, then, that there is not an Inquisition in Spain; that, just now, no one can be thrown "into the Inquisition;" and whoever speaks of such an event shows himself ignorant of one of the most interesting passages of recent European history: but it must also be borne in mind, that they who refer to Spain to prove that the Inquisition of heresy has ceased, and conceal the fact that there are Tribunals appointed for that purpose, with power to deliver over their victims to the secular arm, to be burnt alive or hung, are guilty of gross dishonesty. Although there be not an Inquisition in name, there is one in *reality*. It is perpetuated, by the renewal of old laws, in the Tribunals of the Faith.

CHAPTER XIX.

PORTUGAL.

HAPPILY for Portugal in the fifteenth century, the sway of the "Catholic Sovereigns," Ferdinand and Isabella, did not extend into that kingdom, neither did the Inquisition of Torquemada. But the spirit of persecution cannot be excluded from a province where the Romish priesthood officiate. In Portugal, as in Spain, the Jews had long been oppressed; and although multitudes who left the latter country in 1492 were allowed to remain in Portugal, it was only under conditions of extreme severity; and, at length, they were reduced to the same terrible alternative of exile, or compulsory profession of Christianity. They who submitted to the latter took upon themselves, not the easy yoke of Christ, of whom they had been taught nothing, but an insufferable bondage to the Church of Rome. Under the usual designation of New Christians, they were obnoxious to suspicion, contempt, and the most vexatious vigilance of the Priests: although the King Emanuel had granted them a promise, in 1497, that they should be exempt from inquisition for twenty years. Whether there was any Tribunal there it is not easy to say; but that there was formal prosecution for heresy, as in every other country of Popedom, is unquestionably certain. The same exemption was renewed in 1507; and in 1521 John III. again renewed it for another twenty years, with a clause, that even after the term appointed, their descendants should not be tried for heresy without being confronted with their accusers, and that the property of persons put to death for heresy should, nevertheless, descend to their heirs. These privileges, like all others, must have been *purchased* by the New Christians for themselves and their children. But, six years before the expiration of the term, Pope Clement VII. sent an Inquisitor-General, Fray Diego de Silva, to set up an Office in Lisbon; and this he did, not of his own motion, but in compliance with earnest representations and entreaties from King John III., who complained that those New Christians were receiving the doctrines of Luther, which then began to find acceptance in all parts of the Peninsula. After some reluctance, it is said, Clement consented to absolve the King from his obligation, and sent the Friar, invested with full authority, to introduce the Holy Office. Don Diego came, but encountered the execrations of the inhabitants; and the New Christians expostulated so strongly, that John was obliged to consent to remit the case to Rome for a reconsideration. Clement died about that time; and his successor, Paul III., struggling with a sense of honour, hesitated to confirm the act of his predecessor. But the ferocious importunity of John, and the prevailing spirit of the Church, overcame his scruples; and he issued a Bull (March 23d, 1536) that satisfied the importunity of fifteen years, and enabled King John fully to avenge the contempt which he said those Judaisers had shown to ceremonies of the mass and to images of the saints. His Holiness named three Bishops as Commissaries, or sub-Inquisitors, with Silva, to whom he gave the title of Chief Inquisitor, and commanded them to proceed, in conjunction with the Ordinary of the diocese, but for three years to follow the practice of criminal courts, and proceed according to common right. He also prohibited confiscation of property; thus adapting, as he conceived, the odious institution to the circumstances of the country. In due time a Supreme Council was formed in Lisbon, which sat twice every week.

Thus began the Inquisition of Portugal, as the documents quoted by Antonio de Sousa* demonstrate. Some writers, following Páramo, attribute it to one Juan Perez de Saavedra, a clever impostor, who forged a Bull, in the year 1540, to the purport that the Tribunals of Portugal should be assimilated to those of Spain, came to Badajoz with a splendid equipage, assumed the dress and title of a Cardinal, acted as Papal Nuncio, received all the honours rendered to such a personage, visited the Holy Houses, instructed the Inquisitors, heard appeals, redressed grievances, levied contributions, accepted presents, suffered his attendants to receive fees, did much "good," as he afterwards pleaded, by diminishing the odium of the Inquisition through such acts of lenity as were never known to be performed by a true Inquisitor, took money, indeed, but, unlike real Inquisitors, did not take life. He learned Inquisitorial secrets, but divulged none of them; deserved, as he thought, praise and reward for the skilful management of so beneficial a fraud; but was detected,

* Aphorismi Inquisitorum.

arrested, and sent to expiate his offences against Pontifical and Inquisitorial dignity by nineteen years' labour in the galleys. His fraud, it might have been expected, and the presumption of heresy which always attends offences against the Inquisition, should have sent him to the stake. But it was not so. Thither go the confessors of Christ. Fraud is too familiar with the defenders of Romish faith to be classed with mortal sins; and even Philip II. of Spain, severely zealous as he was, sent for "the false Nuncio of Portugal" after his release from punishment, and complacently bade him relate his adventures. He did so, but adorned the narrative with romance enough to provide material for a novel, and to mislead those who do not critically examine dates and cannot detect improbabilities.

The partition of Portugal into Inquisitorial districts soon took place. The Tribunal of Evora was erected by De Silva in the year 1537, with Juan de Mello, afterwards Archbishop of Evora, for its first Inquisitor. In 1539 Cardinal Henry, second Inquisitor-General, established that of Lisbon, whither he transferred De Mello, to make beginning there also. And the same Cardinal created a third at Conimbra, in 1541, under the administration of two "Commissary-Inquisitors," Bernardo da Cruz, a Dominican, and Alfonso Gomez, a Canonist.

If we had the correspondence that passed between the true Nuncio and King John and the Court of Rome, an insight into the history of the early Portuguese Inquisition might, perhaps, be gained; and the veil which now covers most of the proceedings of the Inquisition and Government of Lisbon might be withdrawn. But enough is published to show that those proceedings were atrocious. From a Brief of Paul III. to the King (June 16th, 1545), we learn that Simon de Vega, his Ambassador, had taken a letter to Rome, five months before, relating the case of the Inquisition in Portugal, and complaining, at great length, and in no very respectful terms, of a former Brief, wherein the Pope had forbidden that neophytes then imprisoned should be subjected to any further trial or punishment until Giovanni Ricci, Bishop elect of Sipento, had further informed him concerning some of them. The Pontiff complained that the King had demanded, with an air of bitterness very unbecoming in a Christian, permission to inflict vengeance on the Jews, and full severity on heretics. But he proceeded to tell him that he had received many and sore complaints of the conduct of the Inquisitors, who were accused of having burnt many persons unjustly, and of having kept very many more in custody, in order to burn them, also, unjustly; and that therefore he had commanded judgment to be suspended, and a report of the doings of those Ministers of the Holy Office to be transmitted to himself, that he might see whether they had been just or unjust. The truth is, that the Pontifical authority had been resisted by the Inquisition. When Paul III. confirmed the appointment of his predecessor, he did so under a compromise with the agent of the New Christians in Rome, who obtained, by the usual method, an order for the release of his brethren then in the prisons of the New Inquisition in Lisbon. But the Inquisitors, headed by the King, refused to open the prisons; and the Nuncio, resolved to maintain the dignity of the Pope, caused the proclamation of pardon to be affixed to the church-doors, and himself went to the prisons, saw them opened, and released one thousand eight hundred persons from durance, and many of them, no doubt, from death. But the King persisted in placing his forces at the service of the Inquisitors, who furiously renewed the persecution; and the agent of the persecuted people, Duarte de Paz, a Knight of St. John, had been actively engaged at Rome in moving the Court to enforce the favourable orders they had purchased. Gold, given by the persecuted while under the pressure of suffering, procured Briefs to mitigate the violence of their persecutors; and it would seem that Papal authority overcame the fury of John III. Paul commanded the Cardinal Henry of Portugal, head of the Inquisition, both as Chief Inquisitor and by virtue of his dignity as Legate, to see that the Ministers proceeded cautiously, and bade him exhort the King, his brother, to refrain from unchristian severity. And to "his son," the King, the Pope sent another Brief, exhorting him to be careful that, while the Inquisition was *free*, it should also be *moderate;* to remember that those neophytes were as yet but babes in Christianity, and that both nature and Scripture teach us to treat babes with soft words rather than with threatenings.* For Lutheran heretics, however, Paul had

* These Briefs are given by Raynaldus, A.D. 1545, LVIII.; 1547, CXXXI., CXXXII.

not been moved to exhortation; and they were left to be burnt without pity. Doubtless he would allow *their* condemnation to be "just."

A veil of obscurity hides those victims from our knowledge; and, although we find it everywhere stated that Autos were no less frequent than in Spain, we do not find authentic narratives to yield material for a consecutive sketch, and must therefore be content to mark a few instances, and close our notice of the Inquisition in Portugal.

William Gardiner, a native of Bristol, was "honestly brought up, and by nature given unto gravity; of a mean stature of body, of a comely and pleasant countenance, but in no part so excellent as in the inward qualities of the mind, which he always, from his childhood, preserved without spot of reprehension." Having been respectably educated, he entered into the service of a merchant, who had connexions both in Spain and Portugal, and, when about twenty-six years of age, was sent to Spain for the transaction of business; but, putting into Lisbon, and being there detained for some time, his rapid acquisition of the language, and acquaintance with the commercial relations of his employer, led to his establishment in that port. In those days Englishmen were earnest Protestants, and some such were then in Lisbon, "good and honest men;" and, in their society, with help of good books, and by the blessing of God, he became increasingly earnest in the cultivation of personal religion. On the first day of September, 1552, a son of the King of Portugal was married to a Spanish Princess: the wedding was solemnised with great pomp in the cathedral, "the King first, and then every estate in order," flocked into the church, mass was celebrated with the utmost ceremony, and "the Cardinal did execute." The young Englishman, who had hitherto kept aloof from Romish worship, had gone with the multitude to see the wedding, rather than the mass, which he now saw in its perfection. The Cardinal stood, elevating the host; the people, "with great devotion and silence, praying, looking, kneeling, and knocking." Gardiner felt the horror that seizes on a Christian mind in such a situation, and went home sad. He did not communicate the cause of his heaviness to any one; but, "seeking solitariness and secret places, falling down prostrate before God, with manifold tales he bewailed the neglecting of his duty, deliberating with himself how he might revoke that people from their impiety and superstition." But he reached a determination that could not be executed without putting his life in peril; and, not shrinking from the sacrifice, he deliberately settled all his temporal affairs, paying his debts, and leaving his accounts balanced, and then continued night and day in prayer and meditation in holy Scripture.

In course of the nuptial festivities another mass was to be performed, the King and royal family being present, and the Cardinal officiating. William Gardiner was there, "early in the morning, very cleanly appareled, even of purpose, that he might stand near the altar without repulse." The King and his train came, the crowd filled the church, and Gardiner, as if carried nearer by the press, took a seat almost close to the altar, having a Testament in his hand, which he diligently read, and prayed, heedless of the scene. Mass began. But he sat still. "He which said mass proceeded: he consecrated, sacrificed, lifted up on high, showed his god unto the people. All the people gave great reverence, and, as yet, he stirred nothing. At last they came unto that place of the mass where they use to take the ceremonial host, and toss it to and fro round about the chalice, making certain circles and semicircles.* Then the said William Gardiner, not being able to suffer any longer, ran speedily unto the Cardinal; and, even in the presence of the King and all his nobles and citizens, with the one hand he snatched away the cake from the Priest, and trod it under his feet, and, with the other hand, overthrew the chalice." They were all astounded; but, after the silence of a moment, a great cry rose from all the congregation, nobles and common people ran together to seize him, and one of the latter wounded him on the shoulder with a dagger. But the King commanded him to be saved, and reserved for examination. The tumult having subsided, he was brought before His Majesty, who asked him what countryman he was, and how he dared to commit such an act, in his presence, against the sacraments of the Church. He answered, "Most noble King, I am not ashamed of my country, who am an Englishman, both by birth and religion, and am come hither only for traffic of merchandise. And when I saw, in this famous assembly, so great idolatry committed, my conscience neither ought nor

* In what is called the Lesser Elevation.

could any longer suffer, but that I must needs do that which you have seen me presently do. Which thing, most noble Prince, was not done or thought of by me for any contumely or reproach of your presence, but only for this purpose, as before God I do clearly confess,—to seek only the salvation of this people."

Supposing that he had been instigated by others,—Edward VI. being then on the throne of England,—and anxious to obtain information, they put him into the care of surgeons, and, when his wound was nearly healed, subjected him to the usual process of examination. He persisted in declaring that they, only, who committed such gross idolatry, were the cause of his action. They took possession of his papers, but could learn nothing. They imprisoned all the English that were then in Lisbon, but still could not find that he had any accomplice or adviser. They questioned him as to religion; and, so far was he from attempting to evade their inquisition, that he disputed fearlessly with the theologians, using Latin, which, for such a subject, was more familiar to him than Portuguese. Then they administered various kinds of torture, and, among others, forced a ball down his throat, and drew it up again with such violence, and so often repeated, that death would have been more tolerable. After the tormentors had wearied themselves in vain, and he still declared that he would do the same again, were it possible, to testify against their idolatrous perversion of a holy sacrament, they brought him to the vestry of the cathedral, and chopped off his right hand; which he took up with his left, and kissed. Then they took him to the market-place, cut off his left hand, and mounted him on an ass. From the market-place they thus carried him to the river-side, hoisted him up over a pile of wood, which was set on fire, and, by a rope and pulley, they alternately let him down into it and pulled him up, that the populace might enjoy the sight of his half-roasted body. "In this great torment, for all that, he continued with a constant spirit, and, the more terribly he burned, the more vehemently he prayed." All this time they were exhorting him to repent, and pray to the Virgin; but he preached to them in return, entreating them to leave off such vanity and folly. "When Christ," said he, "ceases to be your Advocate, then I will pray to the Virgin Mary to be mine." Life was ebbing out. But, with his last breath, he prayed,—*Judica me, Deus, et discerne causam meam de gente non sanctâ*: "Judge me, O God, and defend my cause against an ungodly people." He was endeavouring to recite the Psalm, when they drew him up and down with violence, the burning rope broke, he fell into the pile, and was heard no more. One Pendigrace, his fellow-lodger, was kept in the Inquisition for two years, and frequently tortured; but he said nothing that could enable the Inquisitors to proceed against any of his countrymen, and, after his release, returned to England. From his narrative, confirmed by the testimony of other Englishmen, Foxe, our great Martyrologist, derived his information, as we find it in the "Acts and Monuments."

In 1560 the Inquisition of Goa was added to the three of Portugal, Lisbon, Evora, and Conimbra. But of Goa we must speak separately.

In the same year Mark Burges, an Englishman, Master of the ship "Minion," was burnt in Lisbon.

The Inquisitors burnt Protestants at every opportunity; but their business was chiefly with the descendants of Jews who still remained separate from the original Portuguese, and were still called New Christians. Nor was any occasion lost, either at Rome or Lisbon, for making gain of those unhappy people, so long as bigotry was not stronger than cupidity. Thus, in 1579, Sebastian having been beaten by the Moors in a luckless expedition to Africa, they obtained a Bull from Gregory XIII. to exempt them, for ten years, from confiscation of their property by the Inquisitors, in consideration of a sum equal to £250,000, which they had contributed for its outfit. Philip II. of Spain strongly objected to this act of common justice; and when Cardinal Henry, the same man whom Pope Paul III. had been engaged to employ for the protection of that very people, succeeded to his nephew Sebastian on the throne, either forgetting his earlier lessons, or remembering that Papal charity was but venal, he obtained consent of the same Pope to annul the indulgence, three months after its publication. He had consulted learned men, said the crowned Inquisitor, who all agreed that he was bound to make that revocation, which the good of the Faith especially required. Learned men, on subsequent occasions, set their faces against similar compacts with rich heretics, who were fleeced in Portugal as relentlessly as are the Jews, at this day, in Morocco. Yet their great numbers and their industry, superior to that of the Old Christians, always gave them importance; and, in the course of the seventeenth century, they presumed to pray that the Inquisition might be suppressed in Portugal. The King, the Nuncio, and the Pope condescended to receive their petition, but they never gave them anything better than fair words in reply. Clement X. did, indeed, issue a Bull to suppress the Portuguese Inquisition, on petition of the Jesuits, who, at the time, quarreled with it; but the Bull never came into effect.

Clement VIII. (August 23d, 1604) issued a Bull of nominal indulgence, reciting similar documents of Clement VII. and Paul III.; but it only aggravated their condition, by the restrictions with which it was loaded; and De Sousa acknowledges that its intention was, not to relieve the complainants, but, new circumstances having arisen, so to alter the Inquisitorial regulations, as to provide a new remedy. In fact, it was a pardon for past offences under certain conditions; but, after the publication of that pardon, a system of inquisition was to follow, far less easy to be evaded than any that had preceded; and, from that time, similar amnesties with spiritual offenders were not repeated, because, as the Portuguese theologians contended, all the tenderness ever spent on heretics, by Pontiffs and Inquisitors, had been spent in vain. And notable proof of Inquisitorial tenderness was given in the year 1682, when *six* effigies were burnt in an Auto instead of so many persons, who had perished in prison; *eighty-two* were condemned to severe penalties, such as whipping, banishment, and perpetual imprisonment; *three* were burnt alive; and *one* strangled and burnt. The offence charged against most of them was Judaism; some were accused of witchcraft, and others of immorality. A separate company of thirteen did penance for an unnatural crime. Another evidence of the tenderness of Inquisitors towards heretics was furnished in the year 1690, when a deputation from the New Christians of Portugal appeared in Rome, and threw themselves at the feet of Alexander VIII., imploring pity on five hundred prisoners then in the dungeons, of all ranks and ages, arrested without respect of sex or condition. Some of them had lain there fourteen years, some twelve, and none less than seven.

Nor can we wonder at the multitude of captives, nor at

their detention without any final sentence, either of condemnation or acquittal, when we read of such occurrences as that of 1672. A general attack was then made on the neophytes of Lisbon, in consequence of the loss of a few *forms*, or wafers, from one of the churches. There was no one on whom suspicion could be fixed; and the Inquisitors, resolved to profit by the occasion, seized all the neophytes, all who had the misfortune to be of Jewish or Moorish descent, drew on them a flood of popular outrage, and subjected them to the dreadful ordeal of torture. Their sufferings, for once, excited pity, and some Portuguese noblemen, Bishops, Monks, and Doctors, went in a body to the King, and begged him to put an end to those atrocities. His Majesty did not dare to open the dungeons, take out the innocent, and put in the guilty Inquisitors in their stead; but he did refer the matter to the Court of Rome. Before an answer could be had, the thief was detected, not a neophyte, but an Old Christian; and, in common honesty, the prisoners ought to have been all released. But the Inquisitors thought that such an act would be inconsistent with their credit; and therefore they kept the prisoners immured in order to question them further, in presumption that they must have had some correspondence with the criminal. The appeal to Rome was prosecuted; and the Pope, in order that he might judge of their manner of conducting trials, commanded them to send him the records of four. They refused. The Pope insisted. No reports were forthcoming. The Pope, Clement X., threatened excommunication. They began to fear; and, not able to send the reports of four causes, because so many were not on record, they managed to send two. The King, sharing in the indignation of the complainants, prosecuted his application to the Court of Rome for a reform in the rules and administration of the Inquisition, but gained nothing. And after the death of this King, the Inquisitors had the audacity to go to his widow, Donha Luisa, then Queen Regnant, by the law of Portugal, take her to the grave of her late consort, exhume his body, and treat it with brutal insult in her presence. Truly, there was a mingling of political hatred with Inquisitorial bigotry in this instance, as in many others; but that only made their conduct the more abominable.

A foreigner in Spain, who saw a crowd of spectators,

cowled and uncowled, surrounding a *quemadero*, with a pile of faggots blazing, and a human being shrieking and burning in the midst of it, half concealed, however, by fuel and smoke, might suppose them to be men possessed by infernal spirits, and thus impelled to perpetrate a deed, emblematical, as they said, of the last judgment, but certainly presenting a resemblance to hell. In Portugal, the scene would be no less fiendish, and more profoundly brutal. In the Auto itself, the Spanish and Portuguese customs were very similar. The use of the gag, for example, prevailed in both, and was affectingly exemplified to Dr. Michael Geddes, who relates that he saw a prisoner who had been several years shut up in a dungeon, where he could not see clear day, raise his eyes towards the sun, and heard him exclaim in rapture, as if absorbed in the majesty of the object, "How can people that behold that glorious body, worship any other Being than Him who created it?" Instantly the gag was thrust into his mouth, and the Jesuits who attended him to the *Terreiro de Paco*, where the gallery was erected, were not troubled with any more of his reflections. Instead of being marched thence directly to the place of execution, they who were to be burnt were taken to common prisons, kept there for an hour or two, and then brought before the Lord Chief Justice, who asked each of them in what religion he intended to die. If he said, "In the Roman Catholic Apostolic," the sentence was, that he should first be strangled, and then burnt. If he named the Protestant, or any other differing from the Romish, that functionary directed that he should be burnt alive.

At Lisbon, the place of execution was at the water-side. For each person to be burnt, whether alive or dead, a thick stake, or spar, was erected, not less than twelve feet above ground, and within about eighteen inches of the top there was a thick cross-piece, to serve as a seat, and to receive the tops of two ladders. Between those ladders, which were for the use of two Jesuits, was one for the condemned person, whom they compelled to mount, sit on the transverse piece, and there be chained fast. The Jesuits then ascended, delivered a hasty exhortation to repentance, and, that failing, declared that they left him to the devil, who was waiting to receive his soul. On perceiving this, the multitude shouted, "Let the dog's beard be made," that is to say, Let his face be scorched. This was done by tying pieces of furze to the end of a long pole, and holding the flaming bush to his face, until it was burnt black. The disfiguration of countenance, and piteous cries for "mercy, for the love of God," furnished great part of the amusement for the crowd, who, if he had been suffering death in a less barbarous way, for any criminal offence, would have manifested every appearance of compassion. When "the beard" was made, they lit the heap of furze at the foot of the stake, and, if there was no wind, the flame would envelope the seat, and begin to burn the legs; but as there generally is a breeze on the banks of the Tagus, it seldom reached so high as the knees. If there was no wind, he would be dead in half an hour; but the victim generally retained entire consciousness for an hour and a half, or two hours, in dire torment, which the spectators witnessed with such demonstrations of delight as were never produced by any other spectacle. In short, the burning, or rather roasting, to death was so contrived that the sufferer should be exposed to every spectator, and that his cries from that elevation should be distinctly audible. And after such a brutalising education, who can wonder at the degradation of the Portuguese, notwithstanding the ancient wealth and power of Portugal, as the first maritime nation in the world, the fertility of the country, the loveliness of the climate, and the commercial advantages that lie open to the people, especially in relation to Great Britain? But the cause of their disease is evident. The cause is Popery; and until that be removed, the cure cannot be effected.

Now, after the lapse of more than two centuries, we wonder at the mockery of a sermon delivered at an *Auto da Fé* in Evora (A.D. 1637), by a Commissary of the Holy Office, and Prior of the Dominicans. "My well-beloved Portuguese," cried the Monk, "let us render our heartiest thanksgivings to Heaven for the signal favour that has been shown us in this holy Tribunal. If we had not had this, our kingdom would have become a bush without flowers and without fruits, fit only to be burnt.........Let us look on England, France, Germany, and the Low Countries, and see what progress heresy has made, through lack of an Inquisition. We shall have no difficulty in understanding that we should have been like those places, had we been deprived of so great a benefit." *

* Sermon do Padre Frey Antonio Coutinho, impresso em Lisboa, 1638.

The Inquisition of Portugal fell in 1821, amidst the struggle for civil liberty; and the letter of the Portuguese Constitution seems to guarantee freedom of worship to foreigners, and, by fair construction, to leave the Portuguese themselves free to accept the Gospel: but little advantage has been taken of that measure of liberty; British Christians did not enter into the door while it was open. In Madeira, however, an active persecution of Dr. Kalley, and of those converted by his means, demonstrates that, although the external form of the Inquisition has fallen, the spirit yet lives; and present appearances, both in Spain and Portugal, show that if the form and the name be not soon revived, it will not be for want of inclination in the Church of Rome.

CHAPTER XX.

INDIA.

Heroic self-denial in the prosecution of a great object is nowhere exhibited more brilliantly than in the first Indian missions of the Jesuits. This must be acknowledged, notwithstanding the exhibition of vices in the subsequent government of those missions, that were as flagrant as the zeal and sincerity of some of the earliest Missionaries were conspicuous. This, however, is not the place to characterize, much less to describe, the labours of the Propaganda. Our present business is to trace the introduction of the Inquisition into India, and its progress there. If this work were of larger volume, I should indulge in research into this branch of ecclesiastical history, but must now be content to set down just enough to inform the general reader, indicating to the student a field that might be traversed with advantage, although it is covered with obscurity, and pass on to our peculiar object.

Alfonso de Sousa says, that Francisco Xavier, in a letter to John III. of Portugal, dated November 10th, 1545, stated, that "Jewish perfidy was daily spreading in those countries of Eastern India that were subject to Portugal; and earnestly prayed the King to send the Office of the Inquisition into that country as the remedy of so great perfidy." Sousa further states, that the Cardinal Henry, who was at that time Inquisitor-General in the kingdom of Portugal, erected a Tribunal of the Inquisition in Goa, and sent thither Inquisitors, officers, and servants necessary. The first Inquisitor was Alexo Diaz Fulcano, sent thither from Lisbon, March 15th, 1560. But it is not likely that the establishment of the Inquisition in India would, in those days, have depended on the suggestion or the request of any one person; and we cannot gain a more exact view of its origin and progress, than by marking facts as they occurred.

First: there was a bishopric at Goa, established there, as usual in all such cases, on that part of the coast falling into possession of the Portuguese, in 1510.

Then followed an appliance of all the accustomed methods of conversion, under the terror of a strong garrison. Favours and honours were lavished upon the first converts: while the Viceroy and highest functionaries stood sponsors for proselytes at baptism.

Accessions of proselytes along the eastern coast of India, more particularly, and some consolidation of military and civil power, indicated that the time was come for an enlargement of the ecclesiastical platform; but there was still some delay, until more vigorous measures could be taken to sustain a complete hierarchy. The conversion of Gentile Malabars, therefore, was for some years the object chiefly pursued. Adults were persuaded, or intimidated; but children were stolen, baptized, brought up in the Jesuits' houses, and employed afterwards to bring in fresh recruits. They were paraded through the streets, singing Catechism, and every child that could be decoyed to join the processions was taken by the Jesuits and baptized. A great number of these forcible baptisms took place in the year 1557, in spite of the resistance of their parents.*

The flock being multiplied, and somewhat disciplined into subjection, the Bishop of Goa was promoted to be Metropolitan; and two new Bishops were sent out to take possession of the dioceses, created for them, of Malacca and Cochin. This was done in 1559. And as the introduction of a new Romish hierarchy into any country is sure to be followed by correspondent manifestations of authority, the very next year that establishment was followed by the introduction of the "Holy Inquisition."

* "Parentibus quanquam invitis ac renitentibus." (Acostæ Hist. Rerum in Oriente Gestarum. Parisiis, 1572. Fol. 14.)

The Inquisitors were there, preparing and waiting for a pretext. Melchior Carneiro, Bishop-designate of Cochin, was in the mountains of Malabar, on a mission to the Nestorian Christians. Those Christians had been for many centuries in communion with the see of Babylon, or Mosul, and traced a succession of Bishops, as they believed, back to the apostolic age. They were not clear of some corruptions that had overspread Christendom, but had none of the characteristics of Popery; and although reproached on account of the heresy of Nestorius, whose followers do not seem to have entertained a sufficiently exalted view of the person of our incarnate Saviour, they had received from Nestorius a doctrine, on other points, far superior to that of Rome. Their Clergy were married; they knew but of two sacraments,—baptism and the eucharist; they did not pray to saints nor worship images; they knew nothing of auricular confession; they had not heard of purgatory or transubstantiation. They only acknowledged two sacred orders, Diaconate and Presbyterate: * although a member of the latter had always taken the oversight of his brethren within a diocese; and these "Vicars," as they were called, were again associated under a Metropolitan, who acknowledged the superior authority of the Patriarch of Babylon. In their worship they used ancient Syriac liturgies. Of Pope and mass they heard only after the Portuguese invasion of their country; and, to express their abhorrence of idolatry, they shut their eyes when an image or the wafer was produced. Carneiro signalized himself by an assault on that communion. He took possession of one of their churches, and kept possession of it under Portuguese authority for two months. With extreme difficulty he collected hearers, and only by making the most of his position and his means. The people generally fled from him; but he succeeded in persuading a few to submit to anabaptism, under the notion that the Syrian baptism which they had received was no sacrament; and he bound his proselytes to *swear submission* to the Pope of Rome. The Metropolitan concealed himself among the fugitives of his flock, wisely refusing to go down to the coast to hold a disputation with Carneiro. Carneiro, bent on his destruc-

* *Presbyterate*, not priesthood, exactly expresses the Syriac ܩܫܝܫܘܬܐ which agrees with the style of the New Testament.

tion, pursued him into a neighbouring kingdom, and strove to induce the King, or Chief, to put him to death as a propagator of error, and a disturber of peace. In this he failed; but, notwithstanding the provocation he had given to the native Christians, he returned to Cochin without suffering the least violence. But in that place, if his report be true, an arrow struck off his hat; and a note, attributed to some Syrian Christian, and containing expressions disrespectful to Gonsalvo, Principal of the Jesuits at Goa, with blasphemies against our Lord Jesus Christ, was dropped into a charity-box in the principal church. That any Syrian Christian who could write should blaspheme the Saviour whom he acknowledged, and abuse the Jesuits at the same time, whom he hated, is utterly incredible; but such a note, probably written by Carneiro or Gonsalvo, to serve their purpose, was exhibited to show that, while the arrow indicated a murderous intention, another overt act had given proof of heresy. "That thing," says Sacchini, "admonished the fathers that they should see more diligent inquisition made concerning the faith of certain men. And, behold! a vast number of false brethren of the circumcision is discovered. These men, fugitives from various regions of the world, had found means of concealment in India; and, while bearing the name of Christians, secretly practised the rites of Judaism, and propagated the same by stealth." Perhaps the truth may be, that some New Christians, having fled from Europe on account of persecution, were endeavouring to get rid of the spurious Christianity that had been forced upon them. It is not incredible that they would be sometimes overtaken in uniting with the natives to resist the oppression of the Portuguese Governors, or to counteract the schemes of the Jesuits. And, in this instance, they not only suffered the persecution to which their race was universally subjected, but they served as cover for an attack upon the native Christians. "Therefore," according to Sacchini, "if ever the Tribunal of the Holy Inquisition was necessary, the fathers (Jesuits) considered that it was necessary at that time in India, both because of the licentiousness prevalent, and the medley of all nations and superstitions; and having sent urgent letters both to Portugal and Italy, and made representation to those on the spot to whom pertained that care, they demonstrated fully that, in order to preserve that fortress in faith incorrupt, it should be established at Goa." * And a very short time afterwards, (*post paulo,*) in the year 1560, it began its operations.

There can be no doubt that the first proceedings were sufficiently terrific. The "vast number of false brethren" that were detected did not go unpunished. The Inquisitors of Goa would not be less active than their brethren in Portugal; and their victims would be so much the more easily disposed of, as no way of appeal to Rome lay open to them. From the Jewish Christians the "Sacred Searchers of the Faith" proceeded to their work of subjugating the Syrian church. Seven years after the erection of the Tribunal at Goa, Mar Joseph, Syrian Bishop of Cochin, in pursuance of a rescript from Pius V. to Cardinal Henry of Portugal, commanding the Inquisition to prosecute him, stood before it, was declared guilty of the Nestorian heresy, sent prisoner to Lisbon, and thence, in the year following, to Rome, where he died quickly. At that time burnings were common. General baptisms were celebrated with great pomp at Goa, the ecclesiastical metropolis of India, and so were general Acts of Faith. It was deemed an equal evidence of good affection to the Jesuits to attend at either. One Sebastian Fernando, writing to his General, at Rome (November, 1569), applauds the charity of his brethren, the fathers, who constantly attended persons condemned by the Sacred Inquisitors on account of depraved religion, not quitting them from the moment of sentence until the moment when the flames rose round them at the stake.† Such as would not go to mass, and keep their eyes open at the elevation, or in any way showed disaffection to Rome, were burnt for the admonition of the public.

Bishops and Priests disappeared continually, immured at Goa, or sent to Italy or Portugal. Now and then a name transpired. Simeon, a Bishop in the church at Malabar, was seized, sent to Rome, and graciously permitted by Pope Xystus V. to breathe within the walls of a convent of Friars Minors in Portugal, where, in the year 1599, *he perished* (PERIIT).‡ With this significant word Asseman closed a brief

* Sacchini, Hist. Soc. Jesu. Pars secunda, lib. i., 150, 151.

† De Rebus Indicis Epist. Liber. Parisiis, 1572.

‡ Assemanni Dissertatio de Syris Nestorianis CCCCXLVII., where several of these cases are noted.

notice of Simeon: and La Croze* throws light on it, by saying that Meneses, Archbishop of Goa, gained possession of an intercepted letter of his, containing Nestorian errors; that he sent the letter to the chief Inquisitor at Lisbon; that, from that time, no more is heard of Mar Simeon; and that it may therefore be presumed that he was conveyed to the prison of the Inquisition, and then, as one relapsed into heresy, he would be given over to the secular arm.

This same Archbishop, Alexo de Meneses, held a diocesan Synod at Diamper, in Cochin, on the 20th of June, 1599, and six days following. In that Synod a large number of Syrian Priests were present, not by free choice, but by the pressure of Portuguese influence, and were induced, although in the territory of a Pagan Sovereign, to subscribe the following extraordinary Decree, previously written, with all the others, by himself and a Jesuit, in Portuguese, for those poor Malays:—"All the Priests and faithful people of this bishopric, in Synod assembled, submit themselves, with much respect and obedience, to the holy, upright, just, and necessary Tribunal of the Holy Office of the Inquisition of these parts, acknowledging how this Tribunal contributes to the integrity of the faith. They swear and promise obedience to its commands; they desire to be judged according to its laws in matters of faith; and they beseech the Inquisitors to appoint in their place, on account of their distance," (the distance of Goa from the diocese of Cochin,) "the reverend Jesuit Fathers of the College of Vaipicota, or some other learned persons from the number of those who reside in this diocese." (Sess. iii., act. 22.) All the history of Romanism in this part of India contradicts this act. The few Priests who were persuaded to join the Church of Rome, did so with reluctance, and not without reservation; and the majority both of Clergy and laity regarded the strangers with abhorrence. Above all things, the Inquisition was hateful to them; and when the books containing their ancient Syriac liturgies were burnt, and the use of those liturgies forbidden, under peril of excommunication, which was equivalent with death, they conceived a profound indignation, which every successive provocation deepened, until they desperately broke off the yoke.

Long did those Christians refuse obedience to the Roman

* Histoire du Christianisme des Indes, livre i.

Pontiff; but they were lashed into submission; and, after a tedious and humiliating negotiation, a Synod being convened at Amida, a sort of union was effected. Once, during that correspondence, Elijah, their Patriarch, ventured to address Paul V. in such words as these: "We beseech you to send us good letters in consideration of our profession" (of obedience to the Papal See), "to show on our arrival in India," (whither Elijah was going in the new character of one holding authority from the Pope;) "because in Ormus and in Goa, and beyond, the Inquisitors of the Faith sorely trouble us, and the men of our country are not all learned, and therefore they trouble us exceedingly, or else *take money from us, and then let us go*. One Priest of Amida has died in consequence of what they have done to him" (A.D. 1616). But it does not appear that Paul V. condescended to lay any restraint on the Inquisitors, who went on their way, killing some, and ruining others by fines and confiscations, until one too hasty step provoked a part of the people of Malabar to snap their fetters.

Having failed in obtaining any concession from Rome in favour of their Syrian ritual, the Malabar Christians seceded from Francisco García, the Jesuit Archbishop of Cranganore, and applied to the Nestorian Patriarch of Babylon, or the Jacobite at Damascus, for another in his place. He sent them one named Atahalla; but the Inquisitors seized him in Meliapore (St. Thomas), took him to Goa, and there he miserably perished in their hands. Meetings were held in the diocese of Cochin, and, at length, a Nestorian Bishop was ordained (A.D. 1653). From that horrible den at Goa M. Dellon, about thirty years after the murder of Atahalla, withdrew the covering; and, by his assistance, we will look into it for a few moments.

M. Dellon, a French traveller, spending some time at Damaun, on the north-western coast of Hindostan, incurred the jealousy of the Governor and a black Priest, in regard to a lady, as he is pleased to call her, whom they both admired. He had expressed himself rather freely concerning some of the grosser superstitions of Romanism, and thus afforded the Priest, who was also Secretary of the Inquisition, an occasion of proceeding against him as a heretic. The Priest and the Governor united in a representation to the chief Inquisitor at Goa, which procured an order for his arrest. Like all other persons whom it pleased the Inquisitors or their servants to arrest, in any part of the Portuguese dominions beyond the Cape of Good Hope, he was thrown into the common prison, with a promiscuous crowd of delinquents, the place and the treatment being of the worst kind, even according to the colonial barbarism of the seventeenth century. To describe his sufferings there, is not to our purpose, inasmuch as all prisoners fared alike, many of them perishing from starvation or disease. Many offenders against the Inquisition were there at the same time, some accused of Judaism, others of Paganism,—in which sorcery and witchcraft were included,—and others of immorality. In a field so wide and so fruitful, the "scrutators" of the faith could not fail to gather abundantly. After an incarceration of at least four months, he and his fellow-sufferers were shipped off for the ecclesiastical metropolis of India, all of them being in irons. The vessel put in at Bacaim, and the prisoners were transferred, for some days, to the prison of that town, where a large number of persons were kept in custody, under charge of a Commissary of the Holy Office, until a vessel should arrive to carry them to Goa. In due time they were again at sea, and a fair wind wafted their fleet into that port after a voyage of seven days. Until they could be deposited in the cells of the Inquisition with the accustomed formalities, the Archbishop of Goa threw open *his* prison for their reception, which prison, being ecclesiastical, may be deemed worthy of description. "The most filthy," says Dellon, "the most dark, and the most horrible, of all that I ever saw; and I doubt whether a more shocking and horrible prison can anywhere be found. It is a kind of cave, wherein there is no day seen but by a very little hole; the most subtile rays of the sun cannot enter into it, and there is never any true light in it. The stench is extreme........."

On the 16th of January, 1674, at eight o'clock in the morning, an officer came with orders to take the prisoners to "the Holy House." With considerable difficulty M. Dellon dragged his iron-loaded limbs thither. They helped him to ascend the stairs at the great entrance, and, in the great hall, smiths were waiting to take off the irons from all the prisoners. One by one they were summoned to audience. Dellon, who was called the first, crossed the hall, passed through an antechamber, and entered a room, called by the Portuguese "Board of the Holy Office," where the Grand Inquisitor of the Indies sat at one end of a very large table, on an elevated floor in the middle of the chamber. He was a secular Priest about forty years of age, in full vigour, a man that could do his work with energy. At one end of the room was a large crucifix, reaching from the floor almost to the ceiling; and at one end of the table, near the crucifix, sat a Notary on a folding-stool. At the opposite end, and near the Inquisitor, Dellon was placed, and, hoping to soften his Judge, fell on his knees before him. But the Inquisitor commanded him to rise, asked whether he knew the reason of his arrest, and advised him to declare it at large, as that was the only way to obtain a speedy release. Dellon caught at the hope of release, began to tell his tale, mixed tears with protestations, again fell at the feet of Don Francisco Delgado Ematos, the Inquisitor, and implored his favourable attention. Don Francisco told him, very coldly, that he had other business on hand, and, nothing moved, rang a silver bell. The Alcayde entered, led out the prisoner into a gallery, opened and searched his trunk, stripped him of every valuable, wrote an inventory, assured him that all should be safely kept, and then led him into a cell about ten feet square, and shut him up there in utter solitude. In the evening they brought him his first meal, which he ate heartily, and slept a little during the night following. Next morning he learnt that he could have no part of his property; not even was a Breviary, in that place, allowed to a Priest, for they had no form of religion there, and for that reason he could not have a book. His hair was cropped close; and therefore he "did not need a comb."

Thus began his acquaintance with the Holy House, which he describes as "great and magnificent," on one side of the great space before the church of St. Catherine. There were three gates in front; and it was by the central, or largest, that the prisoners had entered, and mounted a stately flight of steps, leading into the great hall. The side-gates provided entrance to spacious ranges of apartments, belonging to the Inquisitors. Behind the principal building was another, very spacious, two stories high, and consisting of double rows of cells, opening into galleries that ran from end to end. The cells on the ground-floor, were very small, perhaps from the greater thickness of the walls, without any aperture from without for light or air. Those of the upper story were vaulted, whitewashed, had a small strongly-grated window, without glass, and higher than the tallest man could reach. Towards the gallery every cell was shut with two doors, the one on the inside, the other on the outside, of the wall. The inner door folded, was grated at the bottom, opened towards the top for the admission of food, and was made fast with very strong bolts. The outer door was not so thick, had no window, but was left open from six o'clock every morning until eleven,—a necessary arrangement in that climate, unless it were intended to destroy life by suffocation.

To each prisoner was given an earthen pot with water wherewith to wash, another full of water to drink, with a cup, a broom, a mat, whereon to lie, a large bason for necessary use, changed every fourth day, and another vessel to cover it, and receive offals. The prisoners had three meals a day; and their health, so far as food could contribute to it in such a place, was cared for in the provision of a wholesome, but spare, diet. Physicians were at hand to render all necessary assistance to the sick, as were Confessors, ready to wait upon the dying; but they gave no viaticum, performed no unction, said no mass. The place was under an impenetrable interdict. If any died,—and that many did die is beyond question,—his death was unknown to all without; he was buried within the walls, without any sacred ceremony; and if, after death, he was found to have died in heresy, his bones were taken up at the next Auto, to be burned. Unless there happened to be an unusual number of prisoners, each one was alone in his own cell. He might not speak, nor groan, nor sob aloud, nor sigh. His breathing might be audible when the guard listened at the grating, but nothing more. Four guards were stationed in each long gallery, open, indeed, at each end, but awfully silent, as if it were the passage of a catacomb. If, however, he wanted anything, he might tap at the inner door, when a jailer would come to hear the request, and would report to the Alcayde, but was not permitted to answer. If one of the victims, in despair, or pain, or delirium, uttered a cry, or dared to pronounce a prayer, even to God, the jailers would run to the cell, rush in, and beat him cruelly, for terror to the rest.

Once in two months the Inquisitor, with a Secretary and

an interpreter, visited the prisons, and asked each prisoner if he wanted anything, if his meat was regularly brought, and if he had any complaint against the jailers. His want, after all, lay at the mercy of the merciless. His complaint, if uttered, would bring down vengeance, rather than gain redress. But in this visitation the Holy Office professed mercy with much formality, and the Inquisitorial Secretary collected notes which aided in the crimination, or in the murder, of their victims.

The officers at Goa were,—the *Inquisidor Mor*, or Grand Inquisitor, who was always a secular Priest; the Second Inquisitor, a Dominican Friar; several Deputies, who came, when called for, to assist the Inquisitors at trials, but never entered without such a summons; Qualifiers, as usual, to examine books and writings, but never to witness an examination of the living, nor be present at any act of the kind; a Fiscal; a Procurator; Advocates, so called, for the accused; Notaries and Familiars. Of these officers enough has been said in preceding chapters. The authority of this Tribunal was absolute in Goa, as in Portugal, except that the Archbishop and his Grand Vicar, the Viceroy and the Governors, could not be arrested without authority obtained, or sent, from the Supreme Council in Lisbon. There does not appear to have been anything peculiar in the manner of examining and torturing at Goa, where the practice coincided with that of Portugal and Spain, as already described.

The personal narrative of Dellon affords a distinct exemplification of the sufferings of prisoners. He had been told that, when he desired an audience, he had only to call a jailer, and ask it, when it would be allowed him. But, notwithstanding many tears and entreaties, he could not obtain one until fifteen days had passed away. Then came the Alcayde and one of his guards. The Alcayde walked first out of the cell; Dellon, uncovered and shorn, and with legs and feet bare, followed him; the guard walked behind. The Alcayde just entered the place of audience, made a profound reverence, stepped back, and allowed his charge to enter. The door closed, and Dellon remained alone with the Inquisitor and Secretary. He knelt; but Don Fernando sternly bade him sit on a bench, placed there for the use of culprits. Near him, on the table, lay a Missal, on which they made him lay his hand, and swear to keep secrecy, and to tell them the truth. They asked if he knew the cause of his imprisonment, and whether he was resolved to confess it. He told them all that he could recollect of unguarded sayings at Damaun, either in argument or conversation, without ever, that he knew, contradicting, directly or indirectly, any article of faith. He had, at some time, dropped an offensive word concerning the Inquisition; but so light a word, that it did not occur to his remembrance. Don Fernando told him that he had done well in *accusing himself* so willingly, exhorted him, in the name of the Lord Jesus Christ, to complete his self-accusation fully, to the end that he might experience the goodness and mercy which were used in that Tribunal towards those who showed true repentance by a sincere and *unforced* confession. The Secretary read aloud the confession and the exhortation, Dellon signed it, Don Fernando rang the silver bell, the Alcayde walked in, and, in a few moments, the disappointed victim was again in his dungeon.

At the end of another fortnight, and without having asked for it, he was again taken to audience. After a repetition of the former questions, he was asked his name, surname, parentage, baptism, confirmation, place of abode, in what parish?—in what diocese?—under what Bishop? They made him kneel down, make the sign of the cross, repeat the Pater Noster, Hail Mary, Creed, Commandments of God, Commandments of the Church, and Salve Regina. He did it all cleverly, and even to their satisfaction; but the Grand Inquisitor exhorted him, by the tender mercies of our Lord Jesus Christ, to confess without delay, and sent him to the cell again.

His heart sickened. They required him to do what was impossible,—to confess *more*, after he had acknowledged *all*. In despair, he tried to starve himself to death; but they compelled him to take food. Day and night he wept, and, at length, he betook himself to prayer, imploring pity of "the blessed Virgin," whom he imagined to be, of all beings, the most merciful, and the most ready to give him help. At the end of a month he succeeded in obtaining another audience, and added to his former confessions what he had remembered, for the first time, touching the Inquisition. But they told him that that was not what they wanted, and sent him back again. This was intolerable. In a frenzy of despair he determined to commit suicide, if possible. Feigning sickness, he obtained a physician, who treated him for fever, and ordered him to be bled. Never calmed by any treatment of the physician, blood-letting was repeated often, and each time he untied the bandage, when left alone, hoping to die from loss of blood; but death fled from him. A humane Franciscan came to confess him, and, hearing his tale of misery, gave him kind words, asked permission to divulge his attempt at self-destruction to the Inquisitor, procured him a mitigation of solitude by the presence of a fellow-prisoner, a Negro, accused of magic; but, after five months, the Negro was removed, and his mind, broken with suffering, could no more bear up under the aggravated load. By an effort of desperate ingenuity he almost succeeded in committing suicide, and a jailer found him weltering in his blood, and insensible. Having restored him by cordials, and bound up the wounds he had inflicted on himself, they carried him into the presence of the Inquisitor once more, where he lay on the floor, being unable to sit, heard bitter reproaches, had his limbs confined in iron, and was thus carried back to a punishment that seemed more terrible than death. In fetters he became so furious, that they found it necessary to take them off; and, from that time, his examinations assumed another character, as he defended his positions with citations from the Council of Trent, and with some passages of Scripture, which he explained in the most Romish sense, discovering a depth of ignorance in Don Fernando that was truly surprising. That "Grand Inquisitor" had never heard the passage which Dellon quoted to prove the doctrine of baptismal regeneration: "Except a man be born of water and of the Spirit, he cannot enter into the kingdom of God." Neither did he know anything of that famous passage in the twenty-fifth session of the Council of Trent, which declares that images are only to be reverenced on account of the persons whom they represent. He called for a Bible, and for the Acts of the Council, and was evidently surprised when he found them where Dellon told him they might be seen.

The time for a general Auto drew near. During the months of November and December, 1675, he heard, every morning, the cries of persons under torture; and afterwards saw many of them, both men and women, lame and distorted by the rack. On Sunday, January 11th, 1676, he was surprised by the jailer refusing to receive his linen to be washed,—Sunday being washing-day in the "Holy House." While perplexing himself to think what that could mean, the cathedral-bells rang for vespers, and then, contrary to custom, rang again for matins; and he could only account for that second novelty by supposing that an Auto would be celebrated next day. They brought him supper, which he refused; and, contrary to their wont at all other times, they did not insist on his taking it, but carried it away. Assured that those were all portents of the horrible catastrophe, and reflecting on often-repeated threats in the audience-chamber that he should be burnt, he gave himself up to death; and, overwhelmed with sorrow, fell asleep a little before midnight.

Scarcely had he fallen asleep, when the Alcayde and guards entered the cell, with great noise, bringing a lamp, for the first time since his imprisonment that they had allowed a lamp to shine there. The Alcayde, laying down a suit of clothes, bade him put them on, and be ready to go out when he came again. At two o'clock in the morning they returned, and he issued from the cell, clad in a black vest and trousers, striped with white, and his feet bare. About two hundred prisoners, of whom he was one, were made to sit on the floor, along the sides of a spacious gallery, all in the same black livery, and just visible by the gleaming of a few lamps. A large company of women were also ranged in a neighbouring gallery in like manner. But they were all motionless, and no one knew his doom. Every eye was fixed, and each one seemed benumbed with misery. In a room not very distant, Dellon perceived a third company; but they were walking about, and some appeared to have long habits. Those were persons condemned to be delivered to the secular arm; and the long habits distinguished Confessors busily collecting confessions in order to commute that penalty for some other scarcely less dreadful. At four o'clock, servants of the house came, with guards, and gave bread and figs to those who would accept the refreshment; and one of the guards gave Dellon some hope of life by advising him to take what was offered, which he had refused to do. "Take your bread," said the man; "and if you cannot eat it now, put it in your pocket: you will be certainly hungry *before you return.*" This gave hope that he should not end the day at the stake, but come back to undergo penance.

A little before sunrise, the great bell of the cathedral tolled, and at its sound Goa was aroused. The people ran into the streets, soon lining the chief thoroughfares, and crowding every place whence view could be had of the procession. Day broke, and Dellon saw the faces of his fellow-prisoners, most of whom were Indians. He could only distinguish, by their complexion, about twelve Europeans. Every countenance exhibited shame, fear, grief, or an appalling blankness of apathy, as if dire suffering in the lightless dungeons underneath had bereft them of intellect. The company soon began to move, but slowly, as one by one the Alcayde led them towards the door of the Great Hall, where the Grand Inquisitor sat, and his Secretary called the name of each as he came, and the name of a sponsor, who also presented himself from among a crowd of the bettermost inhabitants of Goa, assembled there for that service. "The General of the Portuguese ships in the Indies" had the honour of placing himself beside our Frenchman. As soon as the procession was formed, it marched off in the order described in a preceding chapter. Poor Dellon went barefoot, like the rest, through the streets of Goa, rough with little flint-stones scattered about; and sorely were his feet wounded during an hour's march up and down the principal streets. Weary, and covered with shame and confusion, the long train of culprits entered the church of St. Francis, where preparation was made for the Auto, the climate of India not permitting a celebration of that solemnity under the burning sky. They sat, with their sponsors, in the galleries prepared; sambenitos, grey zamarras with painted flames and devils, corozas, (or *carrochas*, as the Portuguese call them,) tapers, and all the other paraphernalia of an Auto, made up a woful spectacle. The Inquisitor, the Viceroy, and other personages, having taken their seats of state, the great crucifix being erected on the altar between massive silver candlesticks, with tapers contrasting their glare with the deadly black of dress and skin, the Provincial of the Augustinians mounted the pulpit, and delivered the sermon. Dellon preserved but one note of it. The Preacher compared the Inquisition to Noah's ark, which received all sorts of beasts *wild*, but sent them out *tame*. And the appearance of the hundreds who had been inmates of that ark, certainly justified the figure.

After sermon, two Readers "went up, one after another,

into the same pulpit,"—one person in the same pulpit might at any time suffice,—and, between them, they read the processes, and pronounced the sentences, the person concerned standing before them, with the Alcayde, and holding a lighted taper in his hand. Dellon, in turn, heard the cause of his long suffering. He had maintained the invalidity of *baptismus flaminis*, or desire to be baptized, when there is no one to administer the rite of baptism by water. He had said that images ought not to be adored, and that an ivory crucifix was a piece of ivory. He had spoken contemptuously of the Inquisition. And, above all, he had an ill intention. His punishment was to be confiscation of his property, banishment from India, and five years' service in the galleys in Portugal, with penance, as the Inquisitors might enjoin. As all the prisoners were excommunicate, the Inquisitor, after the sentences had been pronounced, put on his alb and stole, walked into the middle of the church, and absolved them all at once. Dellon's sponsor, who would not even answer him before when he spoke, now embraced him, called him brother, and gave him a pinch of snuff, in token of reconciliation. But there were two persons, a man and a woman, for whom the Church had no more that they could do; and these, with four dead bodies, and the effigies of the dead, were taken to be burnt on the Campo Santo Lazaro, on the river-side, the place appointed for that purpose, that the Viceroy might see justice done on heretics, as he surveyed the execution from his palace-windows.

The remainder of Dellon's history adds nothing to what we have already heard of the customs of the Inquisition. He was taken to Lisbon, and, after working in a gang of convicts for some time, was released on the intercession of some friends in France with the Portuguese Government. With regard to his despair, and attempts at suicide, when in the Holy House, we may observe, that, as he states, suicide was very frequent there. The contrast of his disconsolate impatience with the resignation and constancy of Christian confessors in similar circumstances, is obvious; and affords valuable illustration of the difference between those who suffer without a consciousness of Divine favour, and those who can rejoice with joy unspeakable and full of glory.

CHAPTER XXI.

INDIA—(CONCLUDED).

The Inquisition of Goa continued its Autos for a century after the affair of Dellon. That at which he was present followed an interval of two years, or rather more; but so long an interval was unusual; and an aged Franciscan Friar, whom Dr. Buchanan found there, stated that from the years 1770 to 1775 he had witnessed five annual celebrations. In the last year the King of Portugal, in "humanity and tender mercy," as the same Friar said, abolished the Tribunal. But immediately after his death, the power of the Priests acquired the ascendant; and the Queen-Dowager re-established it, after a bloodless period of five years, in 1779, subject, indeed, to certain restrictions, but not in the slightest degree better than the former. One of them was, that a greater number of witnesses should be required to convict a criminal. There were to be seven, indeed, in the time of Dellon; but as any one, irrespective of character, might witness against a criminal accused of heresy, and as it required great courage to refuse to testify according to the wish of the Inquisitors, and as the Notary made the utmost of every word that might be condemnatory, that departure from the established rule of the Church concerning Inquisitorial examinations availed very little on the side of humanity. Another restriction was, "that the *Auto de Fé* should not be held publicly, as before, but that the sentences of the Tribunal should be executed privately, within the walls of the Inquisition." This only made the secret perfect, and augmented the power, while it diminished the odium, of the institution "in the presence of British dominion and civilisation."

In the summer of 1808 Dr. Claudius Buchanan visited that city, and had been unexpectedly invited by Joseph à Doloribus, second and most active Inquisitor, to lodge with him during his visit. Not without some surprise, Dr. Buchanan found himself, "heretic, schismatic, and rebel" as he was, politely entertained by so dread a personage. Regarding his English visiter merely as a literary man, or professing so to do, Friar Joseph, himself well educated, seemed to enjoy his company, and was unreservedly communicative on every subject not pertaining to his own vocation. When that subject was first introduced by an apparently incidental question, he did not scruple to return the desired information, telling Dr. Buchanan that the establishment was nearly as extensive as in former times. In the library of the Chief Inquisitor he saw a register containing the names of all the officers, who still were numerous.

On the second evening after his arrival the Doctor was surprised to see his host come into his apartment clothed in black robes, from head to foot, instead of white, the usual colour of his order (Augustinian). He said that he was going to sit on the Tribunal of the Holy Office; and it transpired that, so far from his "august office" not occupying much of his time, he sat there three or four days every week. After his return, in the evening, the Doctor put Dellon's book into his hand, asking if he had ever seen it. He had never seen it before, and, after reading aloud and slowly *Relation de l'Inquisition de Goa*, began to peruse it with eagerness. While Dr. Buchanan employed himself in writing, Friar Joseph devoured page after page; but, as the narrative proceeded, betrayed evident symptoms of uneasiness. Then he turned to the middle,—looked at the end,—skimmed over the table of contents,—fixed on principal passages, and at one place exclaimed, in his broad Italian accent, *Mendacium! Mendacium!* The Doctor requested him to mark the passages that were untrue, proposed to discuss them afterwards, and said that he had other books on the subject. The mention of *other books* startled him: he looked anxiously on some books that were on the table, and then gave himself up to the perusal of Dellon's "Relation" until bed-time. Even then he asked permission to take it to his chamber.

The Doctor had fallen asleep under the roof of the Inquisitor's convent, confident, under God, in the protection at that time guaranteed to a British subject, his servants sleeping in a gallery outside the chamber-door; and, about midnight, he was "waked by loud shrieks and expressions of terror from some one in the gallery." In the first moment of surprise, he concluded it must be the Alguacils of the Holy Office seizing his servants to carry them to the Inquisition. But, on going out, he saw the servants standing at the door, and the person who had caused the alarm, a boy of about fourteen, at a little distance, surrounded by some of the Priests, who had come out of their cells on hearing the noise. The boy said he had seen a spectre; and it was a considerable time before the agitations of his body and voice subsided. Next morning, at breakfast, the Inquisitor apologised for the disturbance, and said the boy's alarm proceeded from a *phantasma animi*,—'phantom of the imagination.'"

It might have been so. Phantoms might well haunt such a place. As to Dellon's book, the Inquisitor acknowledged that the descriptions were just; but complained that he had misjudged the motives of the Inquisitors, and written uncharitably of Holy Church. Their conversation grew earnest; and the Inquisitor was anxious to impress his visiter with the idea that "the Inquisition had undergone a change in some respects, and that its terrors were mitigated." At length Dr. Buchanan plainly requested to *see* the Inquisition, that he might judge for himself as to the humanity shown to the inmates,—according to the Inquisitor,—and gave, as a reason why he should be satisfied, his interest in the affairs of India, on which he had written, and his purpose to write on them again, in which case he could scarcely be silent concerning the Inquisition. The countenance of his host fell; and, after some further observations, he reluctantly promised to comply with the request.

Next morning, after breakfast, Joseph à Doloribus went to dress for the Holy Office, and soon returned in his black robes. He said he would go half an hour before the usual time, for the purpose of showing him the Inquisition. The Doctor fancied that he looked more severe than usual, and that his attendants were not so civil as before. But the truth was, that the midnight scene still haunted him. They had proceeded in their palankeens to the Holy House, distant about a quarter of a mile from the convent; and the Inquisitor said, as they were ascending the steps of the great entrance, that he hoped the Doctor would be satisfied with a transient view of the Inquisition, and would retire when he should desire him so to do. The Doctor followed, with "tolerable confidence," towards the Great Hall aforementioned, where they were met by several well-dressed persons, familiars, as it afterwards appeared, who bowed very low to the Inquisitor, and looked with surprise at the stranger. Dr. Buchanan paced the hall slowly, and in thoughtful silence;

the Inquisitor thoughtful too, silent and embarrassed. A multitude of victims seemed to haunt the place; and Dr. Buchanan could not refrain from breaking silence. "Would not the Holy Church wish, in her mercy, to have those souls back again, that she might allow them a little further probation?" The Inquisitor answered nothing, but beckoned him to go with him to a door at one end of the Hall. By that door he conducted him to some small rooms, and thence to the spacious apartments of the Chief Inquisitor. Having surveyed those, he brought him back again to the Great Hall, and seemed anxious that the troublesome visiter should depart; and only the very words of Dr. Buchanan can adequately describe the close of this extraordinary interview.

"'Now, Father,' said I, 'lead me to the dungeons below: I want to see the captives.'—'No,' said he, 'that cannot be.'—I now began to suspect that it had been in the mind of the Inquisitor, from the beginning, to show me only a certain part of the Inquisition, in the hope of satisfying my inquiries in a general way. I urged him with earnestness; but he steadily resisted, and seemed offended, or, rather, agitated, by my importunity. I intimated to him plainly, that the only way to do justice to his own assertion and arguments regarding the present state of the Inquisition, was to show me the prisons and the captives. I should then describe only what I saw; but now the subject was left in awful obscurity.—'Lead me down,' said I, 'to the inner building, and let me pass through the two hundred dungeons, ten feet square, described by your former captives. Let me count the number of your present captives, and converse with them. *I want to see if there be any subjects of the British Government, to whom we owe protection.* I want to ask how long they have been here, how long it is since they have seen the light of the sun, and whether they ever expect to see it again. Show me the Chamber of Torture, and declare what modes of execution, or of punishment, are now practised inside the walls of the Inquisition, in lieu of the public *Auto da Fé*. If, after all that has passed, Father, you resist this reasonable request, I shall be justified in believing that you are afraid of exposing the real state of the Inquisition in India.'

"To these observations the Inquisitor made no reply; but seemed impatient that I should withdraw. 'My good Father,' said I, 'I am about to take my leave of you, and to thank you for your hospitable attentions; and I wish always to preserve on my mind a favourable sentiment of your kindness and candour. You cannot, you say, show me the captives and the dungeons: be pleased, then, merely to answer this question; for I shall believe your word: How many prisoners are there now below in the cells of the Inquisition?' The Inquisitor replied, 'That is a question which I cannot answer.' On his pronouncing these words, I retired hastily towards the door, and wished him farewell. We shook hands with as much cordiality as we could, at the moment, assume; and both of us, I believe, were sorry that our parting took place with a clouded countenance."

After leaving the Inquisitor, Dr. Buchanan, feeling as if he could not refrain from endeavouring to get another, and perhaps nearer, view, returned to avail himself of the pretext afforded by a promise, from the Chief Inquisitor, of a letter to the British Resident in Travancore, in answer to one which he had brought him from that officer. The Inquisitors he expected to find within, in the "Board of the Holy Office.". The door-keepers surveyed him doubtfully, but allowed him to pass. He entered that Great Hall, went up directly to the lofty crucifix, described by Dellon, sat down on a form, wrote some notes, and then desired an attendant to carry in his name to the Inquisitor. As he was walking across the Hall, he saw a poor woman sitting by the wall. She clasped her hands, and looked at him imploringly. The sight chilled his spirits; and, as he was asking the attendants the cause of her apprehension,—for she was awaiting trial,—Joseph à Doloribus came, in answer to his message, and was about to complain of the intrusion, when he parried the complaint by asking for the letter from the Chief Inquisitor. He promised to send it after him, and conducted him to the door. As they passed the poor woman, the Doctor pointed to her, and said, with emphasis, "Behold, Father, another victim of the Holy Inquisition." The other answered nothing: they bowed, and separated without a word.

When Dr. Buchanan published his "Christian Researches in Asia," in the year 1812, the Inquisition still existed in Goa; but the establishment of constitutional government in Portugal put an end to it throughout the Portuguese dominions.

CHAPTER XXII.

SOUTH AMERICA.

THE Court of Rome is not wont to make gift or grant but for some *consideration.* Accordingly, when Alexander VI. made a pecuniary concession to Ferdinand and Isabella (A.D. 1501), he did so on the consideration that it was their desire "to acquire and recover the islands and countries of the Indies," America being included in the Indies, "that in them, *every condemned sect being cast down*, the Most High might be worshipped and revered." At Rome, however, the Most High—*Altissimus*—is none other than the Pope; and the Bull itself acknowledges that it was not only the desire of the Papacy to extirpate Heathenism in America, even by the extirpation of the Heathen themselves, but to destroy all condemned sects. Even before Luther there were condemned sects; and the document just quoted betrays an apprehension that, in the wildernesses of the New World, sects might flourish which could not be utterly suppressed at home, even by the aid of troops and Inquisitions. In America, therefore, while troops destroyed the natives, Inquisitions were to put down the sects.

The races of New Christians were the objects of earliest pursuit across the ocean. That they might not find refuge in America, the Spanish Inquisitor-General, Cardinal Ximenez de Cisneros, nominated (May 7th, 1516) Fray Juan Quevedo, Bishop of Cuba, to be his delegate in the kingdom of Terra Firma, as the Spanish American territories were then called, and empowered him to appoint the necessary Ministers. Charles I. (or, as Emperor, Charles V.) gave permanence and extended power to the new institution, by desiring the Cardinal Adrian to nominate Inquisitors, to be independent of the Spanish Inquisition; and, on that nomination, he appointed Alonso Manso, Bishop of Puerto Rico, and Pedro de Cordova, Vice-Provincial of the Dominicans, to be "Inquisitors of the Indies and islands of the ocean," with powers for the establishment of an Inquisition there. The Royal Order to that intent was signed on the 20th of May, 1520. The New Christians of America were not only the fugitives from Europe, but natives of those vast regions who had been compelled to submit to baptism so far as the Spanish conquests placed them under the power of the invaders; and as they were no less Heathen than before, and observed forbidden rites of the old idolatry as relics of their ancient state when under Kings of their own, they practised those rites with an enthusiastic attachment, so far as secrecy or hope of impunity encouraged them so to do. The newly-created Inquisition, although not yet stationed within fixed boundaries, but administered by wandering Dominicans from place to place, pushed its power to the utmost, and, after beginning its peculiar work of death, so alarmed the Indians that they retreated by masses into the interior, renounced the profession of Christianity, joined with yet unconquered tribes; and the Viceroys, alarmed at the general desertion, and fearing that the newly-acquired territories would be depopulated, and that combinations of Indians would grow too powerful to be resisted, entreated Charles to put a stop to the proceedings of the Inquisitors. His Majesty, partaking of their apprehension, commanded (October 15th, 1538) the Inquisitors not to interfere, on any account, with aboriginal natives of America, but only with Europeans and their descendants. Yet the Indians were not exempted from inquisition of heresy, but placed under the control of the Bishops, a set of men practically inferior to the Inquisitors, and seldom so murderous as they, and, in this instance, instructed to proceed with gentleness and caution. But the Inquisitors could not so easily be displaced. Still permitted to follow their vocation as to the Europeans by descent, they soon transgressed that limit, evaded the Royal Order by means of their secret, and the evil, after palliation for a few years, became almost as flagrant as before, and the inhibition had to be renewed (October 18th, 1549). The vigilance of the temporal authorities, and the torrent of popular hatred that the barbarous insolence of the Holy Office had drawn forth, made the position of an Inquisitor scarcely less perilous than odious, and few persons could be found willing to undertake the charge.

The humbled Inquisitors then cried out in their turn for succour; and Philip II., even after having renewed the more politic* restrictions of his predecessor, and after having feasted

* I would gladly write *more humane*, but the efforts of Charles V. to establish the Spanish Inquisition in the Netherlands, at the same time

his eyes on the martyrdoms of Spain, as he had gloated over those of England, issued a Royal Order (January 25th, 1569), complaining that the heretics, by books and conversation, introduced their new doctrine into America; said that the Council of the Supreme, with the Inquisitor-General at their head, had resolved to name Inquisitors and Ministers, not to perambulate the country, as formerly, but to be intrenched amidst palaces and prisons, and obeyed, as in Spain, by the Magistrate and the soldier, and commanded accordingly. Then in Panamá (June 20th, 1569), and next in Lima (January 29th, 1570), Inquisitors were installed as chiefs of districts. The Inquisitors made solemn entries into those places, and the authorities, again reduced to abject submission, received them with every demonstration of honour that could be devised. Mexico followed next (August 18th, 1570); and the process of organization reached yet another stage, when it was ordained that at three central Tribunals, in Lima, Mexico, and Cartagena de Indias, Inquisitors-General should preside, and guide the operations of secondary establishments (December 26th, 1571), subject, however, to the Supreme Council at Madrid. There is reason to believe that persecutions were renewed on a very large scale, although, through poverty of record, they cannot be reduced to history.

It is known, however, that in the very year that Hernan Cortes, conqueror of Mexico, died (1574), the first Auto was celebrated in that capital with extreme pomp, and was not inferior in grandeur, unless by the absence of royalty, to that of Valladolid, where Philip, as the reader may remember, so rigidly and ostentatiously fulfilled his vow to take vengeance on the heretics. At this first Mexican Auto, it is related that a Frenchman, who had probably escaped the Bartholomew massacres, and an Englishman were burnt as "impenitent Lutherans," and eighty "penitents" were exhibited, some punished for Judaising, and some for holding the opinions of Luther or of Calvin. A few did penance for bigamy, the sorry Christianity of Spain not having sufficed to overcome the customs of Paganism, customs which the Gospel itself only eradicates with the spread of experimental piety. And a few did sore penance for magic and superstition. As

that his orders mitigated its horrors in America, forbid the employment of that adjective. He was ever noted for a heartless and temporising *policy*.

if the religion of the Reformation were a plague, and as if the plague might be kept within bounds by cutting off communication, infected persons were forbidden to cross the seas. The laws relating to America abound in provisions of the kind; but a Royal Ordinance of the beginning of the seventeenth century may be taken as a pattern of them all. "We ordain and command," says Philip III., "that no one newly converted to our holy faith, from being Moor or Jew, nor his child, shall pass over into our Indies, without our express licence. And we also prohibit and command that no one who has been reconciled," (by the usual Inquisitorial penance,) "nor the child or grandchild of any one who has publicly worn a sambenito, nor the child or grandchild of a person burnt or condemned as a heretic, for the crime of heretical pravity, through male or female descent, shall pass over to the Indies, under penalty of loss of goods for our chamber and fisc, and their persons to be placed at our mercy, and to be perpetually banished from our Indies: and, if he have no property, let them give him a hundred lashes, publicly." * Lashes were given, doubtless, and property confiscated; but as a way of egress might be opened by means of a royal licence, Spanish merchants of impure blood might pay their fees of office, and pass beyond the ocean; or through petty bribery to underlings, persons of inferior class could effect an embarkation; and thus a rapidly-increasing population of New Christians is found to have mingled with the Spanish Americans. These provided constant work for the Inquisitors, who not only demanded aid of the secular arm, but were ever encroaching on the jurisdiction of the Magistrates, which rendered it necessary for the Court of Madrid to interpose by the gentler method of agreement, under sanction of the Crown, between the rival powers beyond sea, or by the mandate of the Sovereign.

This rivalry served one good end. It diminished the power of the Inquisition; for Viceroys, in their jealousy of ecclesiastical pretension, were not sorry to see public indignation burst on those Holy Officers, who were obliged to content themselves with *Particular* Acts of Faith, where they alone officiated, the civil authorities taking no part. And here, again, an authentic document affords description. It is a small volume, printed in Mexico in 1648, intituled,

* Ordenanzas Reales para la Contratacion de Sevilla, &c. Valladolid, 1604.

"Relation of the third Particular *Auto de Fé* that the Tribunal of the Holy Office of the Inquisition of the Kingdoms and Provinces of New Spain celebrated in the Church of the professed House of the Sacred Religion of the Company of Jesus, on the thirtieth of March, 1648, the very illustrious Lords Doctor Don Francisco de Estrada y Escovedo, Doctor Don Juan Saenz de Mañozca, and Licentiate Don Bernabé de la Higuera y Amarilla, being Inquisitors therein." * This rare volume consists of the Summaries that were published by the Reader on that occasion, and has a preface, equally authentic, of course, from the pen of one of the said Lords, or of a Secretary. This is written in grave, lengthened, and sonorous old Castillian, of which a close translation shall speak in dreary English.

"As indefatigable for vigilance of the care, and awake to the duties of the labour, the upright, just, and holy Tribunal of the Inquisition of this New Spain, always desiring to manifest to the Christian people, amidst the accustomed piety that is an attribute of their profession, and to make known to the world, in view of the clemency that is the boast of their glories, the necessary punishment and inevitable chastisement that is done on the heretical perfidy and rebellious obstinacy of the cruel and sanguinary enemies of our sacred religion; who, blind to its light, deny it, and, deaf to its voice, flee from it. The Lords Inquisitors, who act therein, anxious to gain, in rich perfection," (*en sazonado colmo*,) "the foreseen toil of their wakefulness, and the fruit of their unwearied labour, have celebrated two Particular Acts of Faith in the past years 1646 and 1647, in which, with all attention and good order, were despatched and went forth to public theatre seventy-one causes; the greater part of them of Jews observant of the dead and *detestable* Law of Moses. And now, for particular and convenient ends, not open to the investigation of curiosity," (or we should know what prevented them from burning some of the company,) "and not without well-advised resolution, this Holy Tribunal determined to celebrate another Particular Act of Faith in the church of the Professed House of the Sacred Religion of the Company of Jesus, one of the most capacious and convenient for the purpose that there are in this city, on March 30th, 1648. In which were put to

* It may be found in the British Museum, by referring to he "Old Catalogue" under the head INQUISITION.

penance and punished, (manifesting its severity no less than its clemency and pity,) twenty-eight persons, as well men as women, for the atrocious delinquencies and grave crimes, by them perpetrated, that in this brief and summary relation shall be told. The guilty penitents going out of the prisons of the Inquisition, each one between two Ministers of this Holy Tribunal, at six o'clock in the morning, without any obstruction of the way, or disturbance of good order, from the numerous multitudes of people that were packed close on both sides of the broad streets," (a circumstance sufficiently remarkable to be recorded,) "but who gave good way to the criminals until they reached the said church, where, after the orderly procession of penitents was brought in, and the Lords Inquisitors were seated in their Tribunal," (who afterwards departed in their carriages, attended by their ministers and officers,) "it being then seven o'clock in the morning, the noise of the people that attended being hushed," (yells and hootings, on the appearance of the heretics,) "in good and prescribed order began the reading of the causes, and continued until six o'clock in the evening, and the guilty having abjured, and they with whom that business had to be done being absolved and reconciled, they took them back in the same form and order to the house of the Inquisition, whence they had come by different streets, with the same accompaniment. *And the day following, the justice of lashes was executed, all this kingdom remaining in hope of another more numerous and General Act, for exaltation and glory of our Holy Catholic Faith, punishment and warning of her enemies, edification and instruction of the faithful.*"

The summaries are lively pictures of the moral state of society in Mexico at that time; and some of them have peculiar value as disclosing the manner in which Jews persisted, from generation to generation, in observing that "dead and detestable Law of Moses," as the Doctors were pleased to call it. Others exhibit specimens of clerical depravity, and vulgar superstition.

Among the vagrants who found their way to New Spain, was one *Gaspar de los Reyes*, a layman, who had cleverly acted the part of Priest, said mass, absolved, imposed penance, baptized, married, given extreme unction, buried, and also swindled very extensively. As to the burying and the swindling, there could be no doubt of their being facts accomplished; but seeing that sacramental acts depend for validity on intention, there must have been great perplexity in this case. Did he intend to do as the Church intends? No one could trust in the rectitude of his intentions: therefore transubstantiation, absolution, regeneration, legitimacy of children, and final salvation of penitents, were all sunk into the category of uncertainties under his hands. It was a bad case. The man must have been a heretic. He was contumacious, and should have been burnt. But in default of a secular arm to inflict that penalty, he was made to carry a green taper, a rope round his neck, and a white coroza. Then he was abjured *de vehementi*,—only suspected, although vehemently; for it would have been scandalous to class a living man with convicted heretics,—received three hundred lashes, and was to be shipped off to the galleys of Spain, "perpetual and irremissible." Another case of the same kind was to be punished with two hundred lashes, and five years in the galleys.

Fray Josef de Santa Cruz, forty-three years of age, Monk, Priest, and Confessor, had come to Mexico from Seville without licence, thrown off his habit, changed his name, married twice, become the father of several children, and was in practice as a physician; when, after the lapse of many years, he was discovered, arrested, imprisoned, brought out to this Auto, and sentenced to carry a green candle, be abjured *de vehementi*, save the funds of a hospital in Mexico by serving the sick poor there for four years without pay, and then, from being a prisoner at large, be given up to his Prelates to be dealt with according to the canons and rules. This sentence obviously tended to reserve him for the fire when a General Auto, so earnestly desired by the Inquisition, might be granted for the exaltation and glory of the faith.

Alexo de Castro, eighty-two years of age, native of Manila in the Philippines, a concealed Mohammedan, was accused of Moorish practices in private. As he could not be burnt, he was imprisoned in a monastery, there to *serve*, and there to perish.

The case of *Sebastian Domingo*, sixty years of age, a Negro slave, cannot be read without compassion. He had married when a young man, his wife and he had been separately sold, and his second owner compelled him to marry another woman, supposing that by that means he might be attached to the estate, and prevented from running away to seek his lawful wife. But for this compulsory marriage he was delated, and imprisoned in the Inquisition of La Puebla de los Anjeles. There, in consequence of a large increase in the number of prisoners, he was taken from the dungeon, sworn to fidelity and secrecy, and compelled to be a servant in the Holy House. It would appear from his defence, that he did not understand the extent of his obligation, as to secrecy, but, yielding to a feeling that did him no discredit, spoke to a prisoner through the grating of his prison-door, carried a message to his wife, who was soon imprisoned and punished for receiving it, and brought him letters, with pen, ink, and paper. The grateful woman gave him money for the service, and the receiving it was added to the list of his transgressions. They sentenced him to a green candle, rope, abjuration *de levi*, two hundred lashes, six years' labour in the Spanish galleys, or, if he could not go,—and the Tribunal knew, "in secret," a reason why he could not,—he was to be sold for a hundred dollars, to be applied for the ordinary expenses of the Holy Office, for a time, which would, of course, be long enough to make sure of him for life; and, on the expiration of that time, whatever it might be, he was to be restored to his owner. Suppose him to outlive the infliction of two hundred lashes, or suppose that, not to lower his value, the lashes were forgiven, and that some one would buy him for ten years, and get the utmost possible amount of service from him during that time, how much would he be worth, if alive, at the age of seventy? But this fraud upon his owner was committed by "the upright, just, and holy" Inquisition.

Ana Xuarez, twenty-five years of age, a native of Mexico. Both her parents had been punished as Judaisers. Her marriage with a first husband had been annulled on some account a year before, and he was still alive, in the galleys, for five years, wearing a sambenito, and further sentenced to perpetual confinement to one place of abode. She married a second time; but she and her new husband were soon separated and imprisoned. After a few days' incarceration, she asked for mercy, was admitted to audience, and confessed that, from the age of fourteen, she had observed the fasts and customs of the Law of Moses. Her maternal grandmother is said to have attended at secret meetings in the house of one Simon Vaez, at Seville, to converse concerning the precepts, fasts, rites, and ceremonies of Judaism. At those meetings all present were accustomed to take part, each bringing evidence of his own perseverance, and all encouraging each other to stand fast in the same observance. They formed, says the summary, a sort of *conciliabulum*, or pretended council, where "Catholics" were declared to be under eternal condemnation, and their devotions, processions, and usages spoken of with insolent profanity, showing "the lively hatred that those perfidious and obstinate Jews cherished in their bad hearts." That aged Jewess and "famous dogmatizer" used to take the lead, talk with pride of her children and grandchildren that were good Jews, instructed from childhood by herself, who had made proficiency, fasted admirably, and already attained to high reputation as good Jews and Jewesses throughout the Hebrew nation. Ana Xuarez had been one of her most zealous pupils, and displayed intense enthusiasm in attachment to her religion. She loved her second husband, say they, much better than the first, and married him far more willingly, not because he was a better Jew, but because his father had been burnt in one of the Inquisitions of Portugal. When in prison, she had carried on written correspondence with fellow-prisoners, under a feigned name, and, eluding the vigilance of the Alcaydes, sent messages, received and forwarded messages to other prisoners, made jest about the sambenitos they would have to wear, and agreed with them to make up those garbs of infamy so gay that they would be ornamental, and be rather a credit to the wearers than a disgrace. By this it would seem that the discipline of the prisons in Mexico was not so severe as that of Goa, or that there were classes of prisoners employed in the service of the house, the women to make dresses, and the men sometimes taken from the cell to serve in the kitchen, as was the Negro Sebastian Domingo. Her punishment consisted of appearance in the procession of the Auto in the garb of a penitent, carrying a green candle, confiscation of goods, formal abjuration, perpetual confinement to one place, the sambenito, perpetual banishment from all the West Indies, transportation to Old Spain in the first fleet that might sail from the port of S. Juan de Ulua, perpetual banishment from Sevilla, the home of her family, and from the Court of Madrid, and obligation to present herself at the Inquisition immediately on landing in Spain, that her person might be known, and that she might receive orders for the fulfilment of all particulars of the allotted penance and confinement. If she failed, as to any of those particulars, she would be punished, as an impenitent, with death.

A minute examination of the document before us would elicit proof that the Inquisitors of Mexico fully participated in the spirit of slavery, drawing the utmost possible advantage to themselves from the value of their prisoners, whom they sold, or compelled to labour, so as to meet the current expenses of the Holy House. Equally ingenious in government, in policy, and in trade, they contrived to recover lost ground, and gained the desire of their heart in the revival of General Autos. One they held, certainly, in the year 1659, when William Lambert, an Irishman, was burnt in Mexico, being suspected of the heresies of Luther, Calvin, Pelagius, Wycliffe, and Huss. But renewed favour with the temporal authorities, as it gave them a wider field, and encouraged them to greater insolence, brought them into increased disfavour with the Clergy of the diocese, until the Venerable Palafox, and the Bishop of Cartagena in America, appealed so earnestly against them at Rome, that Clement XI. gave a Bull (January 19th, 1706) for the suppression of the Tribunal. But it soon sprang into life again; and in Mexico, as in all other parts of Spanish America, was numbered with the establishments that were thought to impart honour to those countries, until the political convulsions of Europe spread into the transatlantic world, and, after many alternations of defeat and victory, the institution fell in all the states. The latest efforts of the Inquisitors there were directed against the propagators of new political opinions; and so late as the year 1815, a Priest was put to death in Mexico for having taken part in a movement for separation of the colony from Old Spain. That was his real offence; but it was preferred to throw him into the secret prisons of the Inquisition, and proceed against him for atheism. One proof of the atheism of this Priest, *Josef María Morellos*, was, that he had two children. If having children proves a Romish Priest to be an atheist, few of that body can have the credit of being exempt from the taint of atheism, either in the Old World or the New.

For such atrocities as those of the Papacy, committed through its Inquisition, shall not God be avenged? The denunciations of Prophets, and the events of history, declare that the priesthood cannot escape His avenging retribution; and we have ourselves witnessed their humiliation in countries where they had domineered for ages. In South America, during the struggles of Old Spain for constitutional freedom, after the fall of Bonaparte, and when the Spanish colonies were demanding independence, the Clergy took part against the people on the side of absolute government, and, not content with using the legitimate influence of their position, diminished as it was by their own misconduct, expended the wealth of their churches in carrying on a civil war. Ammunition was laid up in the houses of Priests and Bishops; and Preachers, from their pulpits, assailed those who promoted the new order of things. Then popular fury burst upon the Clergy. The Archbishop of Mexico, Don Juan de la Serna, was banished; the Bishop of Honduras was put to death; and most, if not all the Bishops, were driven from their sees. One brief paragraph translated from the Spanish of the Canon P. A. F. de Cordova, an apologist of their own, may serve to intimate what it remains with political historians to narrate. "The Bishop of the Capital" (Lima), "Don Benito de Lue y Riega, the Lord Archbishop Moxó of Charcas, and Videla, Lord Bishop of Salta, have died in consequence of sufferings in banishment. They" (the Republicans) "obliged Orellana, Bishop of Tucuman, to betake himself to flight through deep forests and trackless wilds. The present Bishop of Paraguay has quite lost his reason through the treatment he suffered. Señor Otondo, Bishop elect of Santa Cruz, lies in prison at Salta; and Rodriguez, Lord Bishop of Santiago of Chile, is exiled in Mendoza." * The Bishop of Truxillo, who had concealed himself in "a solitary place, called Torche," was traced, apprehended, and banished; and the warlike stores found in his palace were transferred to the magazine of artillery in Truxillo. Thus were the weapons of violence which they and their predecessors had used so actively for seven centuries, turned against themselves, and the world saw a solemn exemplification of the Saviour's words: "They that take the sword shall perish by the sword."

* Memorias para servir á la Historia de las Persecuciones de la Iglesia en America. Lima, 1821.

CHAPTER XXIII.

ITALY—THE OLD INQUISITION.

To popular apprehension the Inquisition is rather Spanish than Roman. We have heard so much of Spanish Inquisitors, that we scarcely disengage our thoughts from the association of that particular country with the atrocities of the dungeon and the rack. But the reader of the preceding pages will have seen that this institution is not provincial, but metropolitan, and that if it were to be distinguished by any patronymic, we should most properly call it Roman. Its earliest and its latest operations have been conducted by the Popes and Cardinals; and the Roman See alone gives authority to all its laws, and governs, directly or by delegation, all its operations.

It is true that the earliest act of the Church of Rome that can strictly be called Inquisitorial, was that of the Council of Tours, in France,* and that the first efforts of Dominic were also spent in France; but so far are those facts from suggesting a provincial origin, that they lead us to historical evidence of the contrary. Alexander III., a native of Sienna, an Italian Priest, and afterwards a Roman Cardinal, and Chancellor of "the holy Roman Church," presided at the Council, which would not have been holden in France had he not been driven from Rome. The Cardinals of his party who surrounded him, and with him ruled the Council, were Princes of the Court of Rome; and the French and English Ecclesiastics present, although prepared by the barbarism of the age, were instructed by the doctrine of the Popes to perpetrate any deed of persecution for the exaltation of the Church. And although Dominic was a Spaniard, it must be remembered that he began his career as Inquisitor after attending a Council in the Lateran, and not until he had received a commission from the Pope.

That fiery Pontiff, Innocent III., made persecution of heretics the business of his life. His pontificate was like himself: it was a time of confusion and calamity. A great earthquake shook the Italian peninsula in all its length. A

* See page 2.

hurricane rooted up forests, swept away palaces and churches, and under the ruins of their houses multitudes of people perished. After the hurricane came famine, spreading its horrors chiefly over Lombardy, Tuscany, Romagna, the Campagna di Roma, and the Terra di Lavoro. That year (1202) was long remembered as the year of famine. The Romans, as if persuaded that the wickedness of Innocent had brought down the vengeance of heaven on the land, expelled him from their city: he fled, as Popes have often fled, before the indignation of the people, and took refuge in Ferentino. War followed, and, for the space of seventeen years, irregular bands of Germans and hordes of Italian malcontents ravaged the country, and pillaged the towns. Yet Innocent persisted in his enormities; and, withal, promoted Cardinals, levied troops, waged war, imposed contributions, and feasted luxuriously as ever. After beating the Germans, the soldier-Pope, regardless of the profound wretchedness of the Italians, made a pompous progress from Rome to Anagni, where fifty soldiers were made to entertain him by a gladiatorial exhibition, after which a company of Clergy approached his presence in procession, at Ceccano, singing hymns, and chanting high the responsory, "Thine is the glory." At this stage, according to the chronicler, the Monks bring forth provisions out of their abundance that war and famine have not exhausted, and feast the hungry population, in honour of His Holiness, in the streets of Ceccano, "with bread, and wine, and veal, and beef, and mutton, and pork, and fowls, and geese, and pepper, and cinnamon, and saffron, and honeycomb, and barley, and vegetables." And after the feast Signor Giovanni, Lord of Ceccano, with his knights, play at buffoonery, in presence of Innocent (*burburando*). At another stage he finds accommodation and provender in a convent for himself and two hundred horse. After this manner he prosecuted his imperial progress, distributing benedictions, honours, and privileges, and then returned to Rome, there to spend his winter (A.D. 1208).*

While wielding the sword against the Germans, Innocent spared not the pen; for in epistolary productions he surpassed most Popes, fighting with both sword and pen against the Waldenses. To the Archbishop of Auch, in France, he wrote a Brief, commanding him to engage the help of his

* Chronicon Fossæ Novæ, inter Anecdota Ughelliana.

Bishops to stay the plague of heresy, that was raging, as he said, more fiercely than ever. They were to extirpate all heresies, and those infected by them. They were to expel such from the borders of the province, as well as all who held any sort of communication with them. Any means that the Bishops could find were to be employed, without scruple; and if those means failed, the forces of Princes, and the violence of mobs, were to be called in aid. Princes and people should be incited to coerce heretics with the material sword. A Brief to the Archdeacon of Milan bears us information, that a Cardinal Deacon had gone into Lombardy as Legate, and convened a Council at Verona, where it was determined that no heretic should be admitted to any place of trust or dignity, nor allowed a voice in the election of others. The Legate had deputed the Archdeacon to swear the Magistrates, Consuls, and Councillors of Lombardy to cause that decision to be observed, excommunicating the contumacious, and placing their territories under interdict. Innocent confirmed those powers. Forgetting that our Lord had said, that tares and wheat should grow together in the world until the harvest, he wrote to the Cistertians of Metz an instruction to pluck up the tares, but without hurting the wheat. The tares, in that instance, were a considerable multitude of laymen and of women, who met in secret congregations at Metz and in other parts of the diocese, to read a French translation of the Bible, who troubled the Priests by arguments unanswerable, and who despised them —said the Pope—for their simplicity, trusting in the skilfulness of that new translation. The Bishop and Chapter of Metz he constituted a Board of Inquisition for ascertaining who was the author of that version, what was his intention in translating, what was the faith of those who had read it, and whether they reverenced the Apostolic See and honoured the "Catholic Church." The Bishop had reported that some of the inhabitants openly, and others privately, refused submission to the Pope, and said that they would obey none but God alone. In spite of Bishops and Archbishop, those laymen had presumed to read the French Bible and to preach; and they had also declared, that if the Pope refused them their Bible, they would separate from his Church. Innocent directed that the leaders of those dissidents should be convened, and that, the version having been examined, they should submit to have it corrected, and be punished if they refused.* In the year 1216, this Pope laid the foundation of the horrible Tribunal, by appointing Domingo de Guzman first Inquisitor. Domingo died at Bologna; and after his embalmed body had lain in the grave twelve years, the Dominicans perfumed it, trumpeted a miracle, and had him canonised (A.D. 1233). These Dominicans were now intrusted with the work of making inquisition of heresy.

It is amusing to observe how liberally the historiographers of those times bestowed the honours of sanctity upon their heroes. If those writers tell the truth, we must confess that each Inquisitor was radiant with a halo of purity, that supernatural powers waited on their steps, that they preached with the energy of Apostles, and, like Apostles, to say the least, produced, in every place, miraculous evidences of a Divine commission. The Prince of those sanguinary apostles, next after Dominic, was Friar Peter, of Verona, afterwards distinguished as "Holy Peter, the new Martyr." His demerit, on account of sensual indulgences, which led to a temporary suspension of his functions, with penance in a monastery, was forgotten in consideration of his merits as a defender of the Romish faith. Not less ingenious than severe, he managed, for many years, to parry the blow that, at last, dismissed him to his Judge. Let the reader accept an instance of his wonder-working ability.

In the neighbourhood of Brescia, one of the heretics that then infested Lombardy and Venice had lived for many years, with so great integrity and severity of life, that people said he was raised up to be a second John the Baptist; and when he died, they showed him profound veneration. The Inquisitor of the faith, informed by the testimony of the faithful that he had died in a state of heresy, and separate from the communion of believers, took counsel with the Bishop, and then ordered that his body should be exhumed and given to the fire. The grave was opened. The multitude stood around, witnesses of the disinterment, and followed those who carried it away to the place of burning. The flesh had rotted off the bones, and the corpse was little more than a clammy skeleton, which the bearers hastily threw into the fire. At that instant devils came. They caught out the

* Litteræ Apostolicæ pro Officio Sanctissimæ Inquisitionis; apud Eimeric. Direct. Inquisit. in Appendice.

carcase, climbed on some elevation overhanging the pile, and held it up in the air. The people were astounded, and even the Bishop trembled. Some, incredulous, shouted, "Kill the Bishop;" crying out that he deserved to die for having violated the remains of so good a man. The Inquisitor then suggested that, on the altar erected for the Act,* the Bishop should say a mass to the Virgin Mary. With much trepidation the Bishop proceeded to celebrate, the devils still holding up the bones of the good man, until the elevation of the host, when they cried aloud, "O, Guido di Lacha, we defended thee as long as we could; but a greater than we is here; we cannot now defend thee any longer;" and, thus saying, they dropped the bones of Guido into the fire, wherein they were consumed,—leaving the public to conjecture that the Inquisition was in league with hell, but serving the Church to boast that even devils were in subjection to herself, and paid reverence to "the sacrament of the altar." †

But while the Pope decreed that one Inquisitor should be worshipped, the Italians displayed their hatred of that kind of saintship towards another, and the men of Piacenza gave a salutary example, which other cities often followed, by driving away Fra Rolando, whose operations had rendered him obnoxious to public indignation (A.D. 1234).

Not lingering over the few scattered fragments of intelligence that might be gathered from the scanty histories of the thirteenth century, it may suffice to note that the work of extirpation was carried on with unrelenting rigour. Lombardy was the province most widely occupied by the Preachers of evangelical doctrine, or, at least, of doctrine forbidden at Rome. This is not the occasion for examining the peculiar belief of Cathari, Patarenes, Poor Men of Lyons, Passagines, Josephines, Arnaldists, and Speronists, whom Gregory IX. enumerates in one of his anathemas, archived in the Inquisition of Bologna. There can be no doubt that the injunctions of that document were fulfilled, so far as the Clergy could find secular help to enforce their sentences. To that extent the heretics, whose denominations were notes of infamy, were incapacitated from holding any civil office, possessing property, prosecuting or bearing witness in any

* So early was the custom of placing an altar for the use of the Priest officiating at an Auto.

† Bzovius, A.D. 1233.

court, making bequests, or obtaining civil protection. Even their corpses were denied interment in consecrated ground; and if a Priest, through ignorance or humanity, gave Christian burial to such an one, he was to dig up the body with his own hands, and throw it to the open field, the dunghill, or the ditch. Confessors, too, were required to make inquisition, and report the guilty to their Prelates, notwithstanding the seal of silence which every Confessor was enjoined to keep. And the same Pope, in the eleventh year of his pontificate, advanced on his predecessors by instructing the provincial Prior of the Dominicans, and the other Inquisitors of heretical pravity in Lombardy, the March of Trevigi and Romagna, how to call on the secular Magistrates for assistance. So did Innocent IV.; and their Rescripts or Bulls, with the Constitutions of the latter, constitute no small part of the basis of Inquisitorial rules, as they were afterwards compendiated and enlarged on by Eymeric and his successors.

It is remarkable, that the Constitutions of Innocent were addressed to the Governors, Magistrates, and municipal bodies in the provinces of Italy, who were regarded as children and vassals of the Papal See. They suffered themselves to be so regarded, and condescended so to act; and but one state, the Republic of Venice, refused to accept the ignoble designation, or to allow the Bishop of Rome to control its Magistrates in the exercise of their domestic jurisdiction.

"After that, Pope Innocent IV.," says Fra Paolo Sarpi, "tried to deprive the Emperor, Frederic II., of the empire, kingdoms, and states that he possessed; and a great part of Christendom being thereupon in arms, and all Lombardy in debate with the March of Trevigi and Romagna, then divided into favourers of the Pope and of the Emperor, they were infected with various perverse opinions," (as the Venetian calls evangelical doctrines,) "and, retreating to Venice, there to live in security, the wisdom of this Government, in the year 1249, found a remedy to guard the city from being infected with that contagion that infected the rest of Italy. Wherefore they determined to choose honest, discreet, and Catholic men, to inquire against heretics; and that the Patriarch of Grado, the Bishop of Castello, and the other Bishops of the Doge of Venice, from Grado to Caverzere, should judge of their opinions, and that those that by any of the Bishops were given out to be heretics, should be condemned to the fire by the Duke and Councillors, or the major part of them." * Thus it is evident that the Doge and Councillors of Venice took it for granted, even as a fundamental truth of Christianity, that heretics ought to be punished, and that the punishment should be capital, but said that they would not allow a foreigner to intermeddle either in the sentence or the execution. Neither did they; and although the Venetian territory ceased to afford refuge to the persecuted, inquisition was not made, or death inflicted, by any foreign Prince or Prelate. And the Inquisition there began under an exclusively civil authority and administration.

Where the Magistrates did not resist for the sake of honour, the people resisted for the sake of liberty. Of two Dominicans appointed to conduct the operations of the Lombard Inquisition, one was killed in the execution of his office; and although the record of such a fact ought to be accompanied with a note of disapprobation, it is remembered that Priests were instructed to raise the mob for the purpose of murdering the heretics; and we must acknowledge that if the mob, so taught, and so employed, fell upon their teachers, this was but a merited retribution on those who, as they suffered the consequence of their own doctrine, also deserved the blame. After this event, the Nobles and Magistrates feared to enforce the decrees of the Emperor Frederic against the Patarenes, and others, as Innocent IV. still required them to do; and the Inquisition was therefore empowered, by the Pope, to lay them under ecclesiastical censures until they had inserted the pontifical and imperial statutes—of which copies appear to have been sent to them for that purpose—among the statutes of their "cities and places," and sworn to observe the same, and caused them to be observed with all their might. And as for private persons, against whom the terrors of interdict could not be launched, he commanded his dear sons, the Inquisitors, to exact caution-money from the aiders and abettors of heretics, to be forfeited to the Holy Office, if they were detected in rendering the least succour or encouragement to excommunicated, or even to suspected, persons. This award of prize-money to the scrutators of the faith could not but quicken their diligence, and revive their courage.

* History of the Inquisition of Venice, by Paolo Sarpi. Translated into English. Chap. I.

And now the mandates of the so-called Vicars of Christ breathed defiance against all the world. The empire and the Papacy were in arms against each other, almost dividing Europe between Guelphs and Ghibelines. Italy was divided, state against state; and the general confusion was aggravated by the horrors of a religious war. On the Inquisitors was devolved the conduct of this war on part of the Church of Rome, and Pope after Pope instructed them how to enlist Prelates in the service, and how to raise troops of crusaders to fight against Christians in the name of Christ. Those Inquisitors travelled from place to place, delivering inflammatory harangues, and then enlisting volunteers for the murderous enterprise. For wages they offered plenary indulgences, and the common recompense of marauders in the booty to be found in the dwellings of the persecuted. For honour they gave them crosses, desecrating the sign of human redemption by making it a badge of butchery.

The annals of the thirteenth and fourteenth centuries consist, in great part, of narratives of the conflict between the Inquisition, or its agents, and the civil powers of Europe, but most of all with those of Italy. But the isolation of states, the ignorance of populations, and the perfect organization of the ecclesiastical army, determined the victory, in most cases, to the aggressors. In Genoa, for example, one Anselmo, an Inquisitor-General, persisted in requiring the Governor of the city, Filippo di Torino, to insert the numerous decrees of the Emperors and Constitutions of the Popes, in the tables of civic law, and to publish them throughout the city and state, for universal observance. The Governor, supported by the magistracy in general, refused to do so, and thereby incurred condemnation as a hinderer of the Holy Office, and suspicion of being a favourer of heretics. The Inquisitor summoned him to appear at his Tribunal, there to undergo examination as to his faith; but he indignantly refused to come. Anselmo solemnly excommunicated him, and placed Genoa under interdict. Filippo appealed to Alexander IV. for redress, and His Holiness deigned to suspend the interdict until a certain day, merely to give the recalcitrant Governor space for repentance. Before the appointed day came, he tendered his obedience, caused all the Constitutions that the Inquisitor pleased to specify to be inscribed among the laws of Genoa, and had capital punishment inflicted on all whom the Inquisitor delivered over to him under sentence for heresy. During this unsuccessful effort to cast off the yoke of the Inquisition, some one had written a "Short Tract concerning the Perils of the Last Times," disclosing the abominations of the Dominican and Franciscan Inquisitors; and Alexander employed a mode of suppression which afterwards became general, and still forms the constant business of a Roman Congregation. He commanded three Cardinals to read the book, received their censure, gave that censure sanction, and required the copies that had circulated to be given up to the Inquisitors within eight days, and publicly burnt. Thus Genoa was made quiet for a time; and there can be no doubt that many of the readers of the book, as well as the book itself, were committed to the flames.* Let Genoa be taken as a fair specimen of the state of all Italy.

The silent abjection of Italy, and the Inquisitorial triumphs achieved throughout Europe, gave Alexander leisure to revise the existing code, and to issue new mandates to the Inquisitors and Clergy everywhere, assigning to each class of Ecclesiastics their peculiar part in the general service, and thus imparting uniformity to the administration of the Tribunal, and making the secular Clergy more and more subservient for the general inquisition of heretical pravity. No language can be more sternly imperative than that of Alexander IV. to his "beloved children, the Podestas, Councillors, and communities of the cities and other places of Italy." After health and apostolic benediction, he confirms the orders of his predecessor, Innocent, and proceeds thus: "We command the whole of you (*universitati vestræ*), by apostolic writings, that so far as we have explained to you the laws of the Emperor Frederic against heretical pravity, of which copies are sent herewith, you every one of you cause them to be made known in your capitulars against heretics of all sects whatever, and proceed in conformity thereunto with exact diligence. And we have directed our beloved children, the Friars Inquisitors of heretical pravity, and in our letters to each of them have enjoined, that, if you do not, they compel you by excommunication of your persons, and interdict on your land, without appeal."† It would seem that the civil authorities were not sufficiently

* Bzovius, A.D. 1256. † Litteræ Apostolicæ, ut supra.

prompt in rendering obedience to this mandate, conveyed in terms so general and absolute; and, to leave them without excuse, he sent them, the next year (1259), large and minute instructions, or, in other words, a *law* which they were to execute in all their states, as auxiliaries to the Inquisition. The instructions were, in fact, a transcript of the Constitutions of Innocent IV. And that the Inquisitors might save themselves from any trouble of conscience during the commission of rapine and murder by wholesale, he gave them a Bull, setting forth that "the God of indulgences and Father of mercy," valuing their services in the cause of the faith, had empowered him to refresh them with salutary rewards, and that, therefore, relying on the authority of God, and of the blessed Apostles Peter and Paul, he gave them a full pardon of all sins.* Being thus booted, they could less uncomfortably wade through blood.

Whoever shall write a history of the religious state of Italy under the pontificate of Alexander IV., may find the first suggestions in his Letters Apostolic. In spite of all those fulminations, and in defiance of all the coercion that the Papacy could exert, the laity would not yield general obedience to his pleasure; and the Inquisitors reported, from almost all quarters, that they were not supported to the extent of their necessity, or were prevented, by passive resistance, from rooting the tares out of the field. Some few cities, on the other hand, were made to seem loyal to the Pope; and one of them is marked as worthy of everlasting honour on that account. But that was Viterbo, a place under the preponderation of ecclesiastical influence. At Chiana, in the province of Romagna, Capello di Chiana, as he is called, having been convicted of heresy, and condemned accordingly, but probably supported by his people, had refused to yield, and the Inquisitors could not gain possession of his person. Some of the authorities of Viterbo—doubtless themselves Ecclesiastics—came to the help of the Inquisitors by raising "an army" to march against him; and the "Father of the faithful" hastened to laud their zeal, and exhort them to attack the town without loss of time, and lay his lands waste. The Senators of Viterbo, indeed, had forbidden the troops to march; but Alexander bade them go, notwithstanding, and commanded the Senators to revoke the

* Litteræ Apostolicæ, ut supra.

prohibition. "Be careful thus to obey our admonitions and commands," said he, "that you may increase in merits with God, in grace from us, and in glorious fame with men."* At this rate Alexander proceeded until his death; but I refrain from pursuing further even this brief sketch of his proceedings.

It is important to observe, that in the latter half of the thirteenth century the Papal thunders rolled more widely, the Bulls not being addressed to those provinces only where opinions contrary to the Church of Rome were most prevalent, and the Inquisitors most active, but to "all believers in Christ," under the assumption that the whole world was amenable to them. A Bull of Nicholas III., thus addressed in the year 1280, and archived in the Inquisition of Bologna, as, of course, in other houses of the same kind, was published by Pegna among the documents already quoted.

In Parma, Honorius IV. being our witness, the inhabitants rescued a woman from the stake, whither the chiefs of the city had led her, in pursuance of a sentence of the Holy Office, dispersed the executioners, went to the Franciscan Convent, burst open the doors, battered in the roof of the church, took away vestments and other valuables, and administered such a castigation on the bodies of as many Friars as they could catch,—that fraternity being invested with the office of Inquisitors,—that the whole of them fled, one alone excepted, who died of wounds received. Gladly would the Podesta, the Captain, and other Magistrates of Parma have been released from obligation to burn their fellow-citizens, and for some time they refused to acknowledge the authority of the Bishop, who cited them to answer for the riot; but the usual application of an interdict brought them to the dust again, and, thanking the Pope for his lenity in sparing them from the fury of a crusade, they paid a fine of a thousand marks of silver, that Honorius imposed on the community of Parma. And many persons having emigrated to Sicily, in hope of finding refuge there, the vigilant Pontiff sent a party of Inquisitors to that island, who pursued them into their most remote retreats; nor did they relinquish the pursuit so long as a fugitive could be tracked. But that was not until the lapse of nearly seventy years, when a few survivers escaped into Calabria (A.D. 1353), and there

* Litteræ Apostolicæ, ut supra.

preached Christ with considerable acceptance, rousing again the ire of Rome, whence Innocent VI. dispatched a Dominican Inquisitor to counteract their influence, and subjected the whole kingdom of Sicily to his censure, in revenge for any degree of humanity in the laity who might have connived at the existence of Christians among them.*

The political action of the Inquisition was nowhere more manifest than in the Italian states, all of which retained a strong feeling of national independence, and would certainly have succeeded in casting off the yoke of Papal supremacy if it had not been for the Inquisition. And by the Inquisition we are not only to understand the members of particular Tribunals, but also the entire fraternities of Dominican and Franciscan Monks, who rendered service in Italy, similar to that performed by the familiars in Spain, and who constituted, together with sworn crusaders, a formidable army, strong enough to conquer opposition by main force in any of the weaker states, even without troubling the Pope to enforce the terrors of an interdict.

But Venice, in the thirteenth and fourteenth centuries, was the strongest, most flourishing, and most important state of all, on account of its commercial prosperity, and position as a bulwark of Christendom against the Turks. To subdue Venice by a single stroke was therefore impossible. The Popes used stratagem. Nicholas IV., himself a Minor Friar, on coming to the throne in 1288, besought the Doge and Senate to allow the brethren of his order to exercise their function as Inquisitors within the Republic. The Venetians, foolishly imagining that Popes might be bound by stipulations, and trusting in their own power to resist future encroachments, yielded to his importunity after some reluctance, and suffered the Franciscans to assume the office; but in conjunction with, or, as they fancied, in subordination to, the Doge, to whom was reserved the dignity of Inquisitor-General, inasmuch as he sanctioned the prosecutions, received the spoils, fed the prisoners, and paid the Inquisitors very handsomely. The Pope readily assented. The Doge fancied himself an Alexander, able to mount and rein the Bucephalus that none had mastered. The Venetians were content, and even gloried in being the only people in the world whose Magistrates were permitted to look into the dungeons, and exert

* Bzovius, A.D. 1353.

some influence in managing the affairs, of the Inquisition. Twelve years passed away quietly; the Inquisitors being active, and the Council of State complacent, until Friar Anthony, Inquisitor, issued a monitory to the Doge, requiring him to swear to observe the Papal and imperial Constitutions against heretics; Constitutions, as we scarcely need to repeat, that would have reduced all civil power to a nullity, except for killing victims marked for execution. The Doge refused obedience; but the erection of a lay Inquisition in the first instance, and the subsequent admission of the Friars to share in its administration, laid the foundation of troubles that will soon have to be related.

Among other chiefs of the Ghibelines, or adherents of the Emperor in opposition to the Pope, *Matteo Visconti*, Lord of Milan, incurred his displeasure. To overcome him by crusade was not yet possible; and as for interdict, he had already almost laid an interdict on the Milanese Clergy by preventing no small number of them from performing their ordinary duties. We cannot enter into the history of this quarrel, but merely observe that the Inquisition settled it. Other means having failed, Matteo was accused of heresy, and information taken by the Inquisitors to show that he had been guilty of many wicked actions; and, among them, the following. 2. He had for many years prevented the Inquisitor Placentino from appointing officers to arrest heretics, and had impeded the Office of the Holy Inquisition. 3. He had forcibly arrested the Inquisitor-Bishop Placentino and many other Prelates, and sent them into exile. 11. He had violated the interdict at Milan, by compelling Priests to minister against their will. 17. And he had followed the sect of one Manfreda.* Being now condemned for heresy, Frederic of Austria, Louis of Bavaria, and the Marquis of Monferrato, declared war on Visconti, and, under this plea of heresy, deprived him and his children of their dignity and their dominions.

It is to be regretted that we have no truly religious history of those times, and cannot therefore enliven and hallow the present sketch by reciting the triumphs of our Lord's martyrs. The Inquisitors themselves, however, afford us a slight glimpse into the scenes of murder, by placing some brief notices thereof on record.

* Bzovius, A.D. 1322.

Geraldo Segarelli, a native of some part of the duchy of Parma, of humble parentage, made his appearance in the capital, probably about the year 1270. A Friar Salimbeno, whose manuscript was found in the library of Cardinal Sabelli, "Supreme Inquisitor in the universal Christian republic," describes him as little better than an idiot; which means that he was much like a thorough Monk. He says that he sold his property, went into the city and gave away the money to the rabble, and then devoted himself to preaching, to the delusion, as he says, of the lowest and most licentious of the people. It appears to be certain, however, that his followers multiplied exceedingly, that he was for some time imprisoned by the Bishop in his palace, and then sent away from Parma, but returned, and continued to propagate his doctrine in the city. The Inquisitorial summary of his doctrine is as follows:—

That the Church of Rome has utterly lost the authority received from the Lord Jesus Christ, on account of the wickedness of the Prelates. That the Church governed by Pope, Cardinals, Clerks, and Monks is not the church of God, but is reprobate and barren. That the Roman Church is the apostate harlot, of whom St. John speaks in the Apocalypse. That the authority originally given to the Roman Church has passed over to the Apostolics, as they are called, a spiritual congregation, raised up by God in these last times. That he, Geraldo Segarelli, was divinely commissioned to bring back the Church to its original purity. That the Apostolics are the only Church of God that resembles the Apostles; and therefore they owe no obedience to the Pope, nor to any other person; but they have their law from Christ, the law of a free and perfect life. That the Pope cannot compel them to desert their sect, nor has he power to excommunicate them. That all persons are at liberty to enter their sect, wife without permission of her husband, and husband without consent of his wife; and that in such cases the Pope cannot dissolve the marriage, but, according to the Friar, the Apostolics say they can. That no one can leave them without mortal sin, nor any be saved that is not one of them. That all their persecutors commit mortal sin, and are in danger of perdition. That unless the Pope were as holy as St. Peter, he could not absolve. That all the Popes and Prelates, since the time of Silvester, have been deceivers; and that all the ecclesiastical orders are a detriment to the faith of Christ. That the laity should not pay tithes until the Prelates are as poor as the Apostles. That life is more perfect without a Monkish vow than with it. That God can be worshipped anywhere better than in a (Romish) church. That no man should swear, not even when required to do so by an Inquisitor.—And he is charged, as usual, with immoral opinions and practices.

His doctrine *may* have been unsound in some points; but as the sole object of those summaries was to establish accusations of heresy, even by the admission, if not the invention, of calumnious charges, we may fairly deduct something in allowance for exaggeration. His offence really consisted in denying the holiness and authority of the Church of Rome; and for this he was burnt alive in Parma, on the 18th of July, 1300.

Whatever Geraldo may have taught, the effects of his teaching survived him. Seven years afterwards *Dulcino* and *Margareta* his wife (*consors*), as Eymeric acknowledges her to have been, fled from Milan and took refuge in the mountain-country of Novara. Into those retreats no fewer than six thousand fugitives followed them. The Inquisitor-General of Lombardy sent crusaders to hunt them down; who took many,—how many, our authority does not say,—and brought them to Vercelli, where Dulcino and his wife were torn limb from limb, by direction of the Inquisitors, and their disjointed bodies were then burnt. This brutal execution was followed by a renewed crusade, undertaken by command of Clement V., who offered a plenary indulgence to each crusader. The Bishops and the Dominicans united for the extirpation of the pseudo-Apostolics, as they called them, with perfect unanimity and with terrible success.

Thus did the Inquisition ravage Italy, not so much by the ordinary procedure of its Tribunal, as by making use of every occasion of political disquiet, and by fanning the flames of cupidity and fanaticism. A remnant of those who had been driven from Sicily in the preceding century, sprang up there again, and we find Gregory XI. praising the city of Palermo for having bestowed an annual salary of twelve ounces of gold on their Inquisitor, Simon Pureano (A.D. 1375), while he urges the Bishop of Turin to crush a sect called Bricaraxii who had multiplied in that diocese. The result of this injunction was not very agreeable to the Inquisition. One

Fra Antonio, a Dominican, famous both as Preacher and Inquisitor, in Turin and the neighbourhood, after delivering a sermon and saying mass, on the Sunday after Easter (A.D. 1375), was leaving church, when a party of twelve men surrounded him, plunged their daggers into his body, and left him dead on the spot. Less than two months before, another Inquisitor had been assassinated at Susa; but the avengers of the blood shed by the Inquisition, instead of delivering their countrymen from its oppression, aggravated the evil by providing the Pope and his Clergy with pretence for proclaiming a renewed crusade.

Little more work seemed to remain for the crusaders. The resorts of heretics were broken up in Italy, and the Inquisition gave its attention to those writings that might revive the sects it had suppressed. The writings of the kind most widely circulated at that time, appear to have been those of Raymond Lully, a native of Majorca, by birth a Jew, but, after his conversion to the spurious Christianity of Rome, a Franciscan Friar; a man who had spent his life in striving to convert the Moors in Africa, and to lay the foundation of Oriental studies in Europe, and who had fallen a victim to his zeal for the conversion of the African Mussulmans, some of whom stoned him to death. He had composed twenty-one works, philosophical, religious, and miscellaneous, which appeared too suggestive of new ideas to be allowed to circulate. Nicholas Eymeric, Inquisitor of Aragon and Majorca, author of the famous "Directory of Inquisitors," and eminent for profound knowledge of canon and civil laws, presented the books to Gregory XI., requesting that they might be examined. Twenty-four men of repute for knowledge of theology, with the Bishop of Ostia at their head, were appointed by the Pope to read those books, which they did accordingly, and condemned them as containing many things heretical and blasphemous. This assemblage of Censors at Rome confirmed the precedent, as I should suppose, for the Congregation of the Index subsequently created, and acting in agreement with the Congregation of the Inquisition. Then, as now, it was understood to be a part of the Universal Inquisition, was mentioned as such by Eymeric himself, and ought always to be so considered. The Congregations, indeed, are separate, but their operations are artfully intermingled. That of the Index now serves to cover that of the Inquisition from public observation; and the latter, by exercising an ostensible jurisdiction over books, *seems* to be less occupied with persons. At that time, however, the Roman Censors could not command reverence in Spain; and Peter of Aragon, incensed at the officiousness of Eymeric, banished him from his dominions.

CHAPTER XXIV.

ITALY—THE OLD INQUISITION (CONCLUDED).

DISHONOURED by contentions, and weakened by schism, the Papacy could not act so vigorously against heresy, as in happier times. During a full century neither Pope nor anti-Pope could rouse his adherents to a crusade in Italy. The Waldensian Church in the Alpine and sub-Alpine regions was in a state nearly approaching to repose, except on the side of France, and under the Dukes of Savoy. Martin V. sent forth his fulminations from Rome against the English Lollards, and the Hussites of Bohemia and Moravia, and summoned the Bishops and Inquisitors, wherever the latter were established (*ubilibet constitutis*), to undertake the extirpation of those people; but the bolts passed over Italy, and as for England, Bohemia, and Moravia, there were no Inquisitors, except the Priests and Monks, who proved themselves to be zealous enough, albeit they were not strong enough, to destroy the work of God. The Bull of Martin followed the Council of Constance, and was published in the year 1418.

Calixtus III. did his best to revive the dormant energies of the Italian Inquisition, and to that intent republished (A.D. 1458), with his own sanction, a Bull of Innocent IV., empowering the Inquisitors in Lombardy to publish a crusade, and to confer on the cross-bearers against heretics at home, indulgences equal to those which had been granted to Crusaders against infidel Mussulmans in the Holy Land. But the spirit of that age had changed; and although the scandal of the Cross was undiminished, and the few confessors of Christ still suffered tribulation in the world, there was, in the world, a growing indisposition to fight the battles of the priesthood, and many of the more eminent Clergy, from the time of the Council of Florence,* and the immigration of the Greeks, became more diligent in prosecuting Grecian and Latin studies than in reading theology, censuring religious books, or making inquisition concerning faith.

After the cessation of the great schism, and after the vehement controversy concerning the comparative powers of Popes and Councils had subsided, the Pontifical Government, although no less autocratic in theory than before, underwent considerable modification in practice. We now trace the beginnings of those institutions in the Court of Rome which give it such immense power, and enable the supreme Pontiff, having the concurrence of the College of Cardinals,—a concurrence regulated by a multitude of provisions,—to act with less independence, indeed, but with far greater certainty and power. The revocation of cases to the Pope for ultimate decision, with reservation of certain offences to be absolved by him alone, but, in reality, by the Courts established at Rome for that very purpose, brings a stream of wealth into the Roman coffers from day to day, and raises the administration of discipline above the power of local opposition. One of those reservations is of the power of absolution from "crimes of heresy," which Paul II. made for himself and his successors (A.D. 1468). The law is to be found in the Extravagantes,† is quoted by the Canonists, is acted on at present, and is at the foundation of the supremacy and universality of the Inquisition. Those attributes could not be found in the provincial Tribunals that we have surveyed, but will henceforth become very apparent to the reader of these Italian chapters.

After several ineffectual efforts to establish a regular Inquisition in the Alps, a bold yet cautious and persevering man, John, Archbishop of Embrun (A.D. 1461), undertook to extirpate the Waldensian Church by dint of "monitions, exhortations, and injunctions;" but difficulties arose at every step, and he prudently delayed the employment of any violent measures. Eleven years afterwards a Minorite Friar, deputed, by "apostolic authority," to act as Inquisitor in the Valleys, pursued the usual routine, succeeded so far as to

* Opened at Ferrara in 1438, and closed in Florence the year following.

† Extravagantes Communes, lib. v., cap. ix., tit. 3.

frame a few processes, and thereby arrived at certain knowledge of the doctrines that multitudes of the inhabitants confessed. But he presumed not to go any further, the whole population being hostile to measures of persecution. Again the indefatigable Archbishop, having waited for opportunities during no less a time than twenty-one years, and surrounded himself with ninety "Catholic men," without counting many who aided them secretly, "took new informations," by which it appeared that *all* the inhabitants of the valley of Fraissiniere, and many in the other valleys, were of "most infamous repute," and vehemently suspected to be members of "the said heretical sect." Following out this information, and making the best use of his body of familiars, the Archbishop ventured (A.D. 1486) to publish what we should have called in Spain an Edict of the Faith, commanding all who were conscious of heresy to come with a spontaneous confession within a time appointed. But "they neglected to obey." That monition was published on the 18th day of June. It was repeated on the 29th of the same month, and again on the 9th of July, but without effect. In the month of August "the aforesaid most reverend Lord Archbishop John commanded all that were suspected—mentioning them *by name*—to be cited to answer for their faith, offering them grace if they would return to the bosom of the Church; but they all contumaciously neglected." On the 15th of September the Archbishop "gave letters patent and excommunicatory," on account of their "perfidy and stubborn contumacy." Two days were spent in publishing the excommunication, "which they sustained until the 6th of February, 1487, and continued yet much longer deaf to the excommunication. Among them was one called Angellino Palloni, who now laboured with all his might to conceal the truth with lies. *And this is true*," as the Inquisitor who made the record* asseverates at the close of every paragraph.

On the Italian side the Inquisition had more power. *Giordano Tertian* was burnt at Susa, and *Hippolito Roussiere* at Turin. In the same city *Hugo Champ de Fenestrelles*

* Scriptum Inquisitoris cujuspiam anonymi de Valdensibus, ex Codici M.S.G. in publica Bibliotheca Cantabrigiensi. Given at length by Dr. Allix, in his "Remarks upon the Ecclesiastical History of the Ancient Churches of Piedmont."

was disembowelled, and his mutilated body exposed to public insult. In one valley three thousand persons were murdered, either by the sword, or smothered by fires lighted at the mouths of the caves into which they had gone for refuge.

The report of those butcheries overawed many, no doubt; but it also aroused the indignation of every Italian whose spirit was not utterly broken. This was manifest in Brescia, where the Inquisitor, Antonio di Brescia, in conjunction with the Bishop, "or his Vicar-General," condemned some men and women, as impenitent heretics, to be delivered to the secular arm for burning, "and required the officers of the city of Brescia to fulfil the appointed execution; but the said officers,"—I quote from a Brief of Innocent VIII.,—"to the no small scandal of the orthodox faith, refused to minister justice, and execute the said sentences, unless they might first see the processes which had been carried on by the Bishop and Inquisitor." This drew a mandate from the Pope, who contended that as the crime of heresy was "merely ecclesiastical," and as crimes of the sort should not, on any account, go unpunished, he instructed the Inquisitor and Bishop to command them, under pain of excommunication, to kill the persons condemned within six days. The Brief was dated at Rome, September 30th, 1486. I do not know the effect of this injunction.

My plan does not allow me to narrate the crusade against the Waldenses in the archdiocese of Embrun, conducted by Albertus de Capitaneis, whom Innocent VIII. sent to the Duke of Savoy as Nuncio from the Apostolic See, to demand troops for the intended massacre. For his guidance, however, he was accompanied by an Inquisitor (A.D. 1487); and if the Nuncio and his companion had been demons, not men, they could scarcely have exhibited a more exquisitely malignant and murderous fanaticism.

It happened, when the Jews were driven from Spain, and a remnant that survived the perils and wreck of transport made their appearance on the shore of the Tiber, that the Pope was pleased to allow them to enter on the patrimony of the Church, and live. Some writers, caught by this appearance of charity in the supreme Pontiff, compared his conduct with that of Ferdinand and Isabella, to the great disadvantage of the latter; and many, by repeating the encomium then circulated, and further deceived, perhaps, by a show of comparative lenity in the Inquisitions of the Papal state, have contributed to strengthen an erroneous impression, that the Roman Inquisition has been distinguished from others by a moderation approaching to humanity. A fact or two of history, related by one of their great annalists,* might suffice to remove the false impression.

In the year 1498,—very soon after the extension of Roman hospitality to those poor Jews,—two hundred and thirty Marranos, or Moors who had renounced a compulsory profession of Christianity, so called, in Spain, and were therefore driven from the country, came to Rome, but were soon detected, delated to the Holy Office, and thrown into prisons. At length, however, they once more submitted to make an ecclesiastical confession, and were solemnly received into the Church by Alexander VI. If any of them had persisted in refusing to do so, they would have suffered sudden death by burning, or slow death by perpetual imprisonment. The "reconciliation" was performed thus:—On Sunday, July 29th, a spacious platform being erected before the portico of the Basilica † of the Prince of the Apostles, *de urbe*, between galleries extending from the steps of the said Basilica, the two hundred and thirty exiles were brought out from the dungeons, and exhibited thereon. They sat down on the floor of the platform, in their accustomed Moorish garb. On chairs of state appeared a large company of reverend Lords, whose names and titles it is not necessary to transcribe. All being thus assembled, a certain Master in Theology, of the order of Preachers, delivered a sermon in vulgar Italian concerning the faith, and against the aforesaid Spanish Marranos, amongst whom was one distinguished by the habit of St. Francis, which he had formerly assumed, but afterwards openly cast off. The orator harangued them concerning their notorious errors in faith, pronounced words of reproof, and recited the dogma which they were then required to believe. Sermon being ended, the Marranos, who, at best, could have but a very obscure apprehension of the Italian sentences, prayed for pardon and absolution, uttering piteous cries, no doubt. Then the Master of the Sacred Palace condescended to admonish them, in a Latin sermon, concerning the rules for authorised believing and good living, and at the same

* Bzovius, A.D. 1498.

† *Basilica*,—Royal palace. A name given to a principal church.

time described the punishment they might righteously be made to suffer; and, the oration being finished, pronounced a few hasty words in Spanish, to give them some general notion of what they were at liberty to suppose it might have contained. Having heard this, the whole company fell upon their knees, heard sentence of the penance to be performed, received sambenitos, and, in that livery, walked processionally into the church of St. Peter, there to pray. From St. Peter's they proceeded, in the same order, to the convent of St. Mary on Minerva, whence, laying aside the penitential habit, they might be dismissed to their houses. The Pope saw the ceremony of the theatre from his windows; and, when the Inquisitors had absolved and reconciled the Marranos, he gave them his benediction.

An offender of superior station was at the same time under discipline. *Pedro de Aranda*, Bishop of Calahorra in Spain, and Majordomo of the Pope, lay in prison, under accusation of the heresy of the Marranos. Alexander VI. appointed a board of high Ecclesiastics to hear and determine on his case. Many witnesses were examined on part of the Fiscal, and no fewer than a hundred and one on part of Aranda. From such a multitude of depositions the Judges could easily gather enough to serve their purpose; and, at length, on Friday, September 14th, the day of the Holy Cross, the Commissaries laid their summary before the Pope, as Chief Inquisitor, in secret consistory; the honour of being judged in that Court being rendered to an officer of the apostolic palace. "Which being heard, Alexander, with counsel of the most reverend Lords the Cardinals, deprived Aranda of the episcopal dignity, and of all benefices and offices, and deposed him and degraded him from every order. The said Peter, being thus deprived, deposed, and degraded, was at length thrown into a chamber of the Castle of St. Angelo, there to endure an imprisonment" that was, of course, perpetual. His theology was probably unsound, but his practices were yet more offensive to the licentious Pontiff and his Court. "He laughed at indulgences," says Miravel y Casadevante; "ate flesh on Friday and Sabbath (Saturday); breakfasted before saying mass; and denied purgatory."

During the latter part of the fifteenth century, and the first thirty years of the sixteenth, we find little to relate concerning Italy, beyond what may be summed up in a few words. In Sicily the King of Spain, then Sovereign of the island, endeavoured to introduce the Spanish Inquisition; but his emissaries were obliged to retreat, the inhabitants being united in resistance. The spirit of independence in Italy had been strong enough to obtain seats for the Bishops on the Tribunals, and the Inquisitorial secret, perhaps in consequence of their intervention, was not enforced so rigidly as in Spain. In the Venetian territory, Inquisitors, who attempted to act alone, could not obtain help of the Magistrates, who refused to execute sentences passed without their concurrence; and at Brescia, again, the people, emboldened by the refusal of the Magistrates, had, once at least, cut short the processes by driving away the Inquisitors. Naples, although a realm of Spain, like Sicily, also refused to admit the Spanish Inquisition, or any other Tribunal conducted by a distinct body, apart from the Ordinaries. Lombardy, Piedmont, and the states of northern and central Italy, had been surrendered to the Inquisitorial fury,—renewed after the consolidation of the Papal Government,—and the *aliter credentes*, or persons differing from the dominant religion, hid themselves in the mountains, or, by outward conformity to the rites of Romanism,—an artifice resembling that which is practised by the gipsies in Spain, and perhaps in other countries,—concealed their dissent; and, by a habit of concealment continued from one generation to another, they must have lost the truthful and manly simplicity of their fathers. Nor were they the only sufferers. The confessional and clerical celibacy demoralised Italy, as they have demoralised every other country where they prevail; but the Inquisition induced a reaction against all that bore the name of Christianity, and while a pagan infidelity prevailed among the higher classes,—Pope Leo X., who issued a Bull for the maintenance of orthodoxy in universities (A.D. 1513), not excepted,—the lower classes were pervaded with the grossest superstitions. If the censures of the Clergy were not utterly calumnious, magic, sorcery, witchcraft, infanticide, incest, devil-worship, and every conceivable kind of abomination, was as familiar to the lower classes as was atheism to Leo X., and lewdness to Alexander VI. Nor could it be otherwise. The natural result of an Inquisition is the extinction of all faith.

Leo X., notwithstanding his admiration of excellence in painters, and his disposition to patronise poets, entertained as profound a dislike of innovation on the doctrine of his Church as became a Pope. Acknowledging, indeed, that learning might be easily attained by the reading of books, and that the art of printing might be of great advantage, inasmuch as many printed books might be had for little money, and that even profane literature, which he loved so ardently, might be skilfully made subservient to the cause of Christianity, he said that a complaint had fallen on his ear that certain masters of this art of printing, in various parts of the world, had printed books, translated from Greek, Hebrew, Arabic, and Chaldee into Latin, and that they had dared to publish others, both in Latin and in vulgar tongues, containing errors in faith, and pernicious dogmas contrary to Christianity, and injurious to the fame of persons illustrious in dignity. Lest thorns should choke the good seed, and poisonous herbs grow up together with the medicinal, it behoved him to be vigilant. With the approbation, therefore, of the Fifth Council of Lateran, then sitting, he wished to provide an "opportune remedy," and, that the business of printing books might thenceforth be conducted more happily, determined and ordained "that, in all times to come, no one should print, or cause to be printed, any book or other writing, either in Rome or any other city or diocese whatever, unless it were first approved, if in Rome, by the Pope's Vicar and Master of the Sacred Palace, or, in other cities and dioceses, by the Bishop, or some other person having understanding * of science. Books or writings proposed to be printed were to be diligently examined by the Bishop or his delegate, *and by the Inquisitor of heretical pravity*, in the city or diocese

* A reasonable qualification. But even in the pontificate of Leo X. it must have been easier to prescribe than to administer. But a few years earlier, when the Prince Giovan Pico della Mirandola had maintained nine hundred propositions at Rome, derived from Chaldean, Hebrew, Greek, and Latin authors, and relating to theology, mathematics, natural history, magic, the cabala, and other sciences, real or reputed, the Roman scholars, dazzled and bewildered by his erudition, surmised that he must assuredly be a heretic. The Censors of the Faith laboured hard over his nine hundred propositions, and extracted thirteen which they thought capable of affording witness of heresy. The Prince was censured as temerarious, and suspected; but he presumed to write a defence of himself, and even to put some questions to the Censors. "What," said he, "is cabala?" "Cabala," answered one of the learned Inquisitors, "was a wicked heretic, who wrote against Christ. The Cabalists are a sect who follow him."

where it was to be put to press, and approved by subscription under their own hand, to be given without fee, without delay, and under sentence of excommunication." The penalties of disobedience were loss of the books unlawfully printed, and therefore to be burnt publicly, a fine of a hundred ducats to the fund for building the church of St. Peter, suspension from the exercise of printing for one year, and such other inflictions as he might incur by contumacy. This order was given in public session of the Council on May 12th, 1515. This Fifth of Lateran is acknowledged by the Church of Rome to be a General Council; the regulation then made for placing the universal press at the mercy of Inquisitors was adopted by the Council of Trent, is amplified in the rules of the Indexes of Prohibited Books, published by successive Pontiffs at Rome and by the Spanish Inquisition, and is now cited as the fundamental authority for all such coercive proceedings as the Clergy can venture upon in countries where they have any degree of power. It is a part of canon-law, which the Pope now reigning declares to be binding on his Clergy in these realms, and which they are sworn to enforce, so far as by their influence or their assumed position they may find it practicable.

The last Council of Lateran did not confine itself to approving the Constitution of Leo X. as to printers and books, but also made full provision for the punishment of heretics by the Holy Office, or by the usual substitutes in countries where it did not exist. It ordained as follows:—"That all false Christians, and those who think ill concerning faith, *of whatever people or nation they may be*, as well as heretics, or persons polluted with any stain of heresy, or Judaisers, be utterly excluded from the company of believers in Christ, and expelled *from every place*, and especially from the Roman Court, and punished with due severity. We ordain that proceedings be taken against them with diligent inquisition everywhere, and in the said Court especially, by Judges who shall be deputed by us," (the Pope,) "and they who are guilty of this crime, and legitimately convicted, shall be punished with the penalties due. *But it is our pleasure that the relapsed be dealt with without any hope of pardon or of remission.*" *

* This may be read in the original Latin in the Acts of the Council; or in Raynaldus, A.D. 1514.

Leo X., Adrian VI., and Clement VII., followed up these enactments of the Roman Synod, miscalled Œcumenical, by continuing the struggle of the Papal See with the civil powers of the Popedom, when unwilling, and by flattering them with apostolic letters and blessed trinkets, when willing, to extirpate the followers of Christ. The Bulls of Leo X. against Luther, frustrated though they were at the time, are still documents of high authority in the Inquisition. They were issued in the year 1520; and scarcely had Luther thrown them into the fire when Leo had the audacity to instruct the Inquisitors at Brescia, a Venetian city, to proceed against heretics without so much as allowing the Magistrates to see the processes, much less to be present at the examinations, and to compel the civil officers to kill those whom they might condemn. But, with the Doge and Council, his anathemas and interdicts had no force; and Clement VII. (A.D. 1528), seeing that evangelical doctrines found great acceptance at Brescia, and that the Venetian state would soon be evangelized unless the civil and ecclesiastical authorities were united in persecution, unsaid the previous utterance of the Holy See by instructing the Inquisitors not to refuse to act in conjunction with the Magistrates, and even to allow themselves to be summoned by them to make inquisition into such cases as three lay-Inquisitors, elected by their own lay-constituents, might bring before them for their judgment. Herod and Pilate were again reconciled. We now proceed to survey the Roman Inquisition under its assumed character of "supreme and universal," and to observe how it rose into a position of central power, absorbing, and even rendering less necessary, the provincial courts.

CHAPTER XXV.

ITALY—INQUISITION OF THE CARDINALS.

THE Lutherans in Germany were demonstrating the necessity of a reformation of the head and members of the Church at Rome. Many Princes who yet continued in the communion of that Church demanded such a reformation, and importuned the Roman See for a speedy convocation of a General Council. When the general dissatisfaction was at its height, the Cardinal Farnese, Dean of the Sacred College, was elected Pope, and took the name of Paul III. He had been an active servant of six Popes, he well understood the state of Europe, and was thoroughly imbued with the spirit of the Roman Court. To put the Protestants off their guard, he pretended to be very anxious for the convocation of a Council, and appointed three Cardinals to prepare for its assembling; but those three Cardinals were the most dilatory members of the College. He spoke of the projected Council incessantly in Consistory,* but accompanied his arguments for a Council with distasteful exhortations to his "venerable brethren" to amend their own ways first, and to relinquish the abuses of the Court before sitting in Council to reform the Church. They began to think that he was in earnest, and were perplexing themselves with the question of reform at home, when he dispelled the illusion by promoting two boys to be Cardinals,—Alessandro Farnese, aged fourteen, son of Luigi Farnese his natural son, and Guid' Ascanio Sforza, aged sixteen, son of his natural daughter. From that day the fear of reformation at home no more troubled the Court.

Pursuing the same ambidextrous policy,—doing things contrary to each other at the same time, in order that whatever he did by concession might be undone by another contrary deed of choice,—he published a Bull of indiction, for the assemblage of a Council in Trent, on the 1st day of November, 1542, to which Protestants were invited, under a safe-conduct; and, on the 26th of August, sent three Cardinals to Trent, in order to undertake the necessary correspondence, and receive members as they might arrive; whereas, on the 21st of July, he had set his hand to Constitutions for the appointment and the direction of a new body, whose peculiar duty it should be to crush nonconformity by force, rather than prevent it by counsel. This was THE CONGREGATION OF THE HOLY INQUISITION.

His Bull began by saying that, from the beginning of his pontificate, he had entertained a fixed purpose to drive away all heresy, but that, in spite of all that he could do, bad men

* A *Consistory*, at Rome, is an assembly of Cardinals with the Pope at their head. If the Pope meets them before his coronation, they are only said to form a *Congregation*.

still persisted in their wickedness. Nevertheless, hoping that the authority of a General Council might awe them into submission to the faith, he had "put off the business of Inquisition of that kind of heretical pravity" (Protestantism) "until that day." Why he was that day in so great haste to take the matter out of the hands of the expected Council, he did not condescend to say; but all the world knows that a majority of the Council of Trent, even under Italian influences, would hardly have been found that would agree to a universal Inquisition, governed by the Curials at Rome, or to any court of similar pretensions; and it is further notorious that the Pope's Legates at that Council *proposed* every subject of deliberation, determining afterwards to manage the debate, or to stop it when they could not guide, and that this subject of Inquisition was one of those that they never ventured to introduce. He lost sight, then, of the Council, after merely observing that it could not yet be convened; * and, "lest, while a Council was expected, all things should grow worse and worse," and being himself unable to transact all business, especially while under the pressure of so many arduous cares, he named and appointed six Cardinals to be Commissaries and Inquisitors General and Most General (*generalissimos*), in all cities, towns, lands, and places of the Christian Republic, on both sides of the Alps, to act, under apostolical authority, as his delegates. Whoever wandered "from the way of the Lord," and from the paths of "Catholic Faith," *thinking* evil of that faith, or were in any way, or in any degree, suspected of heresy, together with their followers, abettors, or defenders, who gave them aid or counsel, directly or indirectly, publicly or privately,—all persons, of whatever state or dignity, low or high,—were to be subject to their universal jurisdiction. And lest persecution should be delayed, or Inquisitorial fury mitigated, lest the Clergy in any "city, town, land, or place," should interpose to shield their flocks from the incursion of Roman robbers, Paul ordained that the six Cardinals should act "even without the Ordinaries of places, and that even in causes wherein those Ordinaries had a right to intervene." By his own supreme right, he decreed that the "most general" Inquisitors should proceed officially by way of inquisition, investigation, or otherwise, imprisoning

* More than three years elapsed before the first session, December 13th, 1545.

all guilty or suspected persons, proceeding against them until final sentence, punishing with due penalties those whom they convicted, and, "as was just, taking possession of the property of condemned persons who had suffered death."

The new Universal Roman Inquisition was to have a Fiscal, a Proctor, Notaries Public, and other necessary officers, who might be Priests, or Monks of any order. After they had condemned any Priest or other ordained person as impenitent or as relapsed, it would be their duty to require some Bishop or other dignitary (*antistes*) to degrade him; and, in case of disobedience or delay, they might compel obedience by ecclesiastical censures. For putting condemned heretics to death, Paul armed them with spiritual power—so far as that power could avail—to command and compel the secular arm to slay the victims whom they marked. Their new prerogative extended to the appointment of Inquisitors where, and when, and as often as they pleased, to hear appeals and give ultimate decision,—the graces of absolution and reconciliation being reserved to the Pope himself,—to cite and inhibit in all parts of the world. Then followed a withdrawal of power and authority from all other Judges, and the usual derogation of all Constitutions of preceding Popes to the contrary.

To obviate jealousy, the Spanish Inquisition was exempted from the control of this Congregation; an exemption suggested by the known unwillingness of that body to submit to the dictation of the Court of Rome, and by the spirit of national independence that has often been repressed, but never quenched, in the bosom of the Spaniard. Neither was direct control needed by the Congregation in regard to heretics, so long as the Pope himself appointed the Spanish Inquisitor-General, and so long as the King and Court of Spain were pre-eminent in bigotry. The Pope was the acknowledged head, and was sure to act in agreement with the Congregation.

But the Italian Clergy were not so trustworthy as the Spanish then seemed to be; yet only seemed, for the extension of evangelical doctrine in the parishes and convents of Spain was not yet known. While, therefore, Inquisitorial powers were concentrated within the walls of Rome, new orders were thence communicated to the Inquisitors in the extra-Roman States of Italy. Clement VII. had pointed out the Friars of Lombardy as infected with heresy. It was reported to him that they had preached it openly, and he commanded * the Inquisitors to take active measures against those concealed Lutherans. The Clergy of Bologna and Milan, like the corporate bodies of chartered towns, enjoyed many exemptions from foreign jurisdiction, some granted by Popes, and others, perhaps, in order to obtain their assistance against the laity, by Inquisitors; but Paul III. had opened the way for his universal Inquisition by abolishing those privileges (January 14th, 1542), under the pretence that they had presumed to maintain scandalous and heretical propositions in disputations and in sermons. To extinguish the memory of ancient superstition, and to establish the superstition of his Church more expeditiously in the neophytes, or newly proselyted Jews, he stirred up the Clergy and Inquisitors everywhere to a minute and vigorous examination of their domestic habits (March 21st, 1542). And he induced Charles V., perhaps in return for the gratification of a General Council, to decree the establishment of an Inquisition, after the Spanish model, in Sicily (A.D. 1543). The Sicilians then resisted, but eventually gave way.

But the Cardinal-Inquisitors were not slow in exercising their new powers. Not failing to make inquisition of living heretics, as we shall presently see, they sought to make their ground good by silencing the press, which speaks while authors die. Multitudes of books, pamphlets, and letters were circulated throughout Italy, in spite of all existing prohibitions. There were clandestine presses at work in all parts of Italy, but most of all in the northern States. Printers, when forbidden to carry on their labours, walked abroad during the years of suspension, like men who had no vocation at home; but their wives, and daughters, and servants composed the forms and worked the presses in secret. Books without name of printer or of place were in every hand, and people read them the more attentively because they were forbidden. The public by willing ignorance covered the printers and kept the secret. The Cardinals, unable, as they said, to make perquisition in person, confided that service to the Reverend Father Tommaso María di Bologna, Inquisitor over the cities of Ferrara and Modena. They empowered him and his substitutes to visit all libraries, offices, churches, monasteries and private houses, search for

* In a Brief dated January 15th, 1530.

books, burn the bad ones, and enforce on all booksellers, printers, officers of customs, and other delinquents, the penalties of forfeiture, stripes, fine, suspension from trade, imprisonment or banishment, in proportion to the degree or the number of their offences (July, 1543). It is not improbable that this search after prohibited books was one of the first measures, perhaps it was the chief, that led to the direct inquisition on persons of which we shall find a few examples.

The Venetian Magistrates, flattered by the singular privilege of superintending the inquisition of their fellow-citizens, gave Rome no occasion to deprive them of that honour; yet it was incessantly disputed. The state of things at Venice is thus described in a letter to Luther from Baltassare Altieri, an Italian, attached to the British Legation in that city. He wrote just four months after the appointment of the Roman Congregation, in these words:*—"The fury of Antichrist rages here daily more and more against the elect of God. Many are proscribed, of whom some are said to have gone to the distant provinces, some to Basil and other parts of Switzerland, others into the neighbouring regions" (of the Alps), "and many have been seized and are pining away in perpetual imprisonment; but there is no one to deliver the innocent, none to do justice to the poor man and the orphan, none to maintain the glory of Christ. All conspire together to oppress the Lord and His anointed; and nowhere is this calamity more cruel and more prevalent than in Venice itself, where Antichrist is dominant, and, while using open violence, possesses all his goods in peace. Wicked one that he is, son of perdition, author of sin! That signal thief and most ferocious of wolves slaughters and destroys the Lord's flock at his pleasure, and without restraint. But we cease not to pray the Lord that He would send a stronger than he, who may come and bind him, take away all his weapons, in which he now trusts so confidently, and strip him of the spoils." We further gather from this letter that the Preachers had been silenced, but that many of them were concealed in the city, hoping for the effect of intercession by Protestant Princes of Germany

* I venture to adduce this incidental evidence, although it comes from one whom the Inquisition would have condemned for correspondence with the great heresiarch. His general statement is in perfect consistence with records that no Romanist could reject.

with the Doge and his government, or for some favourable change when the promised Council should assemble.* But no help came from those quarters. From the correspondence of the Cardinals Pole and Contarini, we gather that they had a "sacred piece of work"—*sanctum quoddam negotium*, says Pole—to do at Modena. This is explained, by an Italian editor of Pole's Epistles, to be the suppression of an insurrection in Modena, provoked by the doings of the Inquisitors there. Father Tommaso María did his best, no doubt, and the civil authorities helped him according to the measure of their zeal, or the extent of their ability; but it required an Apostolic Letter from Paul III. to induce them to arrest one whom the Pope describes as the leader of an insurrection against his Inquisitor, to throw him into prison, and to send his books and papers up to Rome.†

In Tuscany the secular arm was uplifted to inflict the sentences of those keepers of the faith. Severe penalties were enacted on the possessors of heretical books, as well as on the printers; and after the usual searchings, arrests, and processes, it was determined to edify the Tuscans by an Act of Faith at Florence, resembling an Auto of Spain. Twenty-two persons were therefore brought out in procession, with the usual apparel of ignominious penance; and it is noted that among them was Bartolommeo Panchiarichi, a gentleman who had served the Duke as Ambassador at the Court of France. They underwent exhibition and reconciliation in the cathedral; and a company of women, by way of giving diversity to the Inquisitorial triumph, appeared in like ceremonial, in the church of S. Simone (A.D. 1556). But commercial prosperity and the Inquisition could not exist on the same ground. Florence was filled with terror and mistrust. Foreigners, being suspected as innovators in religion, and pursued with incessant vexations, ceased to frequent a mart where familiars dogged their steps, and their ships no longer gladdened the course of the Arno. The merchants were impoverished, the inhabitants emigrated, artists and literary men shunned the halls of the Medici, the more eminent Protestants sought refuge in Germany and England, and the less instructed, left without a shepherd, perished for lack of knowledge.

* Seckendorf. Comm. de Luth., lib. iii., sect. 25, § xcvii.

† Gerdes. Spec. Ital. Reform. xxxvii.

The desperate resistance of the Neapolitans to the attempted introduction of the Roman Inquisition into that city in 1547, furnished a terrific episode in Italian history. The Viceroy endeavoured to compel the citizens to accept the Tribunal by military force. He marched a body of three thousand Spanish soldiers into Naples, to quell a riot which his proclamation for the erection of the Tribunal, as a branch of that recently enlarged in Rome, had occasioned. The soldiers fought desperately; but the people were infuriated; and before the bells could ring for evening prayer for the souls in purgatory, the last of the three thousand had fallen, and their bodies, heaped with those of a greater number of Italians, choked the streets. This carnage was to testify at the same time to the brutality of the Inquisitors, and to the horror of the so-called gentle and equitable and holy Roman Inquisition entertained in Italy, where it was too well known to be thought a shade less nefarious than that of Lisbon or Valladolid.

By the indefatigable activity of the Congregation, headed by the Pope, who called on the civil power throughout Italy to support the Inquisition, Lutheranism, as they called it, rapidly died away, and Socinianism, that had for some time been springing up, ate away most of the vitality that remained. Philip II. of Spain outran his predecessor, being yet swifter-footed to shed blood; and the chief men of the island, the very men who twelve years before had driven away the Inquisitor, burnt his papers, and attacked his underlings, were now charmed by privileges offered by the Spanish Nero, became themselves familiars and patrons of the renovated institution, built prisons at their own expense, and salaried the officers. Vain is the help of man! Over violence Romanism can always triumph by violence of its own, combined with greater skill; but when Protestantism degenerates into Socinianism, it becomes a spurious Christianity, that may as well die as live.

A few good men, however, survived the wreck of Protestantism in Italy, and were sacrificed by the Inquisition, one by one. We briefly mention some of them.

On the Pope's demand, *Fannio*, a pious and learned man, was hung at Ferrara, and then burnt. About the same time (A.D. 1550), another, named *Domenico*, suffered violent death at Piacenza, praying for his persecutors. *Galeazzo Treccio*, after enduring imprisonment and questioning, probably with torture, bore witness to the truth as it is in Jesus, and was burnt alive in a town of the Milanese (A.D. 1551). *Giovanni di Montalcino*, an eminent man, once Professor of Metaphysics in the University of Bologna, and a faithful expositor of the New Testament, was burnt alive in Rome (A.D. 1553). *Francisco Gambia*, of Brescia, for having joined in an act of evangelical communion at Geneva, was taken, when crossing the Lake of Como on his way homeward, condemned by the Inquisitors of Como, strangled, and then beheaded, and his body burnt (A.D. 1554). *Pomponio Algieri*, of Capua, a devout Christian, became known in the academy of Padua, was arrested and imprisoned in Venice; but, not being a Venetian, was given up to the Cardinal-Inquisitors, and burnt alive at Rome for their entertainment and that of Paul IV. (A.D. 1555). *Varaglia*, a Capuchin Friar, Inquisitor, and son of an Inquisitor, one who had signalised himself in persecuting and killing Waldenses, while striving to make himself master of the controversy between Rome and the Reformed churches, was converted to the truth and service of the Lord Jesus Christ, and soon fell into the hands of his former brethren, who burnt him in Turin (A.D. 1557). *Luigi Pascal*, an itinerant Preacher among the scattered Christians of Calabria, was taken to Rome, condemned by their Eminences, and burnt outside the castle of St. Angelo, in their presence, the Pope presiding at the ceremony (A.D. 1560). From time to time Inquisitorial spies, at Venice, detected members of the secret societies of worshippers in that city, whom the Inquisition condemned in course. The usual mode of execution there was by drowning in the sea. Gerdes collects the names of four whom they drowned.*

I cannot fully sketch the history of *Pietro Carnesecchi*,† one of the most illustrious victims of the Roman Inquisition, but borrow a few details from an Italian, who, knowing nothing of his religion, cannot be supposed to misrepresent the circumstances of his persecution and death. "The ecclesiastical Tribunal, that is, the Inquisition," says Botta,‡ "also kept a strict eye on those scandalous practices," (of

* Giovanni Guirlanda, Antonio Ricetto, Francesco Sega, Francesco Spinola. From 1562 to 1567.

† But may refer my readers to the "Martyrs of the Reformation," p. 498.

‡ Storia d'Italia, libro xii.

treating Popish ceremonies with disrespect, which it is most unlikely that many persons would have dared to do in such times,) "and thundered processes now on one, and again on another. The Friar who was intrusted with the business, not content with receiving information brought him by persons actuated with sincere zeal for religion, or with malignant revenge, or with cupidity, went about—or sent others to do the same—interrogating simple and ignorant people concerning doctrines of religion; and if any one, perhaps not knowing what he said, answered unsoundly, he forthwith proceeded against him as one suspected." (And in all the Inquisitor only followed his instructions.)

"This came to pass, not only in Tuscany, but in all parts of Italy. Yet, as the Princes wished their deputies to assist at the processes of the Inquisition, and Cosimo" (Duke of Tuscany) "had ordered that the Nuncio should give him an account of them, and that the sentences should not be executed without his consent, the Pope thought that the Tribunal, thus bridled, would not be a sufficient check upon the innovators, and resolved to take another method for the attainment of his end. To strike at the chiefs, in order to terrify their followers, and to draw them from foreign countries to the Inquisition at Rome, seemed the measure most conducive to that end. The lordship of Venice readily gave up into his power Giulio Zanetti, who had fled to Padua when under an accusation of heresy. The Republic excused itself, for an act that was not unlike brutality, by alleging that Zanetti was born at Fano, and was therefore a subject of the Pope. Through almost all the dominions of Italy he sought after such persons, to the alarm of the people, who broke out into riot in some places, as at Mantua, for example. The Princes seconded the will of Pius V., some to seem religious, some through fear of the Pope, and some, after hearing of events in Germany, from fear that reform of religion would bring rebellion into the state.

"Among the principal persons *infected* was Pietro Carnesecchi, whose case affords fearful proof that either one should not vary from general belief, or should flee to some place where it is not professed. He showed, also, by his mournful end, how vain, in such cases, is the friendship of Princes, and how uncertain a protection from the thunders of the Vatican." Carnesecchi is described as a person of high family and great learning. He had been Protonotary at Rome under the reign of Clement VII., but was also a friend of many of the most eminent of the Reformed. On this account he had been once in the hands of the Inquisition; but the Duke of Florence managed to get him released. Then he went to France, and held correspondence with the chiefs of the Reform there. Paul IV. cited him to appear at Rome; but he came not, and was therefore considered contumacious; and his contumacity soon became undoubted when he wrote against the Papacy. Trusting, however, in the friendship of Cosimo, Duke of Florence, he ventured to visit him; but Pio V. commanded the Duke to surrender his guest. The Tuscan would have thought himself bound, as he said, to give up even his own child to the Pope, if he were demanded; and, without a blush, he saw Carnesecchi arrested, when sitting at his table, and carried away by force to Rome.

"On the 26th of August, 1567, he was sentenced to death, having been convicted of thirty-four condemned opinions. The sentence was publicly read to him on the 21st of the month following. Having consigned him to the secular arm, they put on him the *sambenito* painted with flames and devils. At that last stage, Cosimo did not despair of moving the Pontiff to compassion. Pius suspended the execution of the sentence for ten days, promising grace if the condemned would renounce the heretical opinions, and return to the Catholic faith. He also sent a Capuchin to exhort him; but that was in vain; for, so far was he from being converted, that he wished, by disputation, to convert the Capuchin, and he despised death. He was beheaded, and then burnt. To the last he bore the terrible preparation, and the aspect of death itself, with singular constancy. He even chose to walk to the scaffold, as if in pomp, wearing fine linen, and new and elegant gloves, since the *sambenito* did not allow the use of other garments. The ecclesiastical writers, and especially Baronius,* find fault with one who wrote that Carnesecchi was burnt alive; and even affirm that the Roman Inquisition never inflicted such a cruel punishment, which was true, at least, in the case of Carnesecchi. They will have it that the Holy Office, before burning heretics, caused them to be beheaded or hung; but certainly the *sambenito* was burnt before the death of the condemned;

* He means Laderchius, a continuator of Baronius.

and while that was burning, they took off his head, or hanged him. The reader may judge what amount of pity and moderation that was, and whether the Inquisition has reason to boast of it. These are terrible passages of history.

"Great terror, great consternation, followed this tragedy of Carnesecchi, not only in Tuscany, but in all Italy. Every one feared for himself, for his parents, for his friends. Pleasant and confidential conversation was banished, even from the most secret colloquies of families."

And the terror of such executions extended beyond Italy. In the year preceding, an Englishman, named *Thomas Reynolds*, resident or visiting at Naples, had been accused to the Bishop, together with three Neapolitan gentlemen; and Rome being now the Inquisitorial centre of the world, the Bishop sent them all thither. The Cardinals threw the Englishman into prison, and laid him on the rack. From torture, and other sufferings in prison, he died in the month of November.*

The name of *Aonio Paleario* is again familiar to us in England. That great and good man, after many years of persecution, driven from place to place, was teaching Greek and Latin at Milan. The writings by which we know him are of posthumous publication, and had not been seen by the Inquisitors. They condemned him to be hung, and his body burnt, on account only of the following opinions:—1. That there is no purgatory. 2. That the burial of dead in churches was injurious to public health. 3. That Monachism was of pagan origin. 4. "That, as it appeared, he attributed justification to faith alone in the mercy of God, who pardons our sins through Christ." For this he suffered in "the metropolis of Christendom," at the age of seventy, October 5th, 1568.†

The majority of my readers would not thank me for pursuing the series of Papal ordinances for the Inquisition in Italy. I therefore refrain from noticing much that lies before me, and merely observe that the Congregation of Cardinals, from the year 1542 onwards, issued in the name of the Popes a multitude of regulations, either new or else reiterated, all tending to bring the secular Clergy, the regulars, the civil powers, the people, and the press, into utter subjection to themselves.

* Strype, Annals of the Reformation, chap. xlviii.

† Aonii Palearii Epistolæ. Laderchius, A.D. 1568

Paul IV., to the latest hour of his life, displayed an inordinate zeal in the cause of the Inquisition. On that alone, he said, rested his hopes for the continued existence of the Church; and he exhorted the Cardinals who stood around his bed to give it their chief and unremitted care. As soon as he was known to be dead, the inhabitants of Rome, as usual at such times, but then with an extraordinary and resistless vehemence, rejoiced at his departure. The common prisons of the city were opened, according to an ancient custom; but the new prison of the Inquisition was kept strictly shut. Thither the people ran, forced the gates, released the prisoners, and set the building on fire. With great difficulty they were prevented from treating the Dominican convent *della Minerva* in the same manner, and from taking vengeance on the Monks, who, beyond all other orders, were devoted to the service of the Inquisition. The crowd moved towards the capitol, broke down a fine statue of the defunct Pontiff, knocked off its head, and rolled it through the streets during three days, when they dropped the unvisaged boulder into the Tiber. They would have treated the body of Paul in a similar manner, but it was hastily hidden in a vault. The Commissary of the Inquisition was wounded, and his house burnt. The arms of the Caraffe—it was Cardinal Caraffa who advised Paul III. to create the Congregation of the Inquisition—were everywhere torn down (A.D. 1559). But popular tempests lull almost as quickly as they rise, and the Cardinals resumed their legal station without any effectual hinderance. They learnt, however, that the buildings of the Holy Office were not sufficiently substantial; and, in due time, the Princes of the Faith fortified themselves within a more solid edifice.

The indignation of the Romans could scarcely have risen so high, if the Inquisition had not perpetrated many deeds of cruelty. I could cite Protestant authorities to show that, in the year 1568, some were every day burnt, hanged, or beheaded; that the prisons overflowed, and new ones were in course of erection. The character of Pius V., the persecution then raging throughout Europe, every glimpse that the historian can catch of the history of the Italian Inquisition, confirms the probability. But I am willing to sacrifice *effect* to the self-imposed condition of drawing my history out of materials found within the Church of Rome herself.

And if, by any oversight, other witnesses are introduced, let their testimony, however accurate, be set aside. We can do without them. New prisons, and a better-defended establishment, were certainly thought necessary; and the present palace of the Roman Inquisition, erected by Pius V., bears an inscription to attest the year of its foundation, 1569.

CHAPTER XXVI.

ITALY—INQUISITION OF THE CARDINALS (CONCLUDED).

"BLESSED father," said Baronius to Paul V., "the ministry of Peter is twofold, *to feed*, and *to kill*. For the Lord said to him, 'Feed My sheep;' and he also heard a voice from heaven, saying, 'Kill and eat.' To feed sheep is to take care of obedient, faithful Christians, who in meekness, humility, and piety, show themselves to be sheep and lambs. But when he has no longer to do with sheep and lambs, but with lions and other wild, refractory, and troublesome beasts, Peter is commanded to kill them, that is to say, to attack, fight, and slaughter them, until there be none such left." * This notion of killing was not peculiar to Baronius. Pius V. acted up to it thoroughly; and, among many butcher-like doings, confirmed all the privileges and graces granted to crusaders of both sexes, by two Innocents, one Leo, one Julius, one Clement, and other of his predecessors, constituted them a distinct society, for the purpose of helping Inquisitors whenever necessary, and bade them do so without the least scruple or limitation as to means (A.D. 1570). There is reason to believe that the Bartholomew massacre was contrived about this time, partly at Rome, during a visit of the Cardinal of Lorraine, and partly by the instigation of the Inquisitors at Madrid. It is not surprising, therefore, that when intelligence of that crime reached the various Courts of Europe, it should have been celebrated by those of Pius V., his familiars, Cosimo of Tuscany and Philip II., with public rejoicings and Te Deums, whereas it awakened horror in all others.

* Sententia Baronii Card. super excommunicatione Venetiarum, apud "Controversiæ Memorabilis inter Paul V. et Venetos," &c. In Villa Sanvincentiana. 1608.

Of the Maltese Inquisition there is little to be noted, except that when Charles V. gave Malta to the Knights of St. John of Jerusalem in 1522, there was no Inquisition established in Sicily, of which island Malta had been a dependency, and therefore the Inquisition is not mentioned in the Charter; but the Grand Master of Malta was required to send traitors and heretics to the Viceroy of Sicily, and the see of Malta was also to continue in relation to the parent state. But after the Tribunal was established at Palermo, the Inquisitors required heretics, detected in Malta, to be sent to them for punishment. The Grand Master, La Cassiera, resisted this demand, and quarrels between the Order of St. John and the Holy Office became frequent and long-continued. This, however, gave the Court of Rome occasion to extend their Inquisitorial jurisdiction into Malta, so far, at least, as the jealousy of the masters, and the resistance of the people, would allow (A.D. 1574).*

The diocese of Milan, bounding on the territories of reformed Switzerland, was kept under the searching vigilance of the Congregation, of which the acts of a Provincial Synod in the year 1582 are evidence. For the "preservation of the faith," that Synod commanded the inhabitants of the province of Milan, 1. To shun commerce with heretics; 2. And declared it desirable that no person should be admitted into their country who came from lands infected with heresy; or, 3. If that could not be prevented, that no one should be allowed to lodge in a private house, but confined to an inn, or to the house of his agent, if he had one. 4. If any such came into the diocese, "whoever received him should give immediate notice of his arrival and of his habitation to the Bishop, the Inquisitor, or the parish Priest. But no ecclesiastical person whatever should receive him into his house." 5. The stranger was not to enter a church, except at sermon-time. 6. No one was to send his son into a country of heretics, not even for instruction in commerce, while under twenty-five years of age. 7. Nor was any one to go thither without licence obtained from his Bishop or the Inquisitor. 8. A licence only to be obtained by recommendation of the parish Priest. 9. Nor even reside in the neighbourhood of heretics without licence; nor, 10. Sell an estate in order to remove to an infected country,

* Vertot, Histoire de l'Ordre de Malthe, liv. xiv. Malta Illustrata, lib. ii., not. 14.

11. Under peril of being proceeded against according to the canons. And after these regulations were added others for the government of printers and booksellers, and the extirpation of Jewish blasphemy and perfidy. The Swiss, on the other hand, were on the alert to prevent encroachments on their cantons; and on one occasion the Cardinal Borromeo, itinerating in the cause of the Inquisition, very narrowly escaped imprisonment, and had to make speed back to Rome again.*

At Rome the Cardinals were absolute, and, in revenge for being unable to exercise authority in England, cruelly persecuted English heretics, throwing some into prison, and sending others to the galleys.† Gregory XIII., while suffering the Jews to dwell at Rome, for the sake of revenue, compelled them to attend at sermons delivered against Jewish perfidy;‡ and Xystus V. made an onslaught on astrologers,§ whose art had for many centuries been of great authority with both Clergy and laity in Italy.

Passing over entirely the controversy between Rome and Venice,—in which the Inquisition did not fail to take part, by persecuting those who maintained the independence of that state, especially Fra Paolo Sarpi, Theologian of the Senate, whom they censured, and who, wounded at the altar by hired assassins, exclaimed, *Agnosco stylum Romanum*, "I know the Roman style," and narrowly escaped death,—I proceed to notice an important documentary evidence of the control exercised by the Congregation of Cardinals over all the Inquisitions of Italy, in pursuance of the design of its appointment.

In the year 1588, Xystus V. had instituted fifteen Congregations at Rome, placing that of the Inquisition first, as being most important, and enlarged the number of Cardinals to twelve, he being their Prefect, or Inquisitor-General of Christendom; and the officer who would have been called Chief Inquisitor in any other city, was there known only as his "Commissary." Bearing date of 1608, twenty years after this enlargement, a manual was published,—probably one of many similar,—containing, "Brief Instructions in the manner of treating causes of the Holy Office, for the Very Reverend Vicars of the Holy Inquisition, appointed in the Dioceses of Modona" (Módena), "Carpi, Nonantola, and the

* Fra Paolo, Inquis. Venice, chap. i. † Strype, Annals, chap. xvi.
‡ Constitutio, Aug. 29, 1584. § Jan. 5, 1585.

Garfagnana." It was printed at Módena, and bears the signature of F. Michel' Angelo Lerri, Inquisitor of Módena. The manual is very brief, and looks insignificantly small, if compared with the folio of Eymeric and Pegna, to which it refers as the standard authority. It is in Italian, for the benefit of the Very Reverend Vicars, to whom Latin might not have been intelligible; and repeats the directions which I have compendiated at greater length in preceding chapters. Lerri exhorts his Vicars to encourage the denouncers of heretics to persevere, heedless of the reproach of being "spies of the Holy Office," because they would not be discovered, or if by any means they were detected, they ought not to fear the name, since, in time of plague, men would do anything to stay the contagion, regardless of consequences; and for what they do now, in zeal for the Lord, they should be rewarded in heaven. With extreme earnestness he enforces the usual injunctions on all concerned to observe the most profound secrecy, and instructs the Notary how to disguise, or falsify, the summaries of evidence, that the prisoners may not have the slightest clue for conjecturing who has testified against them. As to the methods of self-accusation he is explicit enough, so far as he goes, but stays at the point where torture would be mentioned, as if he wished it to be employed sparingly by the subalterns, and rather inflicted under his own eye. "Many other things," he writes, "have to be observed concerning the defences of the criminal; but as it is our intention that the cases shall be despatched in the Holy Office of this city, and that when they reach this stage, and defences have to be made, processes ended, and sentence given, the criminals be in prison here, we add no more." And, in every case, he reserves to himself the ultimate decision on their reports.

Among the general directions to the Vicars, is one to publish, or cause to be published, the General Edict of the Holy Office three times every year in all places subject to his jurisdiction,—on Corpus-Christi day, on the first Sunday in Advent, and on the first in Lent. They are to send him monthly reports of all their proceedings, omitting no particular, however minute. They are "admonished that, when they have received any information, or formed any process, they are not to speak of it, nor make the slightest allusion to it, to any one except the Notary concerned. If any one comes to ask a question concerning the Holy Office, they are to rebut the question, and reprove the inquirer, telling him that the affairs of the Holy Office cannot be disclosed to any one, and always affirming that they know nothing about it. Above all, they are not to allow it to be known who has given information, or borne witness, or they will be severely punished for divulging what is to be concealed, and of this they must warn their Notaries; and if any one comes to ask favour for any criminal, they are to answer him vaguely, that his case will be disposed of as early as possible, and such mercy as the Holy Office is wont to use will be shown him. And if any person writes letters on behalf of any criminal, they shall, on no account, answer them, except after express permission had from their Lord, Pope Paul V." That is to say, they are to make inquisition on others, but no one is to make it on them.

Clement VIII., be it observed, had said that the Judges and officers of the Inquisition were to do everything gratuitously, and Inquisitor Lerri said something of the same kind. But he appended to this manual, for the government of his Vicars, the table of fees which appears literally translated at the foot of our page. In the manual it comes under the head of "Instructions from the Congregation at Rome." For payment, he informed them, lands were not to be seized, but the amount of charges might be levied on fruits and rents.* For being torn from the bosom of his family, for

* *To the Notary.*

For making out the summary	scudo 1. of gold.
And, if the process be long, the labour shall be considered.	
For [copying] each page of the summary	bol. 4.
For each letter	bol. 3.
For any citation of witnesses	bol. 2.
For the citation of the criminal	bol. 3.
For the decree of defence	bol. 2.
For each witness in defence	bol. 6.
For any kind of security	bol. 20.
For every page of the copy of the process	bol. 4.
And when a copy of the process itself is not given (to the criminal), for every page of the said process	bol. 2.
For every page of the copy of the defensive process	bol. 5.
For the decree of torture	bol. 2.
For the torture	bol. 10.
For the citation to the sentence	bol. 4.
For the sentence	scudo 1. of gold.
For the copy of the sentence	bol. 20.

each act of malignant accusation, for every stage of suffering, for imprisonment, for torture, and even for being carried to the stake, the victim was to pay! Ruffians and tormentors were to be bribed at his own cost, to murder him by piecemeal, and then to keep the secret. Who can wonder, after this, at assassinations done, in Italy, for hire?

The perusal of this, as of all documents relating to the Inquisition, and of incidental allusions to it, occurring in other writings, leaves the impression that it was very active, and meddled with all the affairs of political, domestic, and social life. But it is also certain, that popular and tumultuary resistance had given place to another kind of reaction, and that the acts and pretensions of Inquisitors were canvassed in relation to the controversy between the secular and ecclesiastical powers,—a controversy which contributes abundantly to the history of Europe in the seventeenth and eighteenth centuries.

Paul V. had excommunicated the Venetians (April 17th, 1606), and, notwithstanding a superficial reconciliation, the disagreement between Rome and Venice, real but latent,

For the relaxation (delivery to the stake)............. bol. 10.
For the Congregation.................................... bol. 10.
For the visit to the house of the criminal.............. bol. 20.

To the Signor Fiscal.

For any witness, at instance of the criminal .... bol. 12.
For the torture .... bol. 20.
For the Congregation.................................. bol. 20.
For the visit to the house .... bol. 40.
For the sentence...................................... scudo 1. of gold.

To the Serjeants.

For the capture of the criminal in the city .... scudo 1. of gold.
When this takes place out of town, regard must be had to the distance.
For the torture .... bol. 40.
For the visit to the house .... bol. 20.
For accompanying the criminal to the sentence ...... bol. 40.
And for this regard shall be had to their trouble and danger.

As for the Jailer, that is left to the discretion of the Inquisitor, and in the said list of fees (*tassa*) there is not any mention made of it. That the Inquisitors, or Vicars, for the future, may not apply pecuniary penalties for the benefit of the Holy Office, or of any other places, without first giving a statement of the same to the sacred Congregation of Rome. And this is by order of the said sacred Congregation.

And let this suffice for the present, &c.

was revived; when the senate, complying with a request of the English Ambassador, opened the prison of the Inquisition in their city, without a word of previous notice or demand, either to the Inquisitor or the Nuncio, and released *Lodovico Castelvetro*, a very learned man who lay there condemned for heresy, and doomed to perpetual imprisonment, if not to fire (A.D. 1612). He had translated into Italian a work of a German heresiarch.* Such a direct attack on the Tribunal had never been made before at Venice; and it showed that, thenceforth, the Doge was resolved to be Chief-Inquisitor in the State of St. Mark, leaving the Pope to exercise a similar prerogative elsewhere, so long as his power over States and Princes might continue.

The case of *Galileo* is too notorious to be passed over without notice. Urban VIII., by the fires he kindled in the squares of Milan, was already the terror of Italy; and public dread was by no means diminished when men saw that the Inquisition not only meddled with religious opinions, but extended its vigilance into the domain of natural science. At Florence, still a great city, in spite of the persecution that spoiled its commerce, Galileo Galilei taught mathematics, under the patronage of the Grand Duke. During many years he had endeavoured, both from the professorial chair and by the press, to prove that the earth revolves around the sun, and not the sun around the earth. The Friars declared his theory to be absurd, false, and heretical. The Holy Office caught this rumour of heresy, and the Congregation of Cardinals at Rome, by command of the Pope, required their Consultors to report on the writings of Galileo. Their sentence was condemnatory, of course; and Galileo was summoned to Rome, there to receive the censure or endure the consequence. He went. Cardinal Bellarmino called him into his presence, and commanded him to abandon the suspected "doctrine" under pain of imprisonment, and never more to teach it by word or by writing. He promised, and the Sacred Congregation seemed to be satisfied. But Galileo could not keep his promise. He applied himself to the composition of a dialogue between three persons; one in doubt, a second addicted to the Ptolemaic system, and a third believing in

* Botta, lib. xvi. The liberation of captives from other Italian Inquisitions by civic authority or military power became, at this time, not unfrequent.

the Copernican. He trusted that by venturing an hypothesis rather than propounding a theory, he might escape the charge of dogmatising. The interlocutors merely inclined to the speculations of Copernicus; and the author feared not to present himself at Rome, and ask licence of the Master of the Sacred Palace to print the dialogues. And, by special intercession of the Grand Duke of Tuscany, he obtained it.

But no sooner did his book see the light, than the Monkhood was in uproar, and the Congregation were on the point of condemning the Master as a heretic for having given the licence. To Urban they pointed out that the Tuscan philosopher had caricatured the Pope himself in the person of "Simplicius" the Peripatetic; and his Holiness kindled into wrath against the insolent contemner of the Apostolic chair. Galileo was then summoned to present himself before the Holy Office in Rome, within the month of October, 1632. Thither he prepared to go, poor, old, sickly, and appalled with recollection of the fate of Carnesecchi; but, overwhelmed with fear, he fell sick, and appeared to be on the point of death. Nicolini, Ambassador of the Grand Duke, interceded earnestly with the Pope for a prorogation of the cause, and physicians certified that he was unable to travel from Florence to Rome. The Cardinals treated the certificates as untrue, and insisted on his appearance. The Grand Duke, Ferdinand, being reminded of the perfidy of Cosimo I. towards Carnesecchi, at first refused to give him up; but the Grand Duchess, Christina, ruled by Priests, implored her husband to gratify the Church by surrendering the heretic. The rest is soon told. Galileo was dragged away to Rome (A.D. 1633), where the Congregation of the Holy Office declared him strongly suspected of heresy, prohibited his books, and condemned him to prison and to penance. The great astronomer knelt down * and renounced his "errors," swearing on the holy Gospels; and the Congregation graciously relaxed their severity by confining him to a monastery instead of a dungeon, and eventually permitting him to sojourn in the houses of some of his friends, a prisoner at large, until death withdrew him from their eye.

The Archduke Ferdinand II., who surrendered Galileo to the Cardinals, was a man of extreme and impudent

* But, it is related of him, that on rising from the pavement in the palace of Pius V., burning with shame and indignation, he stamped with his foot, and muttered, *Eppur si muove*,—"But yet it moves."

licentiousness, and a staunch friend of the Inquisitors, whose cruelties he promoted, and whose profligacy he favoured. In his reign an incident occurred which adds another line of deformity to the picture of society in Florence, and contributes an illustration to our review of the Holy Office. One Faustina Mainardi had formed a school of girls, and Pandolfo Ricasoli, a Canon, attended it under the character of master. "Both he and she, being persons of grossly dissolute habits, instead of teaching the children good conduct, taught them, and practised with them, the most infamous obscenities. This became known by the revelation of a Confessor. The Inquisition proceeded against them on the 21st of November, 1641, in the Refectory of the Friars of Holy Cross: a platform was erected, hung with black, like one of the structures prepared for the celebration of a funeral service. Galuzzi relates that there were present at the ceremony the Cardinal Carlo de' Medici, the young Princes, all the Priests of Florence, the nobility and other persons of rank, as many as the place would hold. The two culprits were on the platform, dressed in *pazienze*," (as they call sambenitos in Italy,) "with devils and flames embroidered, kneeling before the Inquisitor, who sat in magisterial state. A Friar in the pulpit read the process aloud, not hesitating nor blushing to relate minutely, and in a loud voice, all the abominations confessed by each of them, so much to the disgust of the audience,—for many young persons of both sexes were there, attracted by the unusual, or rather the usual, spectacle,—that most of them went away more scandalised at the impudence of the Friar than at the impurity of the delinquents. Faustina and Pandolfo were not condemned to the fire, but to die immured in prison; and other accomplices, to suffer punishments in proportion. The Inquisitor was reproved from Rome, not for having conducted himself so indecently, but for having awarded so gentle a sentence." It does not appear that the Inquisitor was either lenient or inactive, but that most of his punishments were terribly severe. But for not burning those two wretched persons, he was displaced by a fiercer agent of the Sacred Congregation.* This single instance of Inquisitorial lewdness must suffice. To collect others would be easy indeed, but could not be justified.

And here it may be said, in confidence that the assertion can be fully sustained, that so long as the Inquisition could

* Botta, lib. xxvii.

keep up its authority by terror, it never cared for morals. True it is, indeed, that at one time it laid some slight restraint on "solicitant Confessors" in Spain; but the delinquents were handled very gently, and that show of Inquisitorial vigilance was absolutely necessary to save the credit of the Church. In reality, there was a collusion between the Inquisitors and their brethren of the confessional, just to blind the public, and fling the veil of discipline over a flagrant scandal.

CHAPTER XXVII.

ITALY—THE INQUISITION AS IT IS.

As cultivation advances, wolves diminish. But there is a district still uncultivated, a region still impervious to that which elsewhere ameliorates the condition of mankind; and intolerance, like the deadly exhalation of the Pontine Marshes, there overspreads the land. The Tibrine wolf yet lingers in its ancient haunts. Humanity and mercy find entrance everywhere else; but at Rome, while there are laws for the government of common prisons worthy of admiration for humanity, those laws do not extend to the cells of the Holy Office, which are under a distinct and awfully secret administration.

A careful examination of Inquisitorial proceedings during the seventeenth and eighteenth centuries would show, as we have already intimated, that the Venetian controversy, with the struggle between the Court of Rome and the King and Clergy in France, and the influence of Protestantism, even in Popish countries, had weakened the agency and contracted the operations of the Holy Office. Castelvetro, as we have seen, was released from the Inquisition in Venice, on the demand of the representative of England; and in the year 1662, two devoted Quakeresses, true Christian heroines, were brought safely to England in a British ship of war, after four years' imprisonment in Malta. The Inquisitor there seems to have had the use of cells in a common prison in Valletta, where heretics, so called, were incarcerated. The Quakeresses, *Catherine Evans* and *Sarah Cheevers*, were thrown into a dark and close dungeon there, where they must soon have perished, if a physician had not certified that it was impossible for them to live in such a place much longer. Their skin became dry as parchment, and the hair fell from their heads, in consequence of extreme heat; while the stench, with stinging of mosquitoes, and an exhausted atmosphere, induced as trying a torture as if they had been racked. Through all this suffering they endured as seeing Him who is invisible, and never ceased to commune with God in prayer, and to preach Christ to their inexorable tormentors. If they had been taken in Italy, instead of Malta, it is not likely that they would have escaped with life; but the Grand Masters generally restrained the ecclesiastical authorities, in jealousy of all that might derogate from their own sovereignty in the island.

The escape of *Archibald Bower* from Macerata, in 1726, is marked by writers on the Inquisition as an interesting event; but there are some details in his account of the constitution and proceedings of the Tribunal there, which seem to require confirmation. That the Inquisition was active, at that time, and that torture and death were frequently inflicted, is notorious; but the statements of Mr. Bower, however accurate, add nothing essential to our knowledge of its customs.

Universal dissatisfaction with the absolutism of the continental Governments encouraged the spread of secret societies, which were spoken of under the general designation of Masonic lodges, and which appear to have been, in reality, political clubs. The Inquisition undertook to disperse those lodges; and some of the "brethren" who suffered persecution in Spain and Portugal, favoured the world with narratives of their experience in the audience-chambers and the cells. The fact that the Inquisition took cognisance of them tends to confirm our persuasion that it is, *chiefly*, a political institution, carrying on its operations under pretence of a spiritual reason, and speaking in the dialect of religion. Freemasonry entered Italy, it is said, at Florence, and there, as in other countries, it was prohibited by the Government. But the institution described on these pages is a society secret above all others; and Clement XII., unwilling, of course, that *two* secret societies should exist side by side, in any part of Popedom, published a condemnatory Bull (A.D. 1738), and in the year following the Cardinal Vicar of Rome issued an edict, denouncing the penalty of death on all Freemasons detected within the Papal State. Such an edict could scarcely have been committed for execution to the Inquisitors without causing many to perish at their hands.

Neither could a new society—ramified throughout Europe,

everywhere professing to be constituted for purposes of mutual benevolence, and sometimes numbering with its members persons of high station, who sought admission for the sake of becoming privy to proceedings that could not otherwise be known, and perhaps of preventing conspiracies against themselves—fail to acquire considerable influence. And such a confederation could not be assailed with great severity without bringing upon the persecutors a return of hatred and revenge. Control of religion, science, and politics besides, was now attempted by the Holy Office, an attempt which quickly verified the truth of an Italian proverb, that *il soverchio rompe il coperchio*—aiming to compass too much, you lose all. And all was quickly lost, except at Rome, and in the Roman State. Suppressions of Inquisitions rapidly succeeded one another. The Inquisitors had plunged into a stream of political partisanship, which, swelling into a torrent, eventually swept them from their footing in every country beyond the territory of the Church.

The Empress Maria Theresa, in common with other Sovereigns, abolished many dangerous ecclesiastical privileges, and in Milan she required the Archbishop and the Inquisitor to refrain from vexatious prohibition of books. She saw that it was no less absurd than troublesome; that good books were suppressed, while demoralising and otherwise hurtful publications were allowed free circulation; and she desired that the Holy Office should cease from prohibitory censure. Archbishop and Inquisitor failing to satisfy so reasonable a desire, Her Majesty took the reins into her own hand, and commanded that the censorship of books should thenceforth be exercised by the Magistrates alone. About the same time (February 21st, 1769), the Duke of Parma published a decree, lamenting that an alien Tribunal, administered by foreigners and Monks, under the title of "Inquisition of the Holy Office," had been introduced into that State; declared that it belonged to him alone, as protector of religion and the Church, to provide for the conservation of sound doctrines; and ordained that, on the death of the Inquisitor of Parma, causes of faith should be brought to the Bishops for decision, none other presuming to interfere therewith. But he promised to afford the Bishops the aid of the secular arm when it became necessary to inflict capital punishment on heretics, and, on the death of the Inquisitor, declared the inmates of the dungeons to be his own prisoners, subject to the ducal jurisdiction.

Similar measures were taken in Tuscany by the Grand Duke Pietro Leopoldo, and his Ministers. The Tuscan Inquisition was eminently hateful on account of iniquitous imprisonments, atrocious cruelties, and a censorship no longer to be suffered. Good and bad were alike the victims, and judgment was given for the profit of the Court of Rome, rather than for the reformation of manners, or conservation of "the faith:" every one declared it to be no longer tolerable. The Regency, during the minority of the Grand Duke, had appointed a civil Delegate to examine books, without the intervention of an Inquisitor. And when the Inquisitors proceeded to exercise jurisdiction over "sinners against the Holy Office," they were commanded to admit two lay-assessors. Rome complained of persecution, the name she always gives to legal restraints. Florence answered by producing facts in justification of those restraints. The Inquisitor of Pisa, they said, by way of example, had attempted to dishonour a young female, whose father protected her against his villany, and in revenge he had caused the man to be flogged until he nearly died. Many other enormities of the same kind had filled the city with disgust. They therefore began by depriving the Inquisitors of their *sbirri*, or familiars. They also abolished conventual prisons, or, in other terms, monastic Inquisitions.*

And it cannot be inopportune to observe in this place, that in whatever country the secret monastic discipline exists, an Inquisition is established there under another name. On this point I say nothing, but leave a celebrated Benedictine † to bear witness. Referring to a work of Mabillon on "the Prisons of Religious Orders," he speaks thus :—"God wills not the death of a sinner, but rather that he should be converted and live. St. Benedict, although he commanded delinquents to be restrained by penalties, with excellent discretion, made no mention of prisons in his sacred rule. Then who first constructed prisons? Matthew, a Prior of St. Martin de Campis, not a bad man in other respects, but one who punished persons in error with extreme severity, and was accustomed to thrust into the blackest dungeon those whom he thought incorrigible. But as examples of that kind are often of most fearful con-

* Botta, lib. xlvii.

† Ziegelbauer, Hist. Rei Literariæ Ord. S. Benedict. pars. iv., cap. iv., sec. 8.

sequence, other Abbots, more inflamed with zeal than with charity, forthwith constructed black, horrid, death-like, sickening, dark, narrow holes, in which they shut up offending Monks with such inhuman severity that Stephen, Archbishop of Toulouse, through his Vicar, complained to John, King of France, of *the horrible rigour that Monks used on Monks offending gravely, shutting them up for life in a dark and concealed prison, a punishment which they call* VADE IN PACE." (Go in peace!) "In consequence of which many lose their reason, or die despairing of salvation. But more, and more distinctly, another time." We cannot here enter into any disquisition on monastic discipline, but must proceed.

Ferdinand VI., King of the Two Sicilies, abolished the Sicilian Inquisition in the year 1782, declaring that it had been ever hateful to the people, disobedient to the Sovereign, and hostile to the laws. His Majesty marked a confession of the Inquisitor-General, that "the inviolable secret is the soul of the Inquisition;" and, after showing that it could no longer be suffered without violation of reason and humanity, he decreed that it was "for ever abolished and extinguished" in that kingdom.*

We now come to Rome.

The reader will remember that Napoleon Bonaparte dispersed the Spanish Inquisitors on his approach towards Madrid in 1808. The French troops entered Rome in 1809; and, whatever mischief they otherwise did, performed an act of humanity in demolishing, in part, at least, the prisons of the Inquisition. And if, as people fancied, the Tribunal had fallen into disuse, or if it could not be revived in this enlightened age, even under shadow of the Pontifical throne they might have been undeceived when another set of prisons, equally numerous and substantial, rose under the direction of Leo XII. in the year 1825. That erection gave evidence to the world that pretensions to unlimited power, which had been made during the interval on behalf of the Court of Rome, were not meant to be an empty boast. Those pretensions, with heartiest concurrence of the Papal Nuncio, and the majority of the Spanish Prelates and Clergy, were put forth in open Cortes at Cadiz, in 1813, by many of the clerical members. They contended† that, "beyond all doubt, the Pontifical authority subsisted entire in Spain,"—as in

* Cited in the Discusion del Proyecto de Decreto, &c., p. 33.

† The words of Don Francisco Riesco are here quoted.

every other country,—"so that it could not be suspended, revoked, nor diminished in the exercise of its functions, by the inhibition of any other Tribunal, without peril of committing notable contempt and scandalous transgression of the decrees and regulations of the Vicar of Jesus Christ, sacred Head of the church militant." They maintained that all authorities, civil and ecclesiastical, were bound to render "the most submissive obedience to the Apostolic Precepts,"—that is to say, the Papal,—and described certain demands for the "prompt reintegration of the Tribunal of the Faith in all its functions" as an evidence of their *Catholicism.*

"The Apostolical Precepts," be it noted, were to come from Rome, or from the Court of Cardinals, wherever that Court might be able to assemble. Soon after these pretensions were made for them in Spain, their Eminences were reinstated at Rome; and the restoration of the prisons was the natural consequence of the resumption of their functions by the Congregation of the Inquisition. A work, authenticated by the Master of the Sacred Palace,* lies before me, printed at Rome in 1824; and I understand that it is still sufficiently exact to serve the Roman Clergy as a manual of ordinary information. It contains an account of this Congregation. Roman Ecclesiastics assure me that it represents the *present* practice of this particular branch of government, and it may now be had to order in the Holy City.

After describing the original constitution of "the Congregation of the Sacred Inquisition," and stating the number of Cardinals to be twelve, unless the Pope shall otherwise determine, our authority proceeds to say, that "this Congregation takes cognisance of all causes that relate to those offences by which suspicion arises of a false belief,—as of heresy, heretical blasphemies, sortileges, abuses of sacraments, and other like foul and wicked maxims; and concerning those persons who maintain fallacious dogmas, or divulge wicked instructions, and bad writings. Hence it is wont to revoke to scrutiny and examination; it proscribes criminal books, *and their authors;* although that properly belongs to the Congregation of the Index, as we shall see in its place; and, finally, takes part in matrimonial dispensations, and

* Relazione della Corte di Roma già pubblicata del Cav. Lunadoro, quindi ritoccata, accresciuta ed illustrata da Fr. Antonio Zaccaria, *ora nuovamente corretta.* Roma, MDCCCXXIV., nella Stamperia de Romanis. Con Licenza di Sup.

treats of all those matters that can in any way relate to the Faith, according to the standard of the many Pontifical Constitutions cited by the Advocate Danielli in his work under this title. *And because the affairs which have to be discussed in the said Congregation are frequent and infinite,* it was holden three times every week, the first on *Monday*, in the Palace of the Holy Office, at which assembled the Consultors, the Assessor, and the Commissary; the processes and the letters of the Inquisitors *in partibus* were read there, and opportune provisions were made. On *Wednesday*, generally, the Second Congregation is in the convent of St. Mary, commonly called the Convent of the Minerva, where the Cardinals attend, to whom the resolutions taken on Monday by the Consultors are referred. And, lastly, the Congregation assembles on *Thursday*, the third time, in the apostolic palace," (either the Quirinal or Vatican,) "where the supreme Pontiff, as head, presides with the Cardinals, and by him, if there be nothing to the contrary, the decrees prepared by the two Congregations are confirmed, *and there is always decided there some particular case.* Let us now speak of the officers of this Congregation.

"Besides the Cardinals, who compose the above-said Congregation, there are other ordinary Ministers who manage this Tribunal, *exercising actual jurisdiction, framing and examining the processes of criminals.* There is the Inquisitor, called Commissary of the Holy Office, who is of the order of St. Dominic. He acts as ordinary Judge of the Congregation. The Assessor is an eminent Prelate and Counsellor of this Court, and renders, so to speak, the same service in its business as does the Commissary; for, indeed, just as many causes are submitted to the judgment of the Assessor, *as there arise civil controversies in respect to the said Tribunal;* and, at one time, the civil and criminal causes that related to persons empowered by letters patent of the said Congregation. It is his duty to report to the Pontiff the resolutions of the Congregation.

"Various theologians and learned canonists, and also members of the secular Clergy, elected by the Pontiff, and called *Consultors* of the Holy Office, also take part in the affairs of the said Congregation. Among the Consultors, the General of the Dominicans, the Master of the Sacred Palace, who is also of the same order, and a Professed of the order of Minors Conventuals of St. Francis, occupy a fixed place. They attend in the Congregations, and give their votes. Sometimes the said Congregation also commits affairs, books, or writings to be examined by some theologian who is not included in the number of Consultors, and has not a place in the Congregation, except on that occasion, when he presents a report on the affairs confided to him. Such a personage has the title of Qualifier (or Reporter).

"Besides these, there is the Depositary, who has care of *the revenues* of this Tribunal; *the Advocate*, who defends the causes of criminals; the Fiscal Proctor, who represents the accuser; and the Notary. And there was also another subaltern minister, commonly called the *Captain*.* All these are persons appointed to the service of the Tribunal."

The Roman Inquisition, therefore, is acknowledged to have an infinite multitude of affairs constantly on hand, which necessitates its assemblage thrice every week. Still there are criminals, and criminal processes. The body of officials are still maintained on established revenues of the Holy Office. So far from any mitigation of severity or judicial improvement in the spirit of its administration, the criminal has now no choice of an Advocate; but one person, and he a servant of the Inquisition, performs an idle ceremony, under the name of advocacy, for the conviction of all. And let the reader, remembering that he is an Englishman, mark that as there are Bishops *in partibus*, so, in like manner, there are Inquisitors of the same class appointed in every country, and chiefly in Great Britain and the colonies, who, sworn to secrecy,† of course, communicate intelligence to this "sacred Congregation" of all that can be conceived capable of comprehension within the infinitude of its affairs. We must, therefore, either believe that the Court of Rome is not in earnest, and that this apparatus of universal jurisdiction is but a shadow,—an assumption which is contrary to all experience,—or we must understand that the spies and familiars of the Inquisition are listening at our doors, and intruding themselves on our hearths. *How* they proceed,

* At Rome, a chief jailer enjoys the honourable title of *Captain*. In relation to these prisons we have hitherto introduced him to the reader under the Spanish, or Saracenic, title of *Alcayde*.

† Every Bishop, as an *Inquisitor natus*, swears to keep secret every counsel intrusted to his confidence. The promise is in terms most absolute: *Nemini pandam*. See the Pontificale Romanum, Forma Juramenti Electi in Episcopum.

and what their brethren at Rome are doing, events may tell; but *we may be sure that they are not idle.*

They were not idle in Rome in 1825, when they rebuilt the prisons of the Inquisition. They were not idle in 1842, when they imprisoned Dr. Achilli, for heresy, as he assures us; nor was the Captain, or some other of the subalterns, who, acting in their name, took his watch from him as he came out. They were not idle in 1843, when they renewed the old edicts against the Jews, of which Dr. Achilli gives us evidence in a decree issued by Fr. Vincenzo Salva, Inquisitor-General of the Holy Office of Ancona, Sinigaglia, Jesi, Osimo, &c. And all the world knows that the Inquisitors on their stations throughout the Pontifical States, and the Inquisitorial agents in Italy, Germany, and eastern Europe, were never more active than during the last four years, and even at this moment, when every political misdemeanour that is deemed offensive to the Pope, is, constructively, a "sin against the Inquisition," and visited with punishment accordingly. A deliberative body, holding formal sessions thrice every week, cannot be idle. And although it may please them to deny that Dr. Achilli saw and examined a Black Book, containing the *praxis* now in use, the criminal code of Inquisitors in force at this day,—as Archibald Bower had an abstract of such a book given to him for his use about one hundred and thirty years ago,—they cannot convince me that I have not seen and handled, and used in the preparation of this volume, the compendium of an unpublished Roman code of Inquisitorial regulations, given to the Vicars of the Inquisitor-General of Modena. They may be pleased to say that the *mordacchia*, or gag, of which Dr. Achilli speaks, as mentioned in that Black Book, is no longer used; but that it is mentioned there, and might be used again, is more than credible to myself, after having seen that the "Sacred Congregation" has fixed a rate of fees for the ordering, witnessing, and administration of *torture*. There was, indeed, a talk of abolishing torture at Rome; but we have reason to believe that the Congregation will not drop the *mordacchia*, inasmuch as, instead of notifying any such reformation to the Courts of Europe, this Congregation has kept silence. For although a continuation of the Bullary has just been published at Rome, containing several decrees of this Congregation of the Inquisition, there is not one that announces a fulfilment of that illusory promise,—a promise imagined by a correspondent to French newspapers, but never given by the Inquisitors themselves. And as there is no proof that they have yet abstained from torture, there is a large amount of circumstantial evidence that they have delighted themselves in death. And why not? When public burnings became inexpedient,—as at Goa,—did they not make provision for private executions?

For a third time, at least, the Roman prisons—I am not speaking of those of the provinces—were broken open, in 1849, after the desertion of Pius IX., and two prisoners were found there, an aged Bishop, and a Nun. Many persons then in Rome reported the event; but, instead of copying what is already before the public, I translate a letter addressed to myself by P. Alessandro Gavazzi, late Chaplain-General of the Roman army, in reply to a few questions which I had put to him. All who have heard his statements in this country—and he has been heard more widely than any other Italian refugee of these times—may judge whether his account of facts be not marked with every note of accuracy. They will believe that his power of oratory does not betray him into random declamation. Under date of "March 20th, 1852," he writes thus:—

"My dear Sir,

"In answering your questions concerning the palace of the Inquisition at Rome, I should say that I can only give a few superficial and imperfect notes. So short was the time that it remained open to the public, so great the crowd of persons that pressed to catch a sight of it, and so intense the horror inspired by that accursed place, that I could not obtain a more exact and particular impression.

"I found no instruments of torture;* for they were

* The gag, the thumb-screw, and many other instruments of severe torture, could easily be destroyed, and others as easily procured. There is reason to believe that the most important records were burnt as soon as the Dominicans apprehended that the Roman people would, once more, make a forcible entrance into the palace. The non-appearance of instruments is not enough to sustain the current belief that the use of them is discontinued. So long as there is a secret prison, and while all the existing standards of Inquisitorial practice make torture an ordinary expedient for extorting information, not even a Bull, prohibiting torture, would be sufficient to convince the world that it has been discontinued. The practice of falsehood is enjoined on Inquisitors.

destroyed at the time of the first French invasion, and because such instruments were not used afterwards by the modern Inquisition. I did, however, find, in one of the prisons of the second court, a furnace, and the remains of a woman's dress. I shall never be able to believe that that furnace was used for the living, it not being in such a place, or of such a kind, as to be of service to them. Everything, on the contrary, combines to persuade me that it was made use of for horrible deaths, and to consume the remains of the victims of Inquisitorial executions. Another object of horror I found between the great hall of judgment and the luxurious apartment of the Chief Jailer (*Primo Custode*), the Dominican Friar who presides over this diabolical establishment. This was a deep trap, a shaft opening into the vaults under the Inquisition. As soon as the so-called criminal had confessed his offence, the second keeper, who is always a Dominican Friar, sent him to the Father Commissary to receive a relaxation * of his punishment. With hope of pardon, the confessed culprit would go towards the apartment of the Holy Inquisitor; but in the act of setting foot at its entrance, the trap opened, and the world of the living heard no more of him. I examined some of the earth found in the pit below this trap: it was a compost of common earth, rottenness, ashes, and human hair, fetid to the smell, and horrible to the sight and to the thought of the beholder.

"But where popular fury reached its highest pitch, was in the vaults of Saint Pius V. I am anxious that you should note well that this Pope was canonised by the Roman Church especially for his zeal against heretics. I will now describe to you the manner how, and the place where, those Vicars of Jesus Christ handled the living members of Jesus Christ, and show you how they proceeded for their healing. You descend into the vaults by very narrow stairs. A narrow corridor leads you to the several cells, which, for smallness and for stench, are a hundred times more horrible than

How, then, could we believe a Bull, or a Decree, if it were put forth to-morrow, to release them from suspicion, or to screen them from obloquy? It would not be entitled to belief.

* In Spain, *relaxation* is delivery to death. In the established style of the Inquisition it has the same meaning. But in the common language of Rome it means *release*. In the lips of the Inquisitor, therefore, if he used the word, it has one meaning, and another to the ear of the prisoner.

the dens of lions and tigers in the Colosseum. Wandering in this labyrinth of most fearful prisons, that may be called 'graves for the living,' I came to a cell full of skeletons without skulls, buried in lime; and the skulls, detached from the bodies, had been collected in a hamper by the first visiters. Whose were those skeletons? and why were they buried in that place, and in that manner? I have heard some Popish Ecclesiastics, trying to defend the Inquisition from the charge of having condemned its victims to a secret death, say that the palace of the Inquisition was built on a burial-ground belonging, *anciently*, to a hospital for pilgrims, and that the skeletons found were none other than those of pilgrims who had died in that hospital. But everything contradicts this Papistical defence. Suppose that there had been a cemetery there, it could not have had subterranean galleries and cells, laid out with so great regularity; and even if there had been such,—against all probability,—the remains of bodies would have been removed on laying the foundations of the palace, to leave the space free for the subterranean part of the Inquisition. Besides, it is contrary to the use of common tombs, to bury the dead by carrying them through a door at the side; for the mouth of the sepulchre is always at the top. And, again, it has never been the custom in Italy to bury the dead, singly, in quick-lime; but, in time of plague, the dead bodies have been usually laid in a grave until it was sufficiently full, and then quick-lime has been laid over them to prevent pestilential exhalations, by hastening the decomposition of the infected corpses. This custom was continued, some years ago, in the cemeteries of Naples, and especially in the daily burial of the poor. Therefore, the skeletons found in the Inquisition of Rome could not belong to persons who had died a natural death in a hospital; nor could any one, under such a supposition, explain the mystery of all the body being buried in lime, with exception of the head. It remains, then, beyond doubt, that that subterranean vault contained the victims of one of the many secret martyrdoms of the butcherly Tribunal. The following is the most probable opinion, if it be not rather the history of a fact.

"The condemned were immersed in a bath of slaked lime, gradually filled up to their necks. The lime, by little and little, enclosed the sufferers, or walled them up all alive.

The torment was extreme, but slow. As the lime rose higher and higher, the respiration of the victims became more and more painful, because more difficult. So that what with the suffocation of the smoke, and the anguish of a compressed breathing, they died in a manner most horrible and desperate. Some time after their death, the heads would naturally separate from the bodies, and roll away into the hollows left by the shrinking of the lime. Any other explanation of the fact that may be attempted, will be found improbable and unnatural.

"You may make any use of these notes of mine, in your publication, that you please, since I can warrant their truth. I wish that writers, speaking of this infamous Tribunal of the Inquisition, would derive their information from pure history, unmingled with romance; for so many and so great are the historical atrocities of the Inquisition, that they would more than suffice to arouse the detestation of a thousand worlds. I know that the Popish impostor-Priests go about saying that the Inquisition was never an ecclesiastical Tribunal, but a laic. But you will have shown the contrary in your work, and may also add, in order quite to unmask those lying Preachers, that the palace of the Inquisition at Rome is under the shadow of the palace of the Vatican; that the keepers of the Inquisition at Rome are, to this day, Dominican Friars; and that the Prefect of the Inquisition at Rome is the Pope in person.

"I have the honour to be

"Your affectionate servant,

"ALESSANDRO GAVAZZI."

The Roman Parliament decreed the erection of a pillar opposite the palace of the Inquisition, to perpetuate the memory of the destruction of that "nest of abominations;" but before that or any other monument could be raised, the French army besieged and took the city, restored the Pope, and with him the Tribunal of the Faith. Not only was Dr. Achilli thrown into one of its old prisons on the 29th of July, 1849; but, the violence of the people having made the building less adequate to the purpose of safe keeping, he was transferred to the Castle of St. Angelo, which had often been employed for the custody of similar delinquents, and there he lay in close confinement until the 19th of January, 1850, when the French authorities, yielding to influential representations from this country, assisted him to escape in disguise as a soldier, thus removing an occasion of scandal, but carefully leaving the authority of the Congregation of Cardinals undisputed. Indeed, they first obtained the verbal sanction of the Commissary, who saw it expedient to let his victim go, and hush an outcry.

Yet some have the hardihood to affirm that there is no longer any Inquisition; and as the Inquisitors were instructed to suppress the truth, to deny their knowledge of causes actually passing through their hands, and to fabricate falsehoods for the sake of preserving the *secret*, because the secret was absolutely necessary to the preservation of their office, so do the Inquisitors *in partibus* falsify and illude without the least scruple of conscience, in order to put the people of this country off their guard.

The writer of an anonymous pamphlet, printed in Glasgow in 1851,* and intended for circulation among the lower classes, whose ignorance he endeavours to abuse, ventures on such denials and affirmations as the following:—"I deny, and fearlessly deny, that there exists at this day any such Tribunal in the length and breadth of Christendom." "The Pope and religious authorities did everything in their power to prevent its establishment, and have ever laboured to restrain its operations within the bounds of *the most scrupulous humanity*." (!) "The Church has not only disavowed its rigours, but opposed them." "St. Dominic never had anything to do with the Inquisition." "Were it not for its forms, it might be held up to the world as a model of equity and humanity." "It took nearly fifty years before the Spanish Government could wring out of the Pope authority to establish the Inquisition." "Nor am I afraid of being called upon to defend the Roman Inquisition, which, like the Spanish, *no longer exists;* but which, when it did exist, can defy the world to show that it ever spilled one drop of blood." And he finishes with the following remarkable profession:—"Whatever old women, whose nerves have been perfectly unhinged by the bugbears held up to them, may think of the Inquisition, or whatever designing, infidel, or immoral rogues, who dread its clear-sightedness in discover-

* Coroner's Inquest and Post-mortem Examination of the Inquisition. Glasgow: Printed by Hugh Margey, 14, Great-Clyde-street, 1851.

ing, and its power of punishing, may say, for my own part, I say, with Count de Maistre, that whether as a Court of Equity, a Court of High Police, or a Censorship of the Press, *its influence would be found most beneficial to society in any country;* that we may roar, 'O! the detestable institution!' but I seek in vain for anything detestable in it. What Count de Maistre says, I likewise say,—that the Inquisition in its nature is *good, mild, and conservative;* to which I add, that, in my humble opinion, never did court of penal justice repress so much crime at the expense of so small an amount of infliction."

This person, who withholds his name because he is too aged, he says, to enter into controversy, must certainly be an Inquisitor *in partibus;* for none other could betray such mendacious earnestness in the cause. As to the character of the Inquisition, it may be left to the abhorrence of the world. As to its past state and proceedings, Romanists themselves have given their witness, and it is their testimony that appeals to my readers. And that the Inquisition really exists, is placed beyond doubt by its daily action as a visible institution at Rome. But if any one should fancy that it was abolished after the release of Dr. Achilli, and that it had ceased to be on the 23d day of May, 1851, when the Glasgow apologist dated the sentences here quoted, let him hear a sentence contradictory from a Bull of the Prefect himself, Pius IX., a document that was dated at Rome just three months later (August 22d, 1851), where the Pontiff, condemning the works of Professor Nuytz, of Turin, says, "After having taken the advice of the Doctors in Theology and Canon-Law, *after having collected the suffrages of our venerable brothers the Cardinals of the Congregation of* THE SUPREME AND UNIVERSAL INQUISITION." And so recently as March 18th, 1852, by letters of the Secretariate of State, he appointed four Cardinals to be "members of the Sacred Congregation of the Holy Roman and Universal Inquisition;" giving incontrovertible evidence that necessary provision is made for attending to the communications of Inquisitors *in partibus* from all parts of the British empire and the world. As the old Cardinals die off, their vacant seats are filled by others. The "immortal legion" is punctually recruited.

After all, have we in Great Britain, Ireland, and the colonies, and our brethren on the foreign Mission-stations, any reason to apprehend harm to ourselves from the Inquisition as it is?

In reply to this question let it be observed:—

1. That there are Inquisitors *in partibus*, is not to be denied. That the letters of these Inquisitors are laid before the Roman Inquisition every week, is equally certain. Even in the time of Leo XII., when the Church of Rome was much weaker and far less active in the British empire than it is now, some particular case was always decided on Thursday, when the Pope, in his character of Universal Inquisitor, presided in the Congregation. It cannot be thought that now, in the height of its exultation, daring, and aggression, this Congregation has fewer emissaries, or that its emissaries are less active or less communicative than they were at that time. We also see that the Congregation is replenished constantly. The Cardinals Della Genga-Sermattei, De Azevedo, Fornari, and Lucciardi have just been added to it.

2. Besides a Cardinal in England, and a Delegate in Ireland, there is, both in England and Ireland, a body of Bishops, "natural Inquisitors," as they are always acknowledged, and have often claimed, to be; and these natural Inquisitors are all sworn to keep the *secret*,—the *soul* of the Inquisition. Since, then, there are Inquisitors *in partibus*, appointed to supply the lack of an avowed and stationary Inquisition, and since the Bishops are the very persons whom the Court of Rome can best command, as pledged for such a service, it is reasonable to suppose that they act in that capacity. An Inquisitor, be it noted, is not, like a Consultor, merely called on to give an opinion or a report on some particular case, perhaps not knowing who are the persons then under Inquisition: but he is, in relation to a distant Tribunal, the Fiscal, or accuser, who must have his own agents to collect information, and to delate the guilty. He is formally appointed by the Congregation to be their Vicar within an allotted province or district. We have read history in vain, if we do not perceive that the appointment of any but Bishops, or persons acting under their jurisdiction, would provoke discontent among the Clergy, and endanger the unity of counsel and action, and the loyalty towards the Court of Rome, which are now essentially necessary to the success of their enterprise in the countries in subjection to

the British crown. Therefore, until other persons are known to be the Inquisitors in these "parts," we must take it for granted that the Bishops, or their nominees, are they who sustain that office.

3. Some of the proceedings of these Bishops confirm the assurance that there is now an Inquisition in activity in England. It is notorious that secret societies have always been subject to persecution by the Inquisition. And, while speaking of *societies*, we cannot here distinguish between good societies and bad, nor forget that, on the continent of Europe, the Popes and the Jesuits have been accustomed to call assemblies for evangelical worship, *lodges*, and that in France and other countries, those assemblies have been dispersed by the police, because it pleased the Priests to denounce them as *clubs*. But the English Inquisitors, like the French, prohibit all associations that displease them. The Bishop of Beverley, for example, in a pastoral just now circulated in his diocese, speaks of cases of sin which are ordinarily reserved to be pardoned by "a higher authority" than that of the Confessor. And a note to that part of the pastoral, (Tablet, April 3d, 1852,) explains that, in the diocese of Beverley, the cases of sin so great that a Confessor cannot absolve one who confesses himself guilty, "are those of Freemasons, Hibernians, and other condemned societies, and also of Catholic parties getting married at a Protestant church." The higher authority, then, must receive communication concerning such cases. I know that the Confessor who applies for an indulgence for a penitent, is not obliged to name that penitent; but what is to be done if the offender does not confess, or will not repent? Not the Confessor, but the Inquisitor, communicates his name. The Bishop of Hexham evidently has offenders of the kind in view, and (Tablet, April 3d) employs language that would be utterly unintelligible, if there were not an Inquisition at work in the land. "We are informed that for some time past a very considerable section of one of those secret societies has assumed the fictitious name of the 'Hibernian Sick Club,' in order to conceal their identity with the 'Hibernian Society,' which we, in common with our episcopal brethren in England and Ireland, have denounced as one of those which have been, and still continue to be, so destructive of the peace and social happiness of Ireland. We would then solemnly warn our

beloved children to avoid all connexion with those dangerous Societies, under whatever denominations they may seek to conceal their real character; and we once more repeat to our Clergy the injunction issued in the first year of our episcopacy: 'That all members of secret Societies, among which we number the Hibernian Societies, the Knights of St. Patrick, Freemasons, &c., &c., are not to be admitted to a participation in the holy sacraments.'" That a Christian Minister should endeavour to dissuade the members of his flock from uniting themselves with secret societies, would be no more than the fulfilment of an obvious duty; and in so doing he could scarcely be too earnest. But that the whole body of Romish Ecclesiastics, to whom the title of Christian Minister does not belong, and who display so little earnestness in showing displeasure at prevalent immorality, except in mere pulpit declamation, should unite in excommunicating the members of associations where political or doctrinal opinions unfriendly to Romanism are maintained, is, to say the very least, an approach towards Inquisitorial discipline. And, after the members are excommunicated, the exercise of discipline upon them does not cease.

4. The marriage of Romanists in Protestant churches is objectionable, no doubt, as would be the marriage of Protestants in mass-houses. But the real object of censure is mixed marriage, over which the Sacred Congregation of the Holy Roman and Universal Inquisition is a board that exercises prerogative. It "takes part in matrimonial dispensations," and must therefore obtain some knowledge of every case of that kind occurring in this country. The vigilance exercised over families, also, the intermeddling of Priests with education, both in families and schools, and with the innumerable relations of civil society, can only be traced back to those Inquisitors *in partibus*, whose peculiar duty, whether by help of Confessors or familiars, is to worm out every secret of affairs, private and public, and to organize and conduct measures of repression or of punishment. Where the secular arm cannot be borrowed, and where offenders lie beyond the reach of excommunication, irregular methods must be resorted to, not rejecting any as too crafty or too violent. Discontented mobs, or individual zealots, are to be found or bought. What part the Inquisitors *in partibus* play in Irish assassinations, or in the general mass of murderous assault that is perpetrated in the lower haunts of crime, it

is impossible to say. Under cover of confessional and Inquisitorial secrets, spreads a broad field of action—a region of mystery—only visible to the eye of God, and to those "most reverend and most eminent" guardians of the Papacy, who sit, thrice every week, in the Minerva and the Vatican, and there manage the hidden springs of Inquisition on the heretics, schismatics, and rebels, no less than on "the faithful," of these realms. Who can calculate the extent of their power over these "religious houses," where so many of the inmates are but neophytes, unfitted by British education for the intellectual and moral abnegation, the surrender of mind and conscience, which monastic discipline exacts? Yet they must be coerced into submission, and kept under penal discipline. Who can tell how many of their own Clergy are withdrawn to Rome, and there delated, imprisoned, and left to perish, if not "relaxed" to death, in punishment of heretical opinions or liberal practices? We have heard of laymen, too, taken to Rome by force, or decoyed thither under false pretences, there to be punished by the Universal Inquisition; and whatever of incredibility may appear in some tales of Inquisitorial abduction, the general fact, that such abductions have taken place, seems to be incontrovertible. But now that Inquisitors *in partibus* are distributed over Christendom,—and that they provide the Roman Inquisition with daily work from year's end to year's end, is among the things most certain,—even the most careless of Englishmen must acknowledge that we have all reason to apprehend much evil from the Inquisition as it is. And no Christian can become aware of this fact, without feeling himself to be more than ever bound to uphold the cause of Christianity, both at home and abroad, as the only counteractive of so dire a curse, the only remedy of so vast an evil.

May God speed the day when that Church, whose episcopate is essentially Inquisitorial, and whose emissaries now pursue their odious and dark vocation throughout all Christendom, shall cease to be, and when, instead of this horrible Tribunal, the kingdom of our blessed Saviour, who destroys the works of the devil, shall be "supreme and universal!"

LONDON:—PRINTED BY JAMES NICHOLS, HOXTON-SQUARE.

MEMORABLE MEN AND MEMORABLE EVENTS.

Each Volume, Price 1*s.*, 18mo., gilt edges.

I.

COLUMBUS;

OR, THE DISCOVERY OF AMERICA.

By the Rev. George Cubitt.

II.

CORTES;

OR, THE DISCOVERY AND CONQUEST OF MEXICO.

III.

PIZARRO;

OR, THE DISCOVERY AND CONQUEST OF PERU.

IV.

GRANADA;

OR, THE EXPULSION OF THE MOORS FROM SPAIN.

Others are in preparation.

THE IRISH CONVERT;

Or, Popish Intolerance illustrated.

By the Rev. William Lupton.

18mo. Price 1*s.* 6*d.*, cambric, gilt-lettered.

HELEN LESLIE; OR, TRUTH AND ERROR.

By Adeline. 18mo., cambric. Price 1*s.* 6*d.*

MEMORIALS OF MISS MARY FISHWICK,

Of Springfield, near Garstang: containing Selections from her Correspondence. With an Introduction, by the Rev. Peter M'Owan.

Third Edition. 18mo. Price 1*s.* 6*d.*, cambric; or, gilt edges, with a Portrait, 2*s.*

ATTRACTIVE PIETY:

Or, Memorials of William B. Carvosso, Grandson of the late Mr. W. Carvosso. By his Father. Second Edition. 18mo. Price 1*s.* 4*d.*

PASTORAL ADDRESSES.

By the Rev. Alfred Barrett.

Volume I., containing Nos. I. to XII.,—Volume II., containing Nos. XIII. to XXIV.,

Cambric, gilt-lettered, Price 1*s.* 6*d.* each; or, with gilt edges, Price 2*s.* each.

THE BOATMAN'S DAUGHTER:

A Narrative for the Learned and Unlearned.

By the Rev. Alfred Barrett.

With a Steel Engraving of the Boat.

18mo., cambric, Price 1*s.* 4*d.*; or, in extra cambric, gilt edges, 1*s.* 8*d.*

HOLY LIVING: EXEMPLIFIED IN

THE LIFE OF MRS. MARY CRYER,

Wife of the Rev. Thomas Cryer, Wesleyan Missionary in India. With Extracts from her Papers and Correspondence.

By the Rev. Alfred Barrett.

With two fine Engravings. 12mo. Price 4*s.*, cambric, gilt-lettered.

SCENES IN THE WEST INDIES, AND OTHER POEMS.

By Adeline. 18mo., gilt edges. Price 1*s.*

NEW EDITIONS OF THE FOLLOWING WORKS:

A COMMENTARY ON THE OLD AND NEW TESTAMENTS:

In which the Sacred Text is illustrated with Copious Notes, Theological, Historical, and Critical; with Improvements and Reflections at the end of each Chapter.

By the Rev. Joseph Sutcliffe, A.M.

Illustrated by Maps and Plates; with a Portrait of the Author. Two Vols,, imperial 8vo., Turkey cambric, gilt-lettered. Price £1. 5*s.*

THE MOTHER AT HOME:

Or, the Principles of Maternal Duty illustrated.

By the Rev. John S. C. Abbott. Edited by the Rev. Daniel Walton.

18mo., cambric. Price 1*s.* 6*d.*

THE INFIDEL'S OWN BOOK.

A Statement of some of the Absurdities resulting from the Rejection of Christianity.
By the REV. RICHARD TREFFRY, JUN.
18mo. cambric. Price 2*s.* 6*d.*

THE SAINTS' EVERLASTING REST.

Extracted from the Works of the REV. RICHARD BAXTER, by the REV. JOHN WESLEY, A.M.
Royal 18mo., cambric. Price 3*s.*

THE IMPORTANCE OF PRAYER-MEETINGS IN PROMOTING THE REVIVAL OF RELIGION.

By the REV. ROBERT YOUNG. 18mo. Price 1*s.*

HYMNS FOR CHILDREN, AND FOR PERSONS OF RIPER YEARS.

By the REV. CHARLES WESLEY, A.M. 24mo. Price 8*d.*

THE WORK OF THE HOLY SPIRIT IN THE HUMAN HEART.

By the REV. JONATHAN EDWARDS, M.A.
Abridged by the REV. JOHN WESLEY, A.M. 18mo., cambric. Price 1*s.* 6*d.*

REVIVALS OF RELIGION:

Their Nature, Defence, and Management.
By the REV. J. EDWARDS, M.A. Abridged by the REV. J. WESLEY, A.M.
18mo., cambric. Price 2*s.* 6*d.*

A SHORT EXPOSITION OF THE TEN COMMANDMENTS.

Extracted from BISHOP HOPKINS, by the REV. JOHN WESLEY, A.M.
18mo., cambric. Price 1*s.* 6*d*

ADMONITORY COUNSELS ADDRESSED TO A METHODIST,

On Subjects of Christian Experience and Practice.
By the REV. JOHN BAKEWELL. 18mo., cambric. Price 2*s.*

PRAYERS FOR THE USE OF CHRISTIAN FAMILIES:

Containing a Morning and Evening Prayer for each Day in the Month, &c.
By SEVERAL WESLEYAN MINISTERS.
8vo., cambric, Price 7*s.*; also in 12mo., Price 4*s.*

A COMPLETE EDITION OF

THE PROSE WORKS OF THE REV. JOHN WESLEY, A.M.

Fourteen Vols. 8vo., Turkey cambric, gilt-lettered. Price £5. 12*s*.

Fourteen Vols. 12mo., cambric, gilt-lettered. Price £3. 3*s*.

⁎ Any Volume may be had separate

ALSO, BY THE SAME AUTHOR,

SERMONS.

3 Vols. 8vo., fine paper, cambric. Price £1. 4*s*.

WITH A SKETCH OF HIS LIFE:
3 Vols. 12mo., cambric, gilt-lettered. Price 10*s*. 6*d*.
3 Vols. 12mo., cambric. Price 8*s*.

JOURNALS.

4 Vols. 8vo., cambric. Price £1. 12*s*.—4 Vols. 12mo., cambric. Price 14*s*.

AN EARNEST APPEAL TO MEN OF REASON AND RELIGION.

Royal 18mo., cambric. Price 3*s*.

A PLAIN ACCOUNT OF CHRISTIAN PERFECTION.

18mo., roan. Price 1*s*. 6*d*.

NOTES ON THE NEW TESTAMENT.

Pocket edition, cambric. Price 5*s*.
8vo., cambric. Price 10*s*.
2 Vols. 8vo, cambric, fine paper. Price 16*s*.

SELECT LETTERS:

Chiefly on Personal Religion.
With a Sketch of his Character, by the Rev. Samuel Bradburn.
12mo., cambric. Price 3*s*.

A PRESERVATIVE AGAINST UNSETTLED NOTIONS IN RELIGION.

18mo., cambric. Price 2*s*.

A NEW AND UNIFORM EDITION OF

THE WORKS OF THE REV. J. W. FLETCHER.

Complete in Eight Volumes Duodecimo, Turkey cambric, gilt-lettered. Price £1. 16*s*.

BY THE SAME AUTHOR,

CHECKS TO ANTINOMIANISM.

2 Vols., 12mo., cambric. Price 6*s*.

POSTHUMOUS PIECES.

Containing his Pastoral and Familiar Epistles, together with Six Letters on the Manifestation of Christ.
12mo., cambric. Price 4*s*.

AN APPEAL TO MATTER OF FACT AND COMMON SENSE.

Or, a Rational Demonstration of Man's Corrupt and Lost Estate.
12mo., cambric. Price 2*s*.

THE LAST CHECK TO ANTINOMIANISM:

A Polemical Essay on the Twin Doctrines of Christian Imperfection, and a Death Purgatory.
12mo., cambric. Price 3*s*. 6*d*.

SELECTIONS FROM THE WORKS OF THE REV. JOHN FLETCHER,

Systematically arranged: with a Life of the Author. By S. Dunn.
12mo., cambric. Price 6*s*. 6*d*.

BY THE REV. JOSEPH BENSON.

A COMMENTARY ON THE OLD AND NEW TESTAMENTS.

6 Vols., imperial 8vo., cambric, Price £5.; or with 112 Illustrations, Price £5. 12*s*.

COMMENTARY ON THE NEW TESTAMENT.

2 Vols., imperial 8vo., cambric. Price £1. 14*s*.

COMMENTARY ON THE NEW TESTAMENT.

2 Vols., imperial 8vo., with Illustrations, cambric. Price £1. 18*s*.

SERMONS ON VARIOUS OCCASIONS.

With a Sketch of the Character of the Author, by the Rev. Jabez Bunting, D.D. 2 Vols., 12mo., cambric. Price 8*s*.

BY THE REV. JONATHAN EDMONDSON, A.M.

SHORT SERMONS ON IMPORTANT SUBJECTS.
2 Vols., 8vo., cambric. Price 10*s.*

A CONCISE SYSTEM OF SELF-GOVERNMENT
In the great Affairs of Life and Godliness. 12mo., cambric. Price 4*s.*

SERMONS ON THE NATURE AND OFFICES OF THE HOLY GHOST.
By the Rev. J. Edmondson, and the Rev. R. Treffry.
12mo., cambric. Price 3*s.* 6*d.*

SCRIPTURE VIEWS OF THE HEAVENLY WORLD.
18mo., cambric. Price 2*s.*

ELEMENTS OF REVEALED RELIGION.
12mo., cambric. Price 5*s.*

AN ESSAY ON THE CHRISTIAN MINISTRY:
Including a General Outline of Ministerial and Pastoral Duties; for the Use of Young Preachers. 12mo., cambric. Price 5*s.* 6*d.*

BY THE REV. RICHARD TREFFRY.

MEMOIRS OF THE REV. RICHARD TREFFRY, JUN.;
WITH SELECT REMAINS,
Consisting of Sketches of Sermons, Essays, and Poetry.
Including Extracts from his Correspondence. With a Portrait.
12mo., cambric. Price 5*s.*

A TREATISE ON SECRET AND SOCIAL PRAYER.
12mo., cambric. Price 3*s.*

A TREATISE ON THE CHRISTIAN SABBATH.
12mo., cambric. Price 3*s.*

A TREATISE ON CHRISTIAN PERFECTION.
18mo., cambric. Price 2*s.* 6*d.*

A PARENTAL PORTRAITURE OF THOMAS H. TREFFRY.
18mo., cambric. Price 1*s.* 6*d.*

MEMOIRS OF MR. RICHARD TREWAVAS, SEN.,
Of Mousehole, Cornwall.
To which is prefixed, An Account of Methodism in Mousehole.
18mo., cambric. Price 1*s.* 6*d.*

BY THE REV. THOMAS JACKSON.

CENTENARY OF WESLEYAN METHODISM.

A brief Sketch of the Rise, Progress, and Present State of the Wesleyan-Methodist Societies throughout the World.
Post 8vo., cambric. Price 5*s.*—Demy 12mo., cambric. Price 2*s.* 6*d.*

An Abridged Edition, for the Use of Schools.
18mo., cambric. Price 1*s.* 4*d.*

THE LIFE OF THE REV. CHARLES WESLEY, M.A.,

Comprising a Review of his Poetry; Sketches of the Rise and Progress of Methodism; with Notices of contemporary Events and Characters. 2 Vols., 8vo., cambric. Price £1. 1*s.*

A LETTER TO THE REV. EDWARD B. PUSEY, D.D.,

REGIUS PROFESSOR OF HEBREW IN THE UNIVERSITY OF OXFORD:

Being a Vindication of the Tenets and Character of the Wesleyan Methodists, against his Misrepresentations and Censures.
8vo. Price 6*d.*—CHEAP EDITION. Price 3*d.*

MEMOIRS OF THE REV. RICHARD WATSON.

Royal 18mo., cambric. Price 5*s.*

JOHN GOODWIN'S EXPOSITION OF THE NINTH CHAPTER OF THE ROMANS;

BANNER OF JUSTIFICATION DISPLAYED, &c. 8vo., cambric. Price 5*s.*

EXPOSITORY DISCOURSES ON VARIOUS SCRIPTURE FACTS AND CHARACTERS.

Post 8vo., cambric. Price 7*s.*

BY THE REV. RICHARD TREFFRY, JUN.

AN INQUIRY INTO THE DOCTRINE OF THE ETERNAL SONSHIP OF OUR LORD JESUS CHRIST.

12mo., cambric. Price 6*s.*

LETTERS ON THE ATONEMENT.

18mo., cambric. Price 2*s.*

LECTURES ON THE EVIDENCES OF CHRISTIANITY.

18mo., cambric. Price 1*s.* 6*d.*

MEMOIRS OF MR. JOHN EDWARDS TREZISE;

With some Account of Methodism in St. Just. 18mo., cambric. Price 2*s.*

THE INFIDEL'S OWN BOOK.

A Statement of some of the Absurdities resulting from the Rejection of Christianity. 18mo., cambric. Price 2*s.* 6*d.*

MISCELLANEOUS.

DELINEATION OF ROMAN CATHOLICISM,

Drawn from the authentic and acknowledged Standards of the Church of Rome: in which her peculiar Doctrines, Morals, Government, and Usages are stated, treated at large, and confuted.
By the REV. CHARLES ELLIOTT, D.D.
A new Edition, corrected and revised throughout, with numerous important Additions.
Imperial 8vo., cambric. Price 15*s.*

SHORT DISCOURSES, PRACTICAL AND EXPERIMENTAL.

By the late REV. RICHARD TREFFRY.
With Biographical Reminiscences of the Author.
12mo., cambric. Price 6*s.*

A HELP TO EXTEMPORE PRAYER.

And an Aid to Private, Domestic, and Public Devotion.
By the REV. JOSEPH WOOD. 18mo. Price 9*d.*

PRACTICAL CONSIDERATIONS ON THE CHRISTIAN SABBATH.

By the REV. PETER M'OWAN.
Third Edition. 18mo., gilt-lettered. Price 1*s.*

A TREATISE ON JUSTIFICATION.

By JOHN GOODWIN. 12mo., cambric. Price 2*s.*

THE SCRIPTURAL DOCTRINE OF JUSTIFICATION.

By the REV. EDWARD HARE.
With a Preface by the REV. THOMAS JACKSON.
12mo., cambric. Price 2*s.* 6*d.*

THE DOCTRINE OF UNIVERSAL RESTORATION EXAMINED AND REFUTED.

By the REV. DANIEL ISAAC. 12mo., cambric. Price 2*s.*

DIALOGUES ON SANCTIFICATION.

By the REV. J. S. PIPE. 18mo., cambric. Price 1*s.* 4*d.*

THE CHRISTIAN MIRACLES;

Or, Conversations on the Miracles of Christ, &c.
By the REV. GEORGE CUBITT.
18mo., cambric, gilt-lettered. Price 2*s.* 6*d.*

WORKS PUBLISHED BY JOHN MASON.

MEMOIRS OF MRS. ELIZABETH MORTIMER.
By Mrs. Agnes Bulmer. 18mo., cambric. Price 2*s*. 6*d*.

JOURNAL AND CORRESPONDENCE OF MRS. M. CLOUGH,
Wife of the Rev. B. Clough, Missionary in Ceylon.
With an Introduction by Dr. Adam Clarke. 18mo., cambric. Price 2*s*.

THE YOUNG CHRISTIAN.
By Jacob Abbott. Revised and corrected by the Rev. D. Walton.
18mo., cambric. Price 2*s*. 6*d*.

YOUTHFUL PIETY;
Being brief Memorials of Children of Wesleyan Ministers.
18mo., cambric. Price 1*s*. 6*d*.

NARRATIVE OF O. M. SPENCER:
Comprising an Account of his Captivity among the Mohawk Indians in North America. 18mo., cambric. Price 2*s*.

SCRIPTURE HISTORIES:
Containing the Histories of Abraham, Isaac, Jacob, Joseph, Moses, Joshua, Elijah, Elisha, and Jeremiah.
By Mrs. Agnes Bulmer. 3 Vols., 18mo., cambric. Price 6*s*.

DIALOGUES, MORAL AND SCIENTIFIC.
2 Vols., royal 18mo., cambric. Price 6*s*.

SKETCHES OF POPULAR ANTIQUITIES.
Designed for the Use of Young Persons. By the Rev. A. E. Farrar.
18mo., cambric. Price 1*s*. 6*d*.

DR. YOUNG'S NIGHT THOUGHTS.
With short Notes by the Rev. John Wesley.
To which is added, Dr. Young's Poem on the Last Day.
With a Preface by the Rev. Thomas Jackson.
32mo., cambric. Price 2*s*. 6*d*.

DR. WATTS'S DEATH AND HEAVEN.
With a Preface by the Rev. Thomas Jackson. 18mo., cambric. Price 2*s*.

SCRIPTURE CONVERSATIONS:
Between George and his Minister. 18mo., cambric. Price 1*s*. 3*d*.

CONVERSATIONS ON THE PARABLES OF CHRIST.
By the Rev. G. Cubitt. 18mo., cambric. Price 1*s*. 6*d*.

www.ingramcontent.com/pod-product-compliance
Lightning Source LLC
LaVergne TN
LVHW020240110826
845151LV00003B/981

9781425530396